PEARSON TEST PREP SERIES
AP EUROPEAN HISTORY

FOR

THE WESTERN HERITAGE
Since 1300

Revised Eleventh Edition
Edition

Written by
Matthew Tippens

PEARSON

Boston   Columbus   Indianapolis   New York   San Francisco   Upper Saddle River
Amsterdam   Cape Town   Dubai   London   Madrid   Milan   Munich   Paris   Montréal   Toronto
Delhi   Mexico City   São Paulo   Sydney   Hong Kong   Seoul   Singapore   Taipei   Tokyo

CONTENTS

About Your Pearson Test Prep Guide **vi**

Part I Introduction to the AP European History Examination   1
The Advanced Placement Program   3
Correlation to *The Western Heritage*   4

Part II Topical Review with Sample Questions and Answers and Explanations   13

CHAPTER 1 The Late Middle Ages: Social and Political Breakdown (1300–1453)   14
Topical Review 14 / AP® Practice Test 17

CHAPTER 2 Renaissance and Discovery   25
Topical Review 27 / AP® Practice Test 28

CHAPTER 3 The Age of Reformation   35
Topical Review 35 / AP® Practice Test 38

CHAPTER 4 The Age of Religious Wars   45
Topical Review 45 / AP® Practice Test 48

CHAPTER 5 European State Consolidation in the Seventeenth and Eighteenth Centuries   55
Topical Review 55 / AP® Practice Test 60

CHAPTER 6 New Directions in Thought and Culture in the Sixteenth and Seventeenth Centuries   69
Topical Review 69 / AP® Practice Test 72

CHAPTER 7 Society and Economy under the Old Regime in the Eighteenth Century   80
Topical Review 80 / AP® Practice Test 84

CHAPTER 8 The Transatlantic Economy, Trade Wars, and Colonial Rebellion   92
Topical Review 92 / AP® Practice Test 96

CHAPTER 9 The Age of Enlightenment: Eighteenth-Century Thought   105
Topical Review 105 / AP® Practice Test 109

CHAPTER 10 The French Revolution   118
Topical Review 118 / AP® Practice Test 121

CHAPTER 11 The Age of Napoleon and the Triumph of Romanticism   128
Topical Review 128 / AP® Practice Test 134

CHAPTER 12 The Conservative Order and the Challenges of Reform   143
(1815–1832)
Topical Review 143 / AP® Practice Test 146

CHAPTER 13 Economic Advance and Social Unrest (1830–1850)   154
Topical Review 154 / AP® Practice Test 158

CHAPTER 14 The Age of Nation-States   167
Topical Review 167 / AP® Practice Test 171

CHAPTER 15 The Building of European Supremacy: Society and
Politics to World War I   181
Topical Review 181 / AP® Practice Test 184

CHAPTER 16 The Birth of Modern European Thought   192
Topical Review 192 / AP® Practice Test 195

CHAPTER 17 The Age of Western Imperialism   202
Topical Review 202 / AP® Practice Test 207

CHAPTER 18 Alliances, War, and A Troubled Peace   216
Topical Review 216 / AP® Practice Test 219

CHAPTER 19 The Interwar Years: The Challenge of Dictators and
Depression   228
Topical Review 228 / AP® Practice Test 232

CHAPTER 20 World War II   240
Topical Review 240 / AP® Practice Test 244

CHAPTER 21 The Cold War Era and the Emergence of the New Europe   252
Topical Review 252 / AP® Practice Test 259

CHAPTER 22 The West at the Dawn of the Twenty-First Century   268
Topical Review 268 / AP® Practice Test 271

Part III Practice Document-Based Questions   279

Part IV Sample AP Practice Test   313

PART I

INTRODUCTION TO THE AP® EUROPEAN HISTORY EXAMINATION

This section overviews the advanced placement program, introduces the types of questions you will encounter on the exam, and provides helpful test-taking strategies. It also explains the grading procedure used by the College Board. Finally, a correlation chart is provided that shows where key information commonly tested on the examination is covered in *The Western Heritage.* Review this section carefully before trying the sample items in the following parts.

THE ADVANCED PLACEMENT PROGRAM

The AP program is sponsored by the College Board, a nonprofit organization that oversees college admissions examinations. (The College Board is composed of college and high school teachers and administrators.) The AP program offers thirty-five college-level courses to qualified high school students. If you receive a grade of 3 or higher on an AP exam, you may be eligible for college credit, depending on the policies of the institution you plan to attend. Approximately 3,000 college and universities around the world grant credit to students who have performed well on AP exams. If you are taking several AP courses and if you score well on multiple AP exams, you may even be eligible to enter college as a sophomore. Some institutions grant sophomore status to incoming first-year students who have demonstrated mastery of many AP subjects. In addition, the College Board confers a number of AP Scholar Awards on students who score 3 or higher on three or more AP exams. Additional awards are available to students who receive very high grades on four or five AP exams.

The College Board appoints committees to develop examinations for each of the nineteen subjects in which it administers AP exams. If you're interested in learning more about how the European History Development Committee designs the AP European History Exam, ask your teacher for a copy of *Advanced Placement Course Description: European History.* You can order a copy directly from the College Board, as well.

Why Take an AP Course?

You may be taking one or more AP courses simply because you are thirsty for knowledge. Of course, the fact that colleges look favorably on applicants who have AP courses on their secondary school transcripts is another powerful incentive! Because AP classes usually involve rigorous lessons, a great deal of homework, and many tests, they signal to college admissions officers that AP students are willing to work hard to get the most from their education. Because AP course work is more difficult than average high school work, many admissions officers evaluate AP grades on a kind of curve—if you receive a *B* in an AP class, for example, it might carry the same weight as an *A* in a regular high school class.

Your AP European History course prepares you for many of the skills you will need in college. For example, your teacher may assign research papers and encourage you to use resources outside the scope of your textbook. Some of these resources may be primary sources that permit you to analyze events as a historian would. Other class assignments may require you to write longer-than-usual essays on historical subjects. The AP European History course will challenge you to gather and consider information in new—and sometimes unfamiliar—ways. You can feel good knowing that your ability to use these methods and skills will give you a leg up as you enter college.

Each college or university decides whether or not to grant college credit for an AP course, and each bases this decision on what it considers satisfactory grades on AP exams. Depending on what college you attend and what area of study you pursue, your decision to take the AP European History Exam could end up saving you tuition money. You can contact schools directly to find out their guidelines for accepting AP credits.

AP European History: Course Goals

One of the central goals of the AP program in European History is to provide students with a basic narrative of the cultural, economic, political, and social developments in Europe that played a fundamental role in shaping our world. In addition, the College Board's stated goals include helping you to develop:

- an understanding of some of the principal themes in modern European history;
- an ability to analyze historical evidence;
- an ability to analyze and to express historical understanding in writing.

- The development of racial and ethnic group identities

The AP European History Exam incorporates artistic, cartographic, and statistical materials. This cross-disciplinary approach reflects the methods used today in colleges and universities to present historical subject matter.

Correlation of AP European History Course Curriculum to The Western Heritage, Revised AP® Edition, 11e

Period 1 c. 1450 - c. 1648		Chapters 2, 3, 4, 5, 6, 7, 8
Key Concept 1.1	The worldview of European intellectuals shifted from one based on ecclesiastical and classical authority to one based primarily on inquiry and observation of the natural world.	Chapters 2, 4, 6
	I. A revival of classical texts led to new methods of scholarship and new values in both society and religion.	pp. 60-68, 70, 77-78, 82
	II. The invention of printing promoted the dissemination of new ideas.	pp. 83-86, 130-132
	III. The visual arts incorporated the new ideas of the Renaissance and were used to promote personal, political, and religious goals.	pp. 68-74, 135, 137, 232-234
	IV. New ideas in science based on observation, experimentation, and mathematics challenged classical views of the cosmos, nature, and the human body, though folk traditions of knowledge and the universe persisted.	pp. 203-211, 215-219, 221-227
Key Concept 1.2	The struggle for sovereignty within and among states resulted in varying degrees of political centralization.	Chapters 2, 3, 4, 5
	I. The new concept of the sovereign state and secular systems of law played a central role in the creation of new political institutions.	pp. 75-82, 115-120, 140-149, 163-165, 170-179

	II. The competitive state system led to new patterns of diplomacy and new forms of warfare.	pp. 143-145, 162-165, 170-172, 174
	III. The competition for power between monarchs and corporate groups produced different distributions of governmental authority in European states.	pp. 170-172, 174-177,
Key Concept 1.3	**Religious pluralism challenged the concept of a unified Europe.**	**Chapters 2, 3, 4, 5**
	I. The Protestant and Catholic Reformations fundamentally changed theology, religious institutions, and culture.	pp. 84-86, 98-107, 110-115, 117, 119-127
	II. Religious reform both increased state control of religious institutions and provided justifications for challenging state authority.	pp. 113-123, 136, 138, 149-153, 154-156
	III. Conflicts among religious groups overlapped with political and economic competition within and among states.	pp. 102-105, 110-112, 116, 134-149, 156-165, 169-170
Key Concept 1.4	**Europeans explored and settled overseas territories, encountering and interacting with indigenous populations.**	**Chapters 2, 4, 8**
	I. European nations were driven by commercial and religious motives to explore overseas territories and establish colonies.	pp. 87-94
	II. Advances in navigation, cartography, and military technology allowed Europeans to establish overseas colonies and empires.	pp. 87, 90, 93
	III. Europeans established overseas empires and trade networks through coercion and negotiation.	pp. 87-94, 277-278
	IV. Europe's colonial expansion led to a global exchange of goods, flora, fauna, cultural practices, and diseases, resulting in the destruction of some indigenous civilizations, a shift toward European dominance, and the expansion of the slave trade.	pp. 89-94, 143-145, 278-290, 303-305
Key Concept 1.5	**European society and the experiences of everyday life were increasingly shaped by commercial and agricultural capitalism, notwithstanding the persistence of medieval social and economic structures.**	**Chapters 3, 4, 5, 6, 7**

	I. Economic change produced new social patterns, while traditions of hierarchy and status persisted.	pp. 97-98, 144, 237-238
	II. Most Europeans derived their livelihood from agriculture and oriented their lives around the seasons, the village, or the manor, although economic changes began to alter rural production and power.	pp. 105, 108-109
	III. Population shifts and growing commerce caused the expansion of cities, which often found their traditional political and social structures stressed by the growth.	pp. 154, 169
	IV. The family remained the primary social and economic institution of early modern Europe and took several forms, including the nuclear family.	pp. 126-130, 231, 244-249
	V. Popular culture, leisure activities, and rituals reflecting the persistence of folk ideas reinforced and sometimes challenged communal ties and norms.	pp. 227-230, 232
Period 2 c. 1648 - c. 1815		**Chapters 5, 6, 7, 8, 9, 10, 11, 12**
Key Concept 2.1	**Different models of political sovereignty affected the relationship among states and between states and individuals.**	**Chapters 5, 7, 8, 9, 10, 11**
	I. In much of Europe, absolute monarchy was established over the course of the 17th and 18th centuries.	pp. 170-174, 179-184, 186-188, 190-191, 196-200, 237-244, 339-351, 376-377
	II. Challenges to absolutism resulted in alternative political systems.	pp. 168-169, 174-177, 190
	III. After 1648, dynastic and state interests, along with Europe's expanding colonial empires, influenced the diplomacy of European states and frequently led to war.	pp. 178, 182-183, 187, 189, 192-196, 273-274, 295-301
	IV. The French Revolution posed a fundamental challenge to Europe's existing political and social order.	pp. 353-390
	V. Claiming to defend the ideals of the French Revolution, Napoleon Bonaparte imposed French control over much of the European continent that eventually provoked a nationalistic reaction.	pp. 393-397, 398-403, 405-413, 426

Key Concept 2.2	The expansion of European commerce accelerated the growth of a worldwide economic network.	Chapters 7, 8, 12
	I. Early modern Europe developed a market economy that provided the foundation for its global role.	pp. 252-253
	II. The European-dominated worldwide economic network contributed to the agricultural, industrial, and consumer revolutions in Europe.	pp. 254-260, 273-290, 456-459
	III. Commercial rivalries influenced diplomacy and warfare among European states in the early modern era.	pp. 189-190, 273-274, 276, 291-295
Key Concept 2.3	The popularization and dissemination of the Scientific Revolution and the application of its methods to political, social, and ethical issues led to an increased, although not unchallenged, emphasis on reason in European culture.	Chapters 5, 6, 7, 9, 11
	I. Rational and empirical thought challenged traditional values and ideas.	pp. 185, 219-221, 311-313, 315-316, 325-331, 333-337, 366
	II. New public venues and print media popularized Enlightenment ideas.	pp. 313-315, 317, 324-325
	III. New political and economic theories challenged absolutism and mercantilism.	pp. 212-215, 325-327, 331-333
	IV. During the Enlightenment, the rational analysis of religious practices led to natural religion and the demand for religious toleration.	pp. 268-270, 318-324, 422-423
	V. The arts moved from the celebration of religious themes and royal power to an emphasis on private life and the public good.	pp. 233-234, 336-339
	VI. While Enlightenment values dominated the world of European ideas, they were challenged by the revival of public sentiment and feeling.	pp. 414-427
Key Concept 2.4	The experiences of everyday life were shaped by demographic, environmental, medical, and technological changes.	Chapter 7, 11
	I. In the 17th century, small landholdings, low-productivity agricultural practices, poor transportation, and adverse weather limited and disrupted the food supply, causing periodic famines. By the 18th century, Europeans began to escape from the Malthusian imbalance between population and the food supply, resulting in steady population growth.	pp. 249-254, 404

	II. The consumer revolution of the 18th century was shaped by a new concern for privacy, encouraged the purchase of new goods for homes, and created new venues for leisure activities.	pp. 254-255, 266
	III. By the 18th century, family and private life reflected new demographic patterns and the effects of the Commercial Revolution.	pp. 260-262
	IV. Cities offered economic opportunities, which attracted increasing migration from rural areas, transforming urban life and creating challenges for the new urbanites and their families.	pp. 263-265, 267-268
Period 3 c. 1815 - c. 1914		**Chapters 7, 11, 12, 13, 14, 15, 16, 17, 18**
Key Concept 3.1	**The Industrial Revolution spread from Great Britain to the continent, where the state played a greater role in promoting industry.**	**Chapters 7, 13, 15**
	I. Great Britain established its industrial dominance through the mechanization of textile production, iron and steel production, and new transportation systems.	pp. 256-260, 462-463
	II. Following the British example, industrialization took root in continental Europe, sometimes with state sponsorship.	pp. 463-465
	III. During the Second Industrial Revolution (c. 1870–1914), more areas of Europe experienced industrial activity, and industrial processes increased in scale and complexity.	pp. 541-547
Key Concept 3.2	**The experiences of everyday life were shaped by industrialization, depending on the level of industrial development in a particular location.**	**Chapters 13, 14, 15**
	I. Industrialization promoted the development of new classes in the industrial regions of Europe.	pp. 467-470, 546, 566
	II. Europe experienced rapid population growth and urbanization, leading to social dislocations.	pp. 463-464, 542-543, 547, 549
	III. Over time, the Industrial Revolution altered the family structure and relations for bourgeois and working-class families.	pp. 471-472, 474-477, 548, 561
	IV. A heightened consumerism developed as a result of the Second Industrial Revolution.	473, 549

	V. Because of the persistence of primitive agricultural practices and land-owning patterns, some areas of Europe lagged in industrialization, while facing famine, debt, and land shortages.	466, 532-533
Key Concept 3.3	**The problems of industrialization provoked a range of ideological, governmental, and collective responses.**	**Chapters 12, 13, 14, 15, 16**
	I. Ideologies developed and took root throughout society as a response to industrial and political revolutions.	pp. 431-439, 442, 446, 456-460, 470-471, 480-487, 566-579, 604-608
	II. Governments responded to the problems created or exacerbated by industrialization by expanding their functions and creating modern bureaucratic states.	pp. 438-441, 443-447, 477-480, 537, 549-553, 581-582
	III. Political movements and social organizations responded to the problems of industrialization.	pp. 443-445, 498-503, 534-536, 538-539, 554-566, 589-590, 593, 609-612
Key Concept 3.4	**European states struggled to maintain international stability in an age of nationalism and revolutions.**	**Chapters 11, 12, 13, 14, 15, 18**
	I. The Concert of Europe (or Congress System) sought to maintain the status quo through collective action and adherence to conservatism.	pp. 410-414, 428-431, 439-441, 443-451, 486, 488
	II. The breakdown of the Concert of Europe opened the door for movements of national unification in Italy and Germany, as well as liberal reforms elsewhere.	pp. 452-456, 488-493, 510-512, 515-535, 576-578
	III. The unification of Italy and Germany transformed the European balance of power and led to efforts to construct a new diplomatic order.	pp. 493-497, 515-526, 530-531, 663-672
Key Concept 3.5	**A variety of motives and methods led to the intensification of European global control and increased tensions among the Great Powers.**	**Chapters 14, 16, 17**
	I. European nations were driven by economic, political, and cultural motivations in their new imperial ventures in Asia and Africa.	pp. 585, 587, 615-618, 620-621, 623-634, 636-644, 648-656
	II. Industrial and technological developments (i.e., the Second Industrial Revolution) facilitated European control of global empires.	pp. 513, 633-635, 645-648, 652-655
	III. Imperial endeavors significantly affected society, diplomacy, and culture in Europe and created resistance to foreign control abroad.	pp. 583, 619, 621-625, 628-633, 636-643, 649-652, 658-662

Key Concept 3.6	European ideas and culture expressed a tension between objectivity and scientific realism on one hand, and subjectivity and individual expression on the other.	Chapters 11, 16
	I. Romanticism broke with neoclassical forms of artistic representation and with rationalism, placing more emphasis on intuition and emotion.	pp. 414-421, 423-426, 591
	II. Following the revolutions of 1848, Europe turned toward a realist and materialist worldview.	pp. 582, 584-590, 592, 608-609
	III. A new relativism in values and the loss of confidence in the objectivity of knowledge led to modernism in intellectual and cultural life.	pp. 592-604
Period 4 c. 1914 to the Present		Chapters 18, 19, 20, 21, 22
Key Concept 4.1	Total war and political instability in the first half of the 20th century gave way to a polarized state order during the Cold War, and eventually to efforts at transnational union.	Chapters 18, 19, 20, 21
	I. World War I, caused by a complex interaction of long- and short-term factors, resulted in immense losses and disruptions for both victors and vanquished.	pp. 672-685, 689, 695
	II. The conflicting goals of the peace negotiators in Paris pitted diplomatic idealism against the desire to punish Germany, producing a settlement that satisfied few.	pp. 690-691, 693-694, 696-702, 704-705, 720, 723
	III. In the interwar period, fascism, extreme nationalism, racist ideologies, and the failure of appeasement resulted in the catastrophe of World War II, presenting a grave challenge to European civilization.	pp. 743-746, 748-761, 763-780
	IV. As World War II ended, a Cold War between the liberal democratic West and the communist East began, lasting nearly half a century.	pp. 780-783, 786-803, 810-812, 815-819, 822-823
	V. In response to the destructive impact of two world wars, European nations began to set aside nationalism in favor of economic and political integration, forming a series of transnational unions that grew in size and scope over the second half of the 20th century.	pp. 862-868

	VI. Nationalist and separatist movements, along with ethnic conflict and ethnic cleansing, periodically disrupted the post–World War II peace.	pp. 823-829
	VII. The process of decolonization occurred over the course of the century with varying degrees of cooperation, interference, or resistance from European imperialist states.	pp. 692-693, 699-700, 803-810
Key Concept 4.2	**The stresses of economic collapse and total war engendered internal conflicts within European states and created conflicting conceptions of the relationship between the individual and the state, as demonstrated in the ideological battle among liberal democracy, communism, and fascism.**	**Chapters 18, 19, 20, 21, 22**
	I. The Russian Revolution created a regime based on Marxist–Leninist theory.	pp. 685-691, 708-716
	II. The ideology of fascism, with roots in the pre–World War I era, gained popularity in an environment of postwar bitterness, the rise of communism, uncertain transitions to democracy, and economic instability.	pp. 716-730, 734-738, 746-747
	III. The Great Depression, caused by weaknesses in international trade and monetary theories and practices, undermined Western European democracies and fomented radical political responses throughout Europe.	pp. 705-709, 731, 734-735
	IV. Postwar economic growth supported an increase in welfare benefits; however, subsequent economic stagnation led to criticism and limitation of the welfare state.	840-842
	V. Eastern European nations were defined by their relationship with the Soviet Union, which oscillated between repression and limited reform, until Mikhail Gorbachev's policies led to the collapse of communist governments in Eastern Europe and the fall of the Soviet Union.	pp. 793, 796-798, 800, 812-813, 815-823
Key Concept 4.3	**During the 20th century, diverse intellectual and cultural movements questioned the existence of objective knowledge, the ability of reason to arrive at truth, and the role of religion in determining moral standards.**	**Chapters 20, 21, 22**

	I. The widely held belief in progress characteristic of much of 19th-century thought began to break down before World War I; the experience of war intensified a sense of anxiety that permeated many facets of thought and culture, giving way by the century's end to a plurality of intellectual frameworks.	pp. 826-832, 854
	II. Science and technology yielded impressive material benefits but also caused immense destruction and posed challenges to objective knowledge.	pp. 765-766, 860-862, 870-875
	III. Organized religion continued to play a role in European social and cultural life, despite the challenges of military and ideological conflict, modern secularism, and rapid social changes.	pp. 802-803, 857-859
	IV. During the 20th century, the arts were defined by experimentation, self-expression, subjectivity, and the increasing influence of the United States in both elite and popular culture.	pp. 847-857
Key Concept 4.4	**Demographic changes, economic growth, total war, disruptions of traditional social patterns, and competing definitions of freedom and justice altered the experiences of everyday life.**	**Chapters 19, 20, 22**
	I. The 20th century was characterized by large-scale suffering brought on by warfare and genocide as well as tremendous improvements in the standard of living.	pp. 730, 766-773, 834-835, 862
	II. The lives of women were defined by family and work responsibilities, economic changes, and feminism.	pp. 730-734, 762, 837-839, 842-846
	III. New voices gained prominence in political, intellectual, and social discourse.	pp. 814, 835-837, 846-848, 851, 853

PART II

TOPICAL REVIEW WITH SAMPLE QUESTIONS AND ANSWERS AND EXPLANATIONS

This section is keyed to chapters 1 through 22 in *The Western Heritage*. Part II overviews important information correlated to the corresponding **AP® key concepts** from the 2015-2016 AP European Curriculum Framework and provides sample questions for every question type using the new AP exam format. Use these practice questions and essays to arm yourself thoroughly for the kinds of test items you will encounter on the AP exam. Answers and explanations are provided for each question for your further review.

CHAPTER 1

The Late Middle Ages: Social and Political Breakdown (1300–1453)

The late Middle Ages were an era marked by major social, religious, and health crises. War, plague, social unrest, and religious schism characterized this era.

THE BLACK DEATH
The Black Death, also known as the bubonic plague, came about as a result of decades of overpopulation, economic depression, famine, and bad health and hygiene in some European regions.
- **The Black Death** was named for the discoloration of the body. The belief is that it was introduced by seaborne rats from the Black Sea area. By the early fifteenth century, Western Europe had lost as much as 40 percent of its population to the plague.
- Lack of sophisticated medicine led to superstitions about the reasons for the plague, including poisoning.

AP® KEY CONCEPTS
1.1 The worldview of European intellectuals shifted from one based on ecclesiastical and classical authority to one based primarily on inquiry and observation of the natural world.
   IV. New ideas in science based on observation, experimentation, and mathematics challenged classical views of the cosmos, nature, and the human body, though folk traditions of knowledge and the universe persisted.

THE HUNDRED YEARS' WAR AND THE RISE OF NATIONAL SENTIMENT
During the late Middle Ages, tremendous violence and political unrest led to the breakdown of European governments. Toward the end of the period, monarchs in England and France began to reassert their power; the Hundred Years' War was the result of their struggle for control.
- The Hundred Years' War (1337–1453) began when the English king Edward III claimed his right to the French throne after the death of Charles IV. The territorial proximity of England and France and their quarrel over the rights to Flanders exacerbated the dispute.
- English success in the war was due to its military superiority and its use of weaponry like the longbow. French weakness was due to territorial infighting and a lack of leadership.
- Fighting consisted primarily of sieges and raids. The battles of Crécy (1346), Poitiers (1356) and Agincourt (1415) were significant victories for the British. The Peace of Brétigny (1360) recognized English holdings in France, in exchange for Edward III renouncing his claim to the French throne.
- Joan of Arc (1412–1431), a peasant from Domrémy who claimed she heard the voices of God, led the French to victory in the Battle of Orléans. Joan served as an inspiration for the

French, who eventually defeated the English and won the war. Joan was later burned at the stake at Rouen as a heretic for refusing to recant her beliefs.

AP® Key Concepts
1.2 The struggle for sovereignty within and among states resulted in varying degrees of political centralization.

    I. The new concept of the sovereign state and secular systems of law played a central role in the creation of new political institutions.

    II. The competitive state system led to new patterns of diplomacy and new forms of warfare.

ECCLESIASTICAL BREAKDOWN AND REVIVAL: THE LATE MEDIEVAL CHURCH

- Pope Innocent III (r. 1198–1216) transformed the church into a secular power, creating a papal monarchy with a political mission that included disposing of *benefices* and declaring saints. Pope Urban IV (r. 1261–1264) continued the secularization of the Church by establishing its own law court, the Rota Romana, and by broadening the distribution of *benefices*. The College of Cardinals became politicized.

- Pope Boniface VIII (r. 1294–1303) refused the English and French efforts to tax the clergy, and issued a bull, *Clericis laicos,* which forbade taxation of the clergy without papal approval. Boniface was forced to make a concession to Philip the Fair of France, but the dispute led the two into further debates. In 1302, Boniface issued the bull *Unam Sanctum,* which declared that temporal authority was subject to the power of the Church. Pope Clement V moved the papacy to Avignon, to avoid the French king and Rome. The time in Avignon was called the "Babylonian Captivity," in an allusion to the biblical bondage of the Israelites.

- Pope John XXII (r. 1316–1334) tried to restore the papacy to Rome. William of Ockham and Marsilius of Padua protested papal power. John Wycliffe and John Huss led the popular lay movements the **Lollards** and the **Hussites (respectively)** that protested the rights of the papacy.

- **The Great Schism** (1378–1417) occurred when Pope Clement VII, a cousin of the French king, was elected by a council of cardinals just five months after they had elected an Italian archbishop, Pope Urban VI. Two papal courts now claimed the right to power.

- Cardinals deposed both popes and elected a new pope, Alexander V. For a time, there were three popes who claimed spiritual authority.

- The Conciliar Movement, an effort to regulate the actions of the pope by councils, grew during this time. In 1414, the council of Constance met. In a document known as the Sacrosancta, the council recognized the Roman pope Gregory XII, and one pope ruled.

AP® Key Concepts
1.2 The struggle for sovereignty within and among states resulted in varying degrees of political centralization.

    III. The competition for power between monarchs and corporate groups produced different distributions of governmental authority in European states.

1.3 Religious pluralism challenged the concept of a unified Europe.

    I. The Protestant and Catholic reformations fundamentally changed theology, religious institutions, and culture.

MEDIEVAL RUSSIA

Prince Vladimir of Kiev (972–1015) chose Greek Orthodoxy as the religion of Russia.

- Kiev was a cultural center that rivaled Constantinople. Three cultural groups —the Great Russians, the White Russians, and the Little Russians (Ukrainians)—developed. Russia's hierarchical social structure divided freemen (clergy, army officers, **boyars**, townspeople, and peasants) from slaves. Debtors made up an intermediate group.
- Mongols, led by Ghengis Khan, ruled Russia in 1223, and Russian cities became parts of the Mongol Empire until their liberation by Grand Duke Dimitri and Ivan the Great.

AP® Key Concepts

1.2 The struggle for sovereignty within and among states resulted in varying degrees of political centralization.

> III. The competition for power between monarchs and corporate groups produced different distributions of governmental authority in European states.

Multiple-Choice Questions

Questions 1–3 refer to the following map.

The Spread of the Black Death

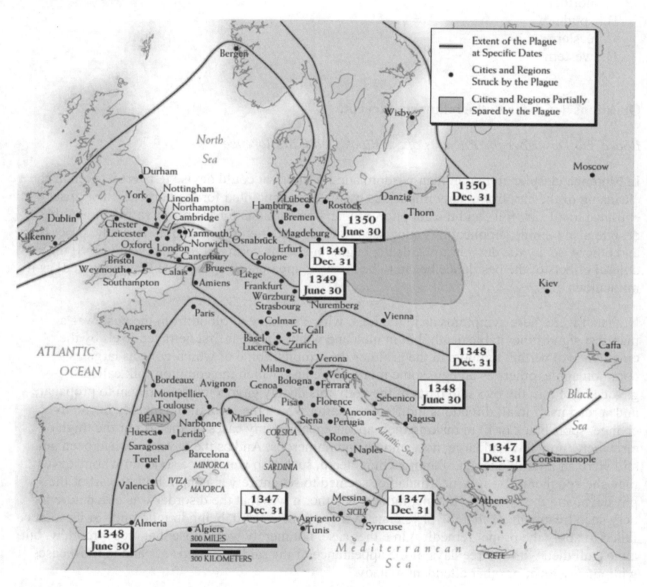

1. Which of these statements is supported by this map?
   A. The Black Death spread directly from Russia to northern Europe.
   B. The Black Death originated in the Americas.
   C. The Black Death spread to Europe via the Mediterranean.
   D. The Black Death originated in Asia.

2. About how long did it take the Black Death to spread across most of France?
   A. one year
   B. five years
   C. three years
   D. two months

3. Which of these regions of Europe was least impacted by the plague?
   A. northern
   B. southern
   C. eastern
   D. western

Questions 4–6 refer to the following excerpt.

Boccaccio Describes the Ravages of the Black Death in Florence

In Florence, despite all that human wisdom and forethought could devise to avert it, even as the cleansing of the city from many impurities by officials appointed for the purpose, the refusal of entrance to all sick folk, and the adoption of many precautions for the preservation of health; despite also humble supplications addressed to God, and often repeated both in public procession and otherwise, by the devout; towards the beginning of the spring of the said year [1348] the doleful effects of the pestilence began to be horribly apparent by symptoms that [appeared] as if miraculous.

Not such were these symptoms as in the East, where an issue of blood from the nose was a manifest sign of inevitable death; but in men and women alike it first betrayed itself by the emergence of certain tumours in the groin or the armpits, some of which grew as large as a common apple, others as an egg, some more, some less, which the common folk called gavoccioli. From the two said parts of the body this deadly gavoccioli soon began to propagate and spread itself in all directions indifferently; after which the form of the malady began to change, spots black or livid making their appearance in many cases on the arm or the thigh or elsewhere, now few and large, now minute and numerous. And as the gavoccioli had been and still were an infallible token of approaching death, such also were these spots on whomsoever they shewed themselves. Which maladies seemed to set entirely at naught both the art of the physician and the virtues of physic; indeed, whether it was that the disorder was of a nature to defy such treatment, or that the physicians were at fault . . . and, being in ignorance of its source, failed to apply the proper remedies; in either case, not merely were those that recovered few, but almost all died within three days of the appearance of the said symptoms . . . and in most cases without any fever or other attendant malady.

4. According to this excerpt, attempts to treat the Black Death were
   A. usually successful.
   B. completely unsuccessful.
   C. often successful.
   D. usually unsuccessful.

5. In the context of medieval medical practice, the remedies described here were
   A. innovative.
   B. crude.
   C. traditional.
   D. radical.

6. Reading this excerpt it appears that for those in charge of Florence, the notion of an infectious disease was
   A. emerging
   B. unknown
   C. well understood
   D. rejected

Questions 7–9 refer to the following image.

Edward III Paying Homage to Philip IV

7. Which of these causes of the Hundred Years' War is illustrated in this image?
   A. commercial conflict
   B. English expansion
   C. nationalist animosity
   D. overlapping jurisdictions

8. This image illustrates the fact that political ties in the Middle Ages were founded on
   A. warfare.
   B. personal relations.
   C. religious doctrine.
   D. clearly defined territories.

Questions 10–12 refer to the following maps.

The Hundred Years' War

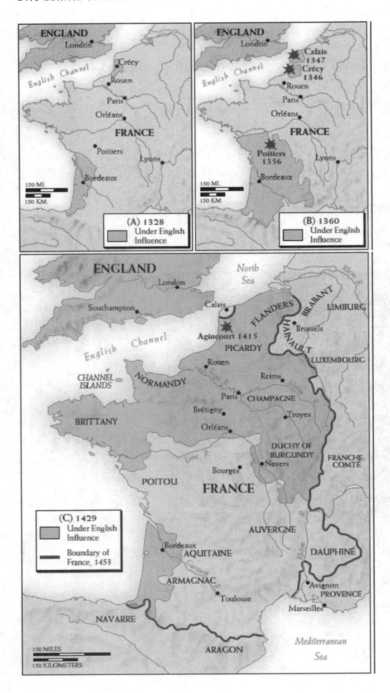

9. According to these maps of the Hundred Years' War, England
    A. won the war.
    B. gained more territory in France during the course of the war.
    C. lost most of the battles in the war.
    D. quickly lost its French territories in the war.

10. In 1429, it would have been reasonable to conclude that the Hundred Years' War would end with
    A. an English victory.
    B. a French victory.
    C. a stalemate.
    D. the devastation of England.

Questions 11–13 refer to the following excerpt.

Giles of Rome, On Ecclesiastical Power (1301)

Hugh of St. Victor . . . declares that the spiritual power has to institute the earthly power and to judge it if it has not been good. . . . We can clearly prove from the order of the universe that the church is set above nations and kingdoms [Jeremias 1:10]. . . . It is the law of divinity that the lowest are led to the highest through intermediaries. . . . At Romans 13 . . . the Apostle, having said that there is no power except from God, immediately added: "And those that are, are ordained of God." If then there are two swords [governments], one spiritual, the other temporal, as can be gathered from the words of the Gospel, "Behold, here are two swords" (Luke 22:38), [to which] the Lord at once added, "It is enough" because these two swords suffice for the church, [then] it follows that these two swords, these two powers and authorities, are [both] from God, since there is no power except from God. But, therefore they must be rightly ordered since, what is from God must be ordered. [And] they would not be so ordered unless one sword was led by the other and one was under the other since, as Dionysius said, the law of divinity which God gave to all created things requires this. . . . Therefore the temporal sword, as being inferior, is led by the spiritual sword, as being superior, and the one is set below the other as an inferior below a superior.

It may be said that kings and princes ought to be subject spiritually but not temporally. . . . But those who speak thus have not grasped the force of the argument. For if kings and princes were only spiritually subject to the church, one sword would not be below the other, nor temporalities below spiritualities; there would be no order in the powers, the lowest would not be led to the highest through intermediaries. If they are ordered, the temporal sword must be below the spiritual, and [royal] kingdoms below the vicar of Christ, and that by law . . . [then] the vicar of Christ must hold dominion over temporal affairs.

11. This author would reject the notion that
    A. the church is superior to secular authority.
    B. spiritual and secular authority can be equal.
    C. spiritual and ecclesiastical authority are the same.
    D. the pope is head of the Catholic Church.

12. What is represented by the "two swords" in this passage?
    A. secular and religious authority
    B. kings and nobles
    C. God and the church
    D. kings and military leaders

13. According to this author, the highest authority in Europe is(are)
    A. a vicar.
    B. princes.
    C. the military.
    D. the pope.

Questions 14–15 refer to the following excerpt.

Propositions of John Wycliffe

That the material substance of bread and . . . wine remain in the Sacrament of the altar.
That Christ is not in the Sacrament essentially . . . in his own corporeal presence.
That if a bishop or priest be in mortal sin he does not ordain [effectively] ordain, consecrate, or baptise . . .
That it is contrary to Holy Scripture that ecclesiastics should have possessions.
That any deacon or priest may preach the word of God apart from the authority of the Apostolic See, or a Catholic bishop.
That no one is a civil lord, or a prelate, or a bishop when he is in mortal sin.
That temporal lords can at their will take away temporal goods from the church, when those who hold them are habitually sinful.
That the people can at their own will correct sinful lords.
That tithes are mere alms, and that parishioners can withdraw them at their will because of the misdeeds of their curates.
That friars are bound to gain their livelihood by the labor of their hands, and not by begging.
That . . . the ordination of clerics [and] the consecration of [holy] places are reserved for the Pope
and bishops on account of their desire for temporal gain and honor.
That the excommunication of the Pope or any prelate is not to be feared, because it is the censure of antichrist.
It is fatuous to believe in the indulgences of the Pope and the bishops.

14. Which of these is most directly attacked in this passage?
    A. the teachings of the Bible
    B. the faith of friars and clerics
    C. the authority of the church
    D. Christianity

15. According to Wycliffe, church leaders are motivated primarily by
    A. competition
    B. material desires
    C. the desire to gain converts
    D. faith

Short-Answer Question

The Black Death spread rapidly through Europe, with high mortality rates.

    a. Choose ONE of the following and explain why your choice represents the key factor leading to this development.

- *Yersinia pestis* was probably the cause of the plague.
- Crop failures in the 1310s weakened the European population.
- Urbanization made Europe vulnerable to the plague.

    b. Contrast your choice against ONE of the other options, demonstrating why that option is not as significant as your choice.

Long-Essay Question

What were the most important causes of the papacy's loss of authority in the fourteenth and fifteenth centuries?

ANSWERS AND EXPLANATIONS: AP® PRACTICE TEST

Multiple-Choice Questions

1. C The Black Death spread most rapidly where it was carried by sea, arriving quickly in Mediterranean regions, and then spreading via the Atlantic and the North Sea.
2. A The plague had reached southern France in 1347, and then spread to the rest of the country in 1348.
3. C As the map indicates, large areas of eastern Europe were not affected by the plague.
4. D Boccaccio says that "almost all died within three days."
5. C The physicians followed the remedies they were familiar with, but without success.
6. A There are indications that city officials attempted to stop the spread of the disease, although it is also clear that the source and spread of the disease were not understood.
7. D Edward III was sovereign in England, but he was also the subject of Philip IV.
8. C The political relations between Edward and Philip were above all personal, as shown in the act of homage.
9. B Although England ultimately lost the war, for much of the war it had the upper hand, and gained a great deal of French territory.
10. A By 1429, England controlled half of France, including its capital and its richest regions.
11. B The author strenuously argues that one authority must be over the other.
12. A The two swords are the competing governments of spiritual and worldly authorities: popes and kings.
13. D The author argues in favor of spiritual authority over temporal authority because the pope is the highest spiritual authority and outranks kings.
14. C These propositions are a harsh condemnation of the practices of the popes and other church authorities.
15. B A common thread in these propositions is the worldliness of church leaders.

Long-Essay Question

What were the most important causes of the papacy's loss of authority in the fourteenth and fifteenth centuries?

(Key topics to focus and elaborate on)
- Crises: Avignon papacy, Schism
- Growing royal authority
- Material distractions of the church
- Challenges of John Huss, John Wycliffe
- Conciliar movement

CHAPTER 2

Renaissance and Discovery

The Renaissance era in European history is associated with Italy, whose city-states were venues for some of the most significant events of the period. Italy's strategic location at the crossroads of the East and the West enabled the country to achieve commercial prosperity during the late Middle Ages. Italian rulers and merchants served as patrons to the arts, government, and education, leading to an unprecedented cultural Renaissance, or rebirth.

THE RENAISSANCE IN ITALY (1375–1527)

The three major city-states in Italy during the Renaissance were Florence, Milan, and Venice.

- The Renaissance was shaped by its emergence in the context of Italian city-states. The merchants of these cities played an important role in Renaissance culture.
- The Treaty of Lodi (1454–1455) was a fragile alliance between the city-states of Naples, Milan, and Florence, and their rivals, Venice and the Papal States.
- Cosimo de' Medici (1389–1464) was a wealthy Florentine who manipulated elections and influenced the local council, the Signoria, in his uncontested control of the city. His grandson, Lorenzo the Magnificent (1449–1492) ruled Florence with a totalitarian regime from 1478–1492. The later Florentine ruler, Piero de' Medici, allied with Naples against Milan in 1494, and he was exiled after handing Pisa and other Florentine possessions over to Charles VIII of France.
- The Visconti family came to rule Milan in 1278, and the Sforza family took over in 1450. Both ruled without constitutional restraint or political competition. A Sforza, Ludovico il Moro appealed to the French in 1494 for aid against Naples and its allies, an appeal that resulted in France's acquisition of Florence.
- In response to the takeover of Florence by Charles VIII of France, in 1495 Ferdinand of Aragon created the League of Venice, a counteralliance designed to protect Venice, Milan, the Papal States, and Emperor Maximilian I from France.
- Girolamo Savonarola (1452–1498), a radical Dominican monk, convinced a mob of Florentines to exile Piero de' Medici and claimed that France's victory was divine justice. Savonarola ruled Florence until his imprisonment and execution in 1498.
- Venice was an exception to the trend of despotic rule. It was ruled by a merchant oligarchy, a 300-member senate, and a judicial council.

AP® KEY CONCEPTS

1.1 The worldview of European intellectuals shifted from one based on ecclesiastical and classical authority to one based primarily on inquiry and observation of the natural world.

    I. A revival of classical texts led to new methods of scholarship and new values in both society and religion.

    III. The visual arts incorporated the new ideas of the Renaissance and were used to promote personal, political, and religious goals.

1.2 The struggle for sovereignty within and among states resulted in varying degrees of political centralization.

    III. The competition for power between monarchs and corporate groups produced different distributions of governmental authority in European states.

    IV. New ideas in science based on observation, experimentation, and mathematics challenged classical views of the cosmos, nature, and the human body, though folk traditions of knowledge and the universe persisted.

1.5 European society and the experiences of everyday life were increasingly shaped by

    I. Economic change produced new social patterns, while traditions of hierarchy and status persisted.

    III. Population shifts and growing commerce caused the expansion of cities, which often found their traditional political and social structures stressed by the growth.

HUMANISM

The growth of humanism, the study and appropriation of the ideals expressed in Latin and Greek classics and other works of antiquity, played an important role in the Italian Renaissance. Humanists were innovative educators who believed in the importance of well-rounded education and in the noble ideals expressed by **Baldassare Castiglione (1478–1529)** in his ***Book of the Courtier***.

- Humanists espoused a program of study that included rhetoric, politics, moral philosophy, poetry, and history, and which embraced classical and biblical sources. In Florence, the Florentine Platonic Academy arose under the patronage of Cosimo de' Medici to enable humanists to devote their attention to Plato and the Neoplatonists.
- Scholars consider Francesco Petrarch (1304–1374) the "father of humanism." Other important works and authors of the era include *The Divine Comedy* by Dante Alighieri (1265–1321) and *The Decameron* by Giovanni Boccaccio (1313–1375).
- In art, new techniques like ***chiaroscuro*** and linear perspective were perfected and implemented by Renaissance artists of extraordinary talent, including Michelangelo Buonarroti (1475–1564), Leonardo da Vinci (1452–1519), and Raphael (1483–1520).

AP® KEY CONCEPTS

1.1 The worldview of European intellectuals shifted from one based on ecclesiastical and classical authority to one based primarily on inquiry and observation of the natural world.

    I. A revival of classical texts led to new methods of scholarship and new values in both society and religion.

    IV. New ideas in science based on observation, experimentation, and mathematics challenged classical views of the cosmos, nature, and the human body, though folk traditions of knowledge and the universe persisted.

THE NORTHERN RENAISSANCE

Northern humanism was stimulated by the learning imported by students returning to the Netherlands from Italy, and the movement was spread further by the effects of the French invasions of Italy.

- Northern humanism was supported by the Brothers of the Common Life, a lay religious movement based in the Netherlands. Northern humanists often had more diverse social backgrounds and were more interested in religious reform than were their Italian counterparts. They were able also to convey their educational ideals to more people as a result of Johann Gutenberg's invention of printing with movable type in 1450.

■ Desiderius Erasmus (1466?–1536), the most famous northern humanist, tried in his writings to unite the classical ideal of civic virtue with Christian ideals. His works embraced anticlerical views and satirized religious superstition. He produced a Greek edition of the New Testament (1516), and then a Latin translation of the Greek edition.

■ The English humanist Thomas More (1478–1535) is best known for *Utopia,* a critique of society that envisioned an imaginary society based on tolerance and communal property.

AP® KEY CONCEPTS

1.1 The worldview of European intellectuals shifted from one based on ecclesiastical and classical authority to one based primarily on inquiry and observation of the natural world.

I. A revival of classical texts led to new methods of scholarship and new values in both society and religion.

II. The invention of printing promoted the dissemination of new ideas.

III. The visual arts incorporated the new ideas of the Renaissance and were used to promote personal, political, and religious goals.

1.2 The struggle for sovereignty within and among states resulted in varying degrees of political centralization.

III. The competition for power between monarchs and corporate groups produced different distributions of governmental authority in European states.

IV. New ideas in science based on observation, experimentation, and mathematics challenged classical views of the cosmos, nature, and the human body, though folk traditions of knowledge and the universe persisted.

VOYAGES OF DISCOVERY AND THE NEW EMPIRE IN THE WEST

Primarily economic motives led western European countries to the exploration of faraway lands. A quest for gold and spices led European explorers to Africa and India.

■ Explorers such as Christopher Columbus (1451–1506), Amerigo Vespucci (1451–1512), Ferdinand Magellan (1480–1521), and Henry the Navigator (1394–1460) sought to conquer unknown worlds and bring riches and supplies back to Europe.

■ The effects of discoveries on the culture and history of conquered peoples frequently involved exploitation and, in some cases, complete destruction.

AP® KEY CONCEPTS

1.4 Europeans explored and settled overseas territories, encountering and interacting with indigenous populations.

I. European nations were driven by commercial and religious motives to explore overseas territories and establish colonies.

II. Advances in navigation, cartography, and military technology allowed Europeans to establish overseas colonies and empires.

III. Europeans established overseas empires and trade networks through coercion and negotiation.

IV. Europe's colonial expansion led to a global exchange of goods, flora, fauna, cultural practices, and diseases, resulting in the destruction of some indigenous civilizations, a shift toward European dominance, and the expansion of the slave trade.

Multiple-Choice Questions

Questions 1–2 refer to the following map.

Renaissance Italy

1. Based on this map, it is most correct to say that Renaissance Italy was
   A. culturally unified.
   B. culturally divided.
   C. politically unified.
   D. politically divided.

2. Relative to other Italian states in the Renaissance, the Papal States were
   A. extremely weak.
   B. among the strongest.
   C. the strongest.
   D. relatively weak.

Questions 3–4 refer to the following excerpt.

Christine de Pisan, **The Treasure of the City of Ladies**

All wives of artisans should be very painstaking and diligent if they wish to have the necessities of life. They should encourage their husbands or their workmen to get to work early in the morning and work until late. . . . [And] the wife herself should [also] be involved in the work to the extent that she knows all about it, so that she may know how to oversee his workers if her husband is absent, and to reprove them if they do not do well. . . . And when customers come to her husband and try to drive a hard bargain, she ought to warn him solicitously to take care that he does not make a bad deal. She should advise him to be chary of giving too much credit if he does not know precisely where and to whom it is going, for in this way many come to poverty. . .

In addition, she ought to keep her husband's love as much as she can, to this end: that he will stay at home more willingly and that he may not have any reason to join the foolish crowds of other young men in taverns and indulge in unnecessary and extravagant expense, as many tradesmen do, especially in Paris. By treating him kindly she should protect him as well as she can from this. It is said that three things drive a man from his home: a quarrelsome wife, a smoking fireplace, and a leaking roof. She too ought to stay at home gladly and not go off every day traipsing hither and yon gossiping with the neighbours and visiting her chums to find out what everyone is doing. That is done by slovenly housewives roaming about the town in groups. Nor should she go off on these pilgrimages got up for no good reason and involving a lot of needless expense.

3. Which of these best reflects the role of women suggested by this excerpt?
   A. Women are primarily mothers.
   B. Women should own their own businesses.
   C. Women can be useful in giving business advice.
   D. Women should be seen and not heard.

4. In this excerpt, it appears that in the Renaissance the home and the workplace
   A. overlapped.
   B. were identical.
   C. were closed to women.
   D. existed in different parts of town.

5. For Christine de Pisan, which of these best characterizes the ideal woman' life?
    A. professional
    B. maternal
    C. domestic
    D. commercial

Questions 6–7 refer to the following excerpt.

Pico della Mirandola, **Oration on the Dignity of Man (ca. 1486)**

The best of artisans [God] ordained that that creature (man) to whom He had been able to give nothing proper to himself should have joint possession of whatever had been peculiar to each of the different kinds of being. He therefore took man as a creature of indeterminate nature and, assigning him a place in the middle of the world, addressed him thus: "Neither a fixed abode nor a form that is thine alone nor any function peculiar to thyself have we given thee, Adam, to the end that according to thy longing and according to thy judgment thou mayest have and possess what abode, what form, and what functions thou thyself shalt desire. The nature of all other beings is limited and constrained within the bounds of laws prescribed by Us. Thou, constrained by no limits, in accordance with thine own free will, in whose hand We have placed thee, shall ordain for thyself the limits of thy nature. We have set thee at the world's center that thou mayest from thence more easily observe whatever is in the world. We have made thee neither of heaven nor of earth, neither mortal nor immortal, so that with freedom of choice and with honor, as though the maker and molder of thyself, thou mayest fashion thyself in whatever shape thou shalt prefer. Thou shalt have the power to degenerate into the lower forms of life, which are brutish. Thou shalt have the power, out of thy soul's judgment, to be reborn into the higher forms, which are divine." O supreme generosity of God the Father, O highest and most marvelous felicity of man! To him it is granted to have whatever he chooses, to be whatever he wills.

6. Which of these best characterizes humanity, based on this excerpt?
    A. essentially weak
    B. animals
    C. powerful
    D. mortal

7. For Mirandola, humans differ from other animals in
    A. being weaker.
    B. having no function.
    C. being divine.
    D. having more freedom.

Questions 8–10 refer to the following excerpt.

Martin Luther, **The Bondage of the Will (1525)**

It is in the highest degree wholesome and necessary for a Christian to know whether or not his will has anything to do in matters pertaining to salvation. . . . We need to have in mind a clear-cut distinction between God's power and ours and God's work and ours, if we would live a godly life. . . . The will, be it God's or man's, does what it does, good or bad, under no compulsion, but just as it wants or pleases, as if totally free. . . . Wise men know what experience of life proves, that no man's purposes ever go forward as planned, but events overtake all men contrary to their expectation. . . . Who among us always lives and behaves as he should? But duty and doctrine are not therefore condemned, rather they condemn us.

God has promised His grace to the humbled, that is, to those who mourn over and despair of themselves. But a man cannot be thoroughly humbled till he realizes that his salvation is utterly beyond his own powers, counsels, efforts, will and works, and depends absolutely on the will, counsel, pleasure, and work of Another: GOD ALONE. As long as he is persuaded that he can make even the smallest contribution to his salvation, he . . . does not utterly despair of himself, and so is not humbled before God, but plans for himself a position, an occasion, a work, which shall bring him final salvation. But he who [no longer] doubts that his destiny depends entirely only on the will of God . . . waits for God to work in him, and such a man is very near to grace for his salvation. So if we want to drop this term ("free will") altogether, which would be the safest and most Christian thing to do, we may, still in good faith, teach people to use it to credit man with "free will" in respect not of what is above him, but of what is below him. . . . However, with regard to God and in all that bears on salvation or damnation, he has no "free will" but is a captive, prisoner and bond-slave, either to the will of God, or to the will of Satan.

8. Which of these best characterizes Martin Luther's understanding of free will?
   A. He believes only Christians have free will.
   B. He believes free will was given only to humans.
   C. He believes he alone has free will.
   D. He does not believe humans have free will.

9. According to Luther, Christian salvation comes from
   A. God alone.
   B. humans following the Ten Commandments.
   C. following church ritual.
   D. a holy life.

10. According to this excerpt, which of these is the most important Christian virtue for Luther?
    A. piety
    B. independence
    C. humility
    D. intelligence

Questions 11–13 refer to the following excerpt.

World Map of Nicholas Behaim

Die beiden Erdkugeln nach dem Globus Behaim's.
(Vergl. die Karte Toscanelli's S. 39.)

11. Which of these was not included on this map?
   A. Africa
   B. the Americas
   C. Asia
   D. Europe

12. Which of these theories is illustrated by this map?
   A. It is possible to sail directly from Europe to Asia, traveling west.
   B. Asia is roughly the same size as Europe.
   C. Asia and Europe are separated by a major body of water.
   D. The fastest way to sail to Asia from Europe is around Africa.

13. Looking at this map, upon reaching the Americas, Columbus would have thought he was in
   A. India.
   B. Afrika.
   C. China (Cathaja).
   D. Japan (Cipango).

Questions 14–15 refer to the following excerpt.

Pedro de Alvarado Besieged by Aztec Warriors from the Codex Duran (sixteenth century)

14. Which of these is the most probable message of this image?
    A. The Aztecs far outnumbered the Spaniards.
    B. The Aztecs were defenseless in the face of the Spaniards.
    C. The Aztecs and the Spaniards presented stark contrasts.
    D. The Spaniards were morally superior to the Aztecs.

15. In this image the Spaniards appear to be
    A. victorious.
    B. defeated.
    C. frightened.
    D. on the defensive.

Short-Answer Question

The Northern Renaissance developed a character distinct from the Italian Renaissance.

    a. Choose ONE of the following and explain why your choice represents the key factor leading to this development.

- The political systems of these two regions differed.
- Printing first developed in northern Europe.
- Italian city-states were characterized by great diversity.

    b. Contrast your choice against ONE of the other options, demonstrating why that option is not as significant as your choice.

Long-Essay Question

What were the most important factors that shaped the development of the Renaissance?

ANSWERS AND EXPLANATIONS: AP® PRACTICE TEST

Multiple-Choice Questions

1. D This map shows only political divisions, but it clearly reflects that Italy in this period was made up of many small states.
2. B Assuming territory equals strength, the Papal States were one of the most powerful states.
3. C Christine de Pisan imagines a relatively active role for women in their husbands' business.
4. A In this period, there was no sharp distinction between the home and the workplace.
5. C Although Christine argues that women should take part in their husbands' business affairs, she still suggests that they should spend most of their time at home.
6. C Della Mirandola considers humans to have unlimited potential, unlike other animals.
7. D For this author, humans are distinct from other animals because they have freedom of choice.
8. D Martin Luther clearly argues here that humans do not have free will.
9. A Rejecting the prevailing notion of doing good works to receive salvation, Martin Luther claims that salvation comes from God alone.
10. C Luther's idea of dependence on God—and not good works—goes hand in hand with his notion of humility.
11. B This map was created by Europeans who had not yet discovered the Americas.
12. A According to this map, no major landmasses lay in the way of explorers sailing west from Europe.
13. D According to this map and most authorities of his time, a ship would first reach Japan upon sailing west from Europe.
14. C This image doesn't appear to be strongly biased in favor of either side in this conflict, but does present the two sides as very distinct.
15. D The Aztecs appear to be attacking here, while the Spaniards appear to be defending their position within a fort.

Long-Essay Question

What were the most important factors that shaped the development of the Renaissance?

(Key topics to focus and elaborate on)
- Commercial context
- City-state governments
- Scientific work
- Humanism

CHAPTER 3

The Age of Reformation

The Protestant **Reformation** was a reaction against the traditions, policies, dogma, and abuses of the Catholic Church. Those who opposed the church were called Protestants for the various protests they waged. These protests altered the religious unity of Europe, brought about religious wars, and resulted in the fragmentation of the Christian faith into many different denominations.

THE PROTESTANT REFORMATION

Some of the issues that led to this religious shift away from the Catholic Church include:

- The Great Schism: Two different popes (Clement VII and Urban VI) claimed authority over the Catholic Church; this conflict was not resolved until the Council of Constance in 1414, and the overall result was the weakening of church unity sales of indulgences, nepotism, and simony. These aspects of Catholic life angered Protestants, who believed that they were not scripturally sound. Protestants were alienated by these conditions.
- Humanism: The rise of scholarship during the Renaissance, and humanists' interest in returning to classical texts made study of and access to the Bible of great importance.

AP® KEY CONCEPTS

1.1 The worldview of European intellectuals shifted from one based on ecclesiastical and classical authority to one based primarily on inquiry and observation of the natural world.
    I. A revival of classical texts led to new methods of scholarship and new values in both society and religion.

1.3 Religious pluralism challenged the concept of a unified Europe.
    I. The Protestant and Catholic Reformations fundamentally changed theology, religious institutions, and culture.

PROTESTANT LEADERS

- Martin Luther (1483–1546) was a German theologian who was discontented with the medieval Christian teachings that God required perfect righteousness for salvation. Luther argued on behalf of "justification by faith alone" whereby grace was given freely to those who believed in Jesus Christ. In 1517, Luther famously attacked the Catholic system of indulgences promoted by preachers like John Tetzel, when he posted his ninety-five theses on the door of Castle Church in Wittenberg. Condemned to heresy in 1520, Luther was protected by friends who hid him in a castle, where he translated the New Testament into German, using Erasmus's Greek text and Latin translation.
- Ulrich Zwingli (1484–1531) headed the Reformation in Switzerland. He was opposed to the sale of indulgences and to religious superstition. Zwingli successfully petitioned for the end to clerical celibacy and the clerical right to marry, which was adopted by all Protestant groups. Zwingli believed that anything that lacked literal support in Scripture was not to be believed. He questioned traditional behaviors like fasting, adoration of saints, pilgrimages, and other sacraments. His beliefs translated into a regime of harsh discipline in Zurich, and

made Switzerland an example of puritanical Protestantism. Zwingli and Luther disagreed in the famous Marburg Colloquy (1529) over the presence of Christ's body in the Eucharist.

■ John Calvin (1509–1564) was the leader of the Calvinists, who believed in divine predestination or the concept of "the elect" and the individual's duty to reform society according to God's plan. Calvin's *Institutes of Christian Religion* is a theological statement of the Protestant faith. Calvin believed in the unity of church and state, and he stressed the sovereignty of God over all creation. He instituted a theocracy in Geneva.

AP® KEY CONCEPTS

1.3 Religious pluralism challenged the concept of a unified Europe.

I. The Protestant and Catholic reformations fundamentally changed theology, religious institutions, and culture.

II. Religious reform both increased state control of religious institutions and provided justifications for challenging state authority.

THE ENGLISH REFORMATION

Protestant ideas did not take hold in England until the sixteenth century. Important figures are listed below.

■ Martin Bucer, a Strasbourg reformer who influenced Calvin, was forced into exile during the Augsburg Interim and helped to draft the religious texts of the English Reformation.

■ William Tyndale (1492–1536) translated the New Testament into English in 1524–1525, and it began to circulate in England in 1526.

■ Cardinal Thomas Wolsey (1475–1540) and Sir Thomas More (1478–1535), chief ministers to King Henry VIII, guided the royal response to English Protestantism.

■ Henry VIII (r. 1509–1547), married to Catherine of Aragon, who did not produce an heir; in order to divorce her and then to marry Anne Boleyn, he converted himself (and the rest of England) to Anglicanism.

■ Thomas Cranmer (1489–1556) and Thomas Cromwell (1485–1540), Lutheran sympathizers who helped Henry VIII declare himself supreme ruler over English affairs, which enabled him to take charge of the Church of England and put an end to Catholic interference with his policies.

■ Edward VI (r. 1547–1553), Henry's son, presided over the flourishing of Protestantism in England. Oversaw all vestiges of Catholicism removed from churches and English life.

AP® KEY CONCEPTS

1.3 Religious pluralism challenged the concept of a unified Europe.

I. The Protestant and Catholic reformations fundamentally changed theology, religious institutions, and culture.

III. Conflicts among religious groups overlapped with political and economic competition within and among states.

THE COUNTER-REFORMATION

The Catholic Counter-Reformation consisted of both reforms that sprang from within the church, and reforms that emerged in reaction to the Protestant Reformation.

■ The Society of Jesus, the Jesuits, was one of the most influential Counter-Reformation groups, organized by Ignatius of Loyola in the 1530s. Loyola's *Spiritual Exercises* embodied a program of spiritual disciplines that encouraged believers to transform their spiritual selves through discipline and practice.

- The Council of Trent, the result of an effort by Emperor Charles V to force Pope Paul to reassert church doctrine, met from 1545–1563, and was attended predominantly by Italians. The council made reforms in internal church affairs (including restricting the selling of church offices and religious relics), strengthened the authority of local bishops, and subjected them to new rules requiring them to reside in their dioceses and be visible and accessible to their congregations.

AP® KEY CONCEPTS

1.3 Religious pluralism challenged the concept of a unified Europe.

I. The Protestant and Catholic reformations fundamentally changed theology, religious institutions, and culture.

III. Conflicts among religious groups overlapped with political and economic competition within and among states.

1.5 European society and the experiences of everyday life were increasingly shaped by commercial and agricultural capitalism, notwithstanding the persistence of medieval social and economic structures.

IV. The family remained the primary social and economic institution of early modern Europe and took several forms, including the nuclear family.

V. Popular culture, leisure activities, and rituals reflecting the persistence of folk ideas reinforced and sometimes challenged communal ties and norms.

Multiple-Choice Questions

Questions 1–3 refer to the following map.

The Empire of Charles V

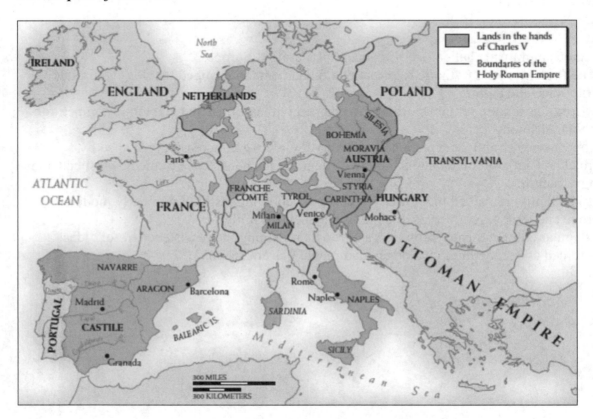

1. In this map, which of these countries was most threatened by the power of Charles V?
    A. England
    B. Portugal
    C. France
    D. Poland

2. Which of these best characterizes the power of Charles V in the Holy Roman Empire?
    A. weak
    B. limited
    C. negligible
    D. complete

3. Which of these was the most likely barrier to the power of Charles V in Italy?
   A. the papacy
   B. Naples
   C. France
   D. Castile

Questions 4–5 refer to the following excerpt.

Calvin on Predestination

No one who wishes to be thought religious dares outright to deny predestination, by which God chooses some for the hope of life, and condemns others to eternal death. But men entangle it with captious quibbles; and especially those who make foreknowledge the ground of it. We indeed attribute to God both predestination and foreknowledge; but we call it absurd to subordinate one to the other. When we attribute foreknowledge to God we mean that all things have always been and eternally remain before God's eyes so that to his knowledge nothing is future or past, but all things are present; and present not in the sense that they are reproduced in imagination (as we are aware of past events which are retained in our memory), but present in the sense that he really sees and observes them placed, as it were, before his eyes. And this foreknowledge extends over the whole universe and over every creature. By predestination we mean the eternal decree of God, by which he has decided in his own mind what he wishes to happen in the case of each individual. For all men are not created on an equal footing, but for some eternal life is preordained, for others, eternal damnation . . .

4. According to Calvin, divine "foreknowledge" and predestination are
   A. part of the same idea.
   B. mutually exclusive.
   C. the same thing.
   D. erroneous doctrines.

5. For Calvin, humans cannot affect their own salvation because
   A. they are inherently evil.
   B. they are already saved.
   C. they lack faith.
   D. their fates are already determined.

Questions 6–8 refer to the following map.

Religions in Europe c. 1560

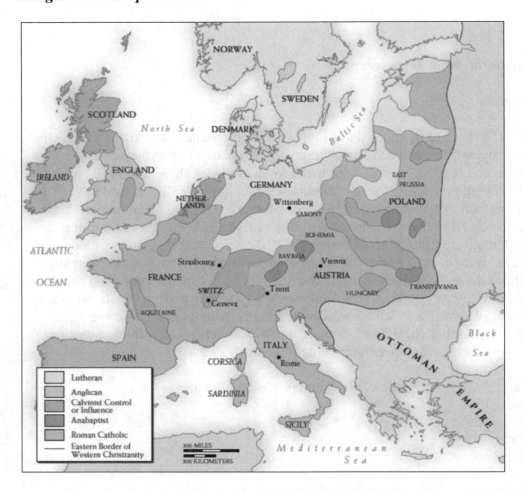

6. Looking at this map, which area of Europe remained predominantly Catholic?
   A. northern
   B. central
   C. southern
   D. eastern

7. Which of these nations was most divided by the Protestant Reformation?
   A. Spain
   B. Poland
   C. Italy
   D. Spain

8. Where was Lutheranism strongest in this period?
   A. France
   B. Poland
   C. England
   D. Germany

Questions 9–10 refer to the following excerpt.

The Power of the Jesuits

Let us with the utmost pains strain every nerve of our strength to exhibit this virtue of obedience, firstly to the Highest Pontiff, then to the Superiors of the Society; so that in all things, to which obedience can be extended with charity, we may be most ready to obey his voice, just as if it issued from Christ our Lord . . . directing to this goal all our strength and intention in the Lord, that holy obedience may be enjoined on us with great readiness, with spiritual joy and perseverance; by persuading ourselves that all things [commanded] are just; by rejecting with a kind of blind obedience all opposing opinion or judgment of our own. . . . And let each one persuade himself that they that live under obedience ought to allow themselves to be borne and ruled by divine providence working through their Superiors exactly as if they were a corpse which suffers itself to be borne and handled in any way whatsoever; or just as an old man's stick which serves him who holds it in his hand wherever and for whatever purpose he wishes to use it . . .

9. Which of these is the main characteristic expected of Jesuits?
   A. independence
   B. intelligence
   C. submission
   D. creativity

10. The phrase "just as an old man's stick" likens the members of the Jesuit order to
    A. slaves.
    B. priests.
    C. tools.
    D. the sick.

Questions 11–12 refer to the following excerpt.

Martin Luther, Against Catholicism, *1535*

If the pope were the head of the Christian Church, then the Church were a monster with two heads, seeing that St. Paul says that Christ is her head. The pope may well be, and is, the head of the false Church. Where the linnet is, there is also the cuckoo, for he thinks his song a thousand times better than the linnet's. Even thus, the pope places himself in the Church, and so that his song may be heard, overcrowds the Church. The cuckoo is good for something, in that its appearance gives tidings that summer is at hand; so the pope serves to show us that the last day of judgment approaches. There are many that think I am too fierce against popedom; on the contrary, I complain that I am, alas! too mild; I wish I could breathe out lightning against pope and popedom, and that every word were a thunderbolt.

11. According to this passage the position claimed by Catholic popes is
    A. well founded.
    B. falsely taken.
    C. merited.
    D. too humble.

12. Which of these best summarizes Luther's message in this passage?
    A. Christians owe no allegiance to the popes.
    B. The Catholic Church and its leaders are in error.
    C. The Catholic Church needs to be reformed.
    D. He hopes to take over as pope.

Questions 13–15 refer to the following excerpt.

Martin Luther, Ninety-five Theses, document posted on door of Castle Church, Wittenberg, 1517

32. Those who believe that they can be certain of their salvation because they have indulgence letters will be eternally damned, together with their teachers.
33. Men must especially be on guard against those who say that the pope's pardons are that inestimable gift of God by which man is reconciled to him.
34. For the graces of indulgences are concerned only with the penalties of sacramental satisfaction established by man.
35. They who teach that contrition is not necessary on the part of those who intend to buy souls out of purgatory or to buy confessional privileges preach unchristian doctrine.
36. Any truly repentant Christian has a right to full remission of penalty and guilt, even without indulgence letters.
37. Any true Christian, whether living or dead, participates in all the blessings of Christ and the church; and this is granted him by God, even without indulgence letters.

13. For Luther, indulgences are
    A. too expensive.
    B. useless.
    C. legitimate.
    D. only for true Christians.

14. For Luther, the way to avoid punishment for one's sins is to
    A. buy indulgences.
    B. seek the pope's forgiveness.
    C. repent.
    D. follow the Catholic Church.

15. In this passage, Luther implicitly challenges the authority of
    A. the Catholic Church.
    B. priests.
    C. the Bible.
    D. Christ.

Short-Answer Question

Several new religious orders—including the Jesuits and Capuchins—emerged in the sixteenth century.

a. Choose ONE of the following and explain why your choice represents the key factor leading to this development.

- The Protestant Reformation began in Germany.
- The Council of Trent met for two decades.
- Lay religious movements grew in popularity in the late Middle Ages.

b. Contrast your choice against ONE of the other options, demonstrating why that option is not as significant as your choice.

Long-Essay Question

What were the most important factors that shaped religious reform as it spread across Europe in the fifteenth and sixteenth centuries?

Answers and Explanations: AP® Practice Test

Multiple-Choice Questions

1. **C** France was threatened by Charles V because it was surrounded by the territories controlled by him. Charles even controlled some territory within France itself.
2. **B** Although Charles V was Holy Roman Emperor, his direct control was limited to his own lands (marked here in purple).
3. **A** The Papal States, centered in Rome, lay across the Italian peninsula, blocking Charles V from uniting his northern and southern Italian territories.
4. **A** For Calvin, predestination is just part of divine foreknowledge.
5. **D** According to Calvin's idea of predestination, humans can do nothing to save or damn themselves because their fates are already determined.
6. **C** Southern Europe—that is Spain, France and Italy—remained predominantly Catholic.
7. **B** Germany was divided into three distinct confessions, although it remained majority Catholic.
8. **D** Not surprisingly, Lutheranism was strongest in the region of its origin: Germany.
9. **C** The Jesuit order was founded on the idea of military discipline and obedience.
10. **C** In this passage, the members of the order should be passive tools in the hands of their superiors.
11. **B** Luther argues forcefully here that the popes claim powers that belong to Christ alone.
12. **D** In this excerpt, as elsewhere, Luther calls the entire Catholic Church false, and especially targets the popes as usurpers, having taken the place of Christ as leaders of the Church.
13. **B** Luther argues that indulgences are useless because all "true Christians" are already saved.
14. **C** For Luther, repentance is all that is needed for all sins to be forgiven.
15. **A** Luther argues against the power of the pope to issue indulgences (pardons) and implies that the Catholic Church has little power to effect salvation.

Long-Essay Question

What were the most important factors that shaped religious reform as it spread across Europe in the fifteenth and sixteenth centuries?

(Key topics to focus and elaborate on)
- Political situations
- Groups involved in reform
- Nationalist sentiments

CHAPTER 4

The Age of Religious Wars

In this era, religious conflict among Protestants and Catholics and dynastic rivalries fueled wars.

THE FRENCH WARS OF RELIGION (1562–1598)

- French Protestants, or **Huguenots**, were under surveillance in France as early as 1520, when Lutheran ideas began to circulate in Paris. Huguenot persecution was essentially a policy under Henry II, and it continued until Henry IV (Henry of Navarre) took the throne in 1589.
- Catherine de Médicis, who served as regent for Charles IX, sought allies among the Protestant factions. In 1562, she issued the January Edict, which granted Protestants freedom to worship publicly outside towns and to hold synods.
- In March of 1562, a duke from the powerful Guise family led a massacre on the Huguenots, starting the French Wars of religion. In the series of wars that followed, Huguenots and their Protestant allies fought against the Guise faction. Catherine de Médicis aligned herself with the Guises, and plotted against Coligny, the leader of the Huguenots. Catherine supported the 1572 St. Bartholomew's Day Massacre, in which 3,000 Huguenots were killed. Within three days, 20,000 Huguenots had been executed.
- The Peace of Beaulieu, led by Henry III in May, 1576, granted Huguenots almost complete religious and civil freedom, but within seven months, the Catholic League forced Henry to back down from these liberties. After Henry III's murder, the Protestant Henry IV (Henry of Navarre) rose to the throne, converted to Catholicism, and proclaimed a formal religious settlement with the Protestants. Called the Edict of Nantes and made on April 13, 1598, this proclamation recognized and sanctioned Huguenots' rights within France. It granted them freedom of worship, right of assembly, and a series of other liberties.

AP® KEY CONCEPTS

1.1 The worldview of European intellectuals shifted from one based on ecclesiastical and classical authority to one based primarily on inquiry and observation of the natural world.

II. The invention of printing promoted the dissemination of new ideas.

1.2 The struggle for sovereignty within and among states resulted in varying degrees of political centralization.

III. The competition for power between monarchs and corporate groups produced different distributions of governmental authority in European states.

1.3 Religious pluralism challenged the concept of a unified Europe.

II. Religious reform both increased state control of religious institutions and provided justifications for challenging state authority.

III. Conflicts among religious groups overlapped with political and economic competition within and among states.

IMPERIAL SPAIN AND THE REIGN OF PHILIP II (R. 1556–1598)

Philip II of Spain was the extremely powerful Catholic ruler of Habsburg lands of Bohemia, Austria, and Hungary, as well as Castile, in Spain.

- Spain dominated the Mediterranean in the Battle of Lepanto, in which the Turkish fleet was brutally put down. Under Philip II, Spain annexed Portugal and gained access to their empires in Africa, India, and the Americas.
- Philip did not see similar success in his attempts to conquer the Netherlands. When Cardinal Granvelle attempted to institute ecclesiastical reform in the Netherlands, William of Orange and the Count of Egmont led the resistance. Egmont was executed, and the resistance was put down by the Duke of Alba, but the Dutch continued their campaign against Spanish governance.
- In 1576, Catholic and Protestant provinces came together in opposition to Spain in what is known as the Pacification of Ghent. True peace with Spain was not achieved until 1609, when the Twelve Years' Truce gave the northern provinces independence. Full recognition was finalized in the Peace of Westphalia in 1648.

AP® KEY CONCEPTS

1.3 Religious pluralism challenged the concept of a unified Europe.
   II. Religious reform both increased state control of religious institutions and provided justifications for challenging state authority.

1.5 European society and the experiences of everyday life were increasingly shaped by commercial and agricultural capitalism, notwithstanding the persistence of medieval social and economic structures.
   I. Economic change produced new social patterns, while traditions of hierarchy and status persisted.
   III. Population shifts and growing commerce caused the expansion of cities, which often found their traditional political and social structures stressed by the growth.

ENGLAND AND SPAIN (1553–1603)

The Catholic Mary Tudor (Mary I) ascended the English throne after challenging the right of Protestant Lady Jane Grey. Mary brought sweeping change to England, restoring the Catholicism of Henry VIII and executing the Protestants Thomas Cranmer, Hugh Latimer, and John Hooper.

- Mary's half-sister, Elizabeth I, was her successor following a 1559 Act of Supremacy that undid much of the anti-Protestant legislation Mary had enacted. The act asserted Elizabeth's right as "supreme governor" over spiritual and secular affairs. Elizabeth strove to maintain a middle ground by not granting too much control to Catholics or Protestants.
- Facing a real threat from Spain, England allied with France in 1571. At this time, explorers Francis Drake and John Hawkins were preying on Spanish ships. Elizabeth's decision to execute Mary Stuart, Queen of Scots, an ardent Catholic and French royal with a legitimate heir to the Scottish throne, aroused Catholic anger.
- Philip II of Spain ordered his Armada to prepare for war with England. This battle resulted in a complete victory for England and encouraged European Protestants.

AP® Key Concepts

1.2 The struggle for sovereignty within and among states resulted in varying degrees of political centralization.

   III. The competition for power between monarchs and corporate groups produced different distributions of governmental authority in European states.

1.3 Religious pluralism challenged the concept of a unified Europe.

   II. Religious reform both increased state control of religious institutions and provided justifications for challenging state authority.

   III. Conflicts among religious groups overlapped with political and economic competition within and among states.

THE THIRTY YEARS' WAR (1618–1648)

The Thirty Years' War was a complicated series of battles in four phases—Bohemian (1618–1625), Danish (1625–1629), Swedish (1630–1635), and the Swedish-French (1635–1648)—between countries with radically opposed political and religious agendas.

■ In the Bohemian Period, Calvinists demanded more freedom from Catholic Habsburg ruler Ferdinand. Protestant nobility responded to Ferdinand's revocation of religious rights by throwing two of his regents out of a window in the "defenestration of Prague."

■ In the Danish Period, King Christian IV of Denmark, tried to bring Protestantism to Germany and was forced to retreat by Maximilian. In 1629, Ferdinand outlawed Calvinism by issuing the Edict of Restitution.

■ In the Swedish Period, military tactics of King Gustavus Adolphus of Sweden helped Protestants win the battle at Breitenfeld. The Swedes refused to join the Peace of Prague Agreement—a compromise between German Protestant states and Ferdinand.

■ The Swedish-French Period, the final phase of the Thirty Years' War, involved French, Swedish, and Spanish soldiers wreaking havoc in Germany. At the most destructive point in the war, religious issues became secondary to political ones.

■ The Treaty of Westphalia of 1648 stopped Ferdinand's Edict of Restitution and recognized Calvinists. The independence of the Swiss Confederacy and provinces of Holland was proclaimed. German princes were acknowledged as the supreme rulers over their principalities. The treaty broadened the legal status of Protestantism in the realm, but it perpetuated Germany's internal division and political weakness.

AP® KEY CONCEPTS

1.2 The struggle for sovereignty within and among states resulted in varying degrees of political centralization.

   III. The competition for power between monarchs and corporate groups produced different distributions of governmental authority in European states.

1.3 Religious pluralism challenged the concept of a unified Europe.

   II. Religious reform both increased state control of religious institutions and provided justifications for challenging state authority.

   III. Conflicts among religious groups overlapped with political and economic competition within and among states.

CHAPTER 4: AP® PRACTICE TEST

Multiple-Choice Questions

Questions 1–3 refer to the following excerpt.

Theodore Beza Defends the Right to Resist Tyranny

It is apparent that there is a mutual obligation between the king and the officers of a kingdom; that the government of the kingdom is not in the hands of the king in its entirety, but only the sovereign degree; that each of the officers has a share in accord with his degree; and that there are definite conditions on either side. If these conditions are not observed by the inferior officers, it is the part of the sovereign to dismiss and punish them. . . . If the king, hereditary or elective, clearly goes back on the conditions without which he would not have been recognized and acknowledged, can there be any doubt that the lesser magistrates of the kingdom, of the cities, and of the provinces, the administration of which they have received from the sovereignty itself, are free of their oath, at least to the extent that they are entitled to resist flagrant oppression of the realm which they swore to defend and protect according to their office and their particular jurisdiction? . . . We must now speak of the third class of subjects, which though admittedly subject to the sovereign in a certain respect, is, in another respect, and in cases of necessity the protector of the rights of the sovereignty itself, and is established to hold the sovereign to his duty, and even, if need be, to constrain and punish him. . . . The people is prior to all the magistrates, and does not exist for them, but they for it. . . . Whenever law and equity prevailed, nations neither created nor accepted kings except upon definite conditions. From this it follows that when kings flagrantly violate these terms, these who have the power to give them their authority have no less power to deprive them of it.

1. For this author, disobedience to a king is characterized as
   A. illegal.
   B. sinful.
   C. a right.
   D. sometimes legitimate.

2. This author implies that political power comes from
   A. God.
   B. the people
   C. magistrates.
   D. the law.

3. According to Beza, which of these describes the obligations of different political groups?
   A. Kings have rights, but not duties towards their subjects.
   B. Kings and magistrates have both powers and responsibilities towards those they govern.
   C. The people have duties, but no rights.
   D. The people are sovereign over monarchs.

Questions 4–6 refer to the following image.

The Milch Cow

Not long time since I saw a cow
Did Flanders represent
Upon whose back King Philip rode
As being Malcontent
The Queen of England giving hay
Whereon the cow did feed

As one that was her greatest help
In her distress and need.
The Prince of Orange milked the cow
And made his purse the pail.
The cow did sh** in monsieurs hand
While he did hold the tail.

4. This political cartoon appears to represent the perspective of
    A. Spain.
    B. France.
    C. England.
    D. Flanders.

5. Which of these best characterizes Flanders as represented in this image?
    A. strongly independent
    B. poor
    C. militaristic
    D. a victim of its more powerful neighbors

6. Which of these is portrayed as Flanders' worst enemy here?
    A. France
    B. Spain
    C. England
    D. the Netherlands

Questions 7–9 refer to the following map.

Germany in 1547

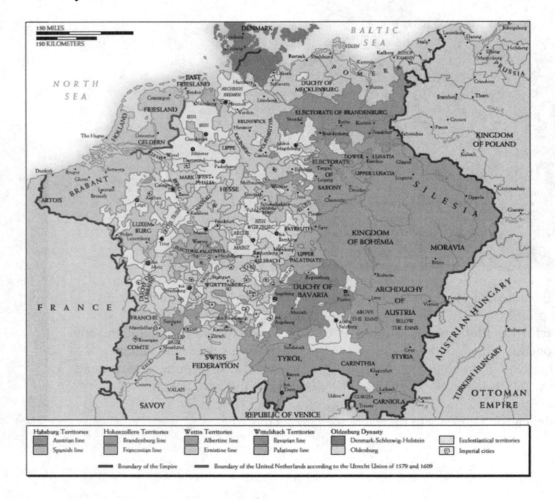

7. Based on this map, Germany is best characterized as
    A. ethnically homogenous.
    B. politically divided.
    C. steadily growing.
    D. religiously united.

8. Which of these appear to be the Holy Roman Emperor's strongest contender for power in Germany in this period?
   A. the Catholic Church
   B. the Swiss
   C. the Netherlands
   D. Saxony

9. What was the main power base of the Habsburgs?
   A. Poland
   B. Saxony
   C. Bavaria
   D. Austria

Questions 10–12 refer to the following map.

The Holy Roman Empire about 1618

10. Which of these best describes the relative strengths of the major religions of the Holy Roman Empire in this period?
    A. Catholicism was far weaker than the Protestant religions.
    B. Lutheranism had spread through most of the empire.
    C. Calvinism and Lutheranism were equally powerful.
    D. Catholicism controlled most of the empire.

11. Which of these patterns in the Holy Roman Empire paralleled the pattern seen in the rest of Europe?
    A. More eastern regions were Protestant.
    B. Catholicism was stronger in the south.
    C. Religious conflicts led to political fragmentation.
    D. Urban areas were more commonly Catholic.

12. The influence of Calvinism on the emergence of Switzerland appears to have been
    A. fatal.
    B. unimportant.
    C. positive.
    D. divisive.

Questions 13–15 refer to the following map.

Religious Divisions about 1600

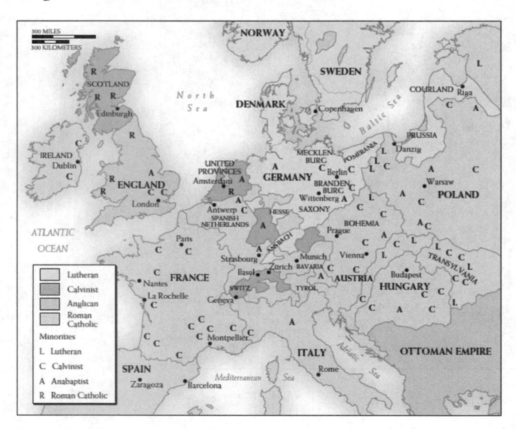

13. Around 1600, which of these was least divided, religiously?
    A. Italy
    B. France
    C. Germany
    D. England

14. According to this map, in France in 1600, Calvinism represented
    A. a dwindling minority.
    B. a serious challenge.
    C. the dominant religion.
    D. southern regions.

15. In this period, in the British Isles religion appeared to be
    A. a unifying factor.
    B. an unimportant issue.
    C. dictated by England.
    D. a source of division.

Short-Answer Question

The Thirty Years' War weakened the Holy Roman Empire.

a. Choose ONE of the following and explain why your choice represents the key factor leading to this development.

- Religious divisions aligned with political divisions in many countries.
- The Habsburgs controlled vast areas of Europe.
- Calvinism had not been protected by the Peace of Augsburg.

b. Contrast your choice against ONE of the other options, demonstrating why that option is not as significant as your choice.

Long-Essay Question

Why did the French Wars of Religion become so bloody?

Multiple-Choice Questions

1. **D** Beza argues that kings rule conditionally, and when those conditions are not met, resistance is allowed.
2. **B** Beza argues that governments exist to serve the people, and that the people give kings and magistrates their authority.
3. **B** For Beza, kings and magistrates have to fulfill their obligations, or risk losing their position.
4. **C** Not only is the caption in English, but the English are seen as most beneficial to the cow (Flanders.)
5. **D** Flanders is depicted as wealthy, but it is preyed upon by the powerful monarchies that surround it.
6. **B** While the other powers are trying to use Flanders to their own advantage, Spain is much more merciless.
7. **B** In this period, Germany was composed of hundreds of independent states, nominally under the authority of the Holy Roman Emperor.
8. **A** The ecclesiastical territories shown here were vast, making the Catholic Church a major threat to the emperor.
9. **D** The Habsburgs were an Austrian dynasty that eventually gained control of the entire Holy Roman Empire.
10. **C** While Catholicism still was prevalent, Lutheranism and Calvinism each controlled perhaps a quarter of the empire.
11. **B** In general, northern Europe was dominated by Protestantism, while southern Europe was dominated by Catholicism.
12. **C** Switzerland emerged not because it was unified by a nationality, but because it was unified by Calvinism and by opposition to imperial rule.
13. **A** Italy was predominantly Catholic with only a very small Calvinist enclave in the north.
14. **B** Calvinism was not only a large minority in France, but it spread throughout the country, representing a serious threat to Catholicism.
15. **D** By this time, the British nations had split along religious and nationalist lines—England, Scotland, and Ireland—although these three nations were nominally all under English rule.

Long-Essay Question

Why did the French Wars of Religion become so bloody?

(Key topics to focus and elaborate on)
- Political factions
- External involvement
- Key Calvinists

CHAPTER 5

European State Consolidation in the Seventeenth and Eighteenth Centuries

In the seventeenth century, England and France moved in different political directions—one toward a constitutional form of government, and the other toward monarchy rule.

THE NETHERLANDS: GOLDEN AGE TO DECLINE

- The United Provinces of the Netherlands were the only new state to appear in Europe during the early modern period. A formal republic, the Netherlands central government exercised its authority through cooperation with the provinces.
- Dutch life was marked by religious toleration and an economic prosperity that derived from the country's extensive trade and overseas commercial empires and its urban consolidation. The highly advanced Dutch capital system financed economic life throughout Europe.

AP® KEY CONCEPTS

1.2 The struggle for sovereignty within and among states resulted in varying degrees of political centralization.
  II. The competitive state system led to new patterns of diplomacy and new forms of warfare.
1.3 Religious pluralism challenged the concept of a unified Europe.
  III. Conflicts among religious groups overlapped with political and economic competition within and among states.
1.5 European society and the experiences of everyday life were increasingly shaped by commercial and agricultural capitalism, notwithstanding the persistence of medieval social and economic structures.
  III. Population shifts and growing commerce caused the expansion of cities, which often found their traditional political and social structures stressed by the growth.
2.1 Different models of political sovereignty affected the relationship among states and between states and individuals.
  II. Challenges to absolutism resulted in alternative political systems.

TWO MODELS OF EUROPEAN POLITICAL DEVELOPMENT

- Monarchy: England's monarchs' efforts to get new sources of income threatened the country's political and economic stability. In France, Louis XIV made the French nobility dependent upon his patronage, but he allowed the Parlement of Paris to oversee his royal decrees and regional parlements to administer local taxation.
- Religion: In England, the Protestant religious movement of **Puritanism** opposed the Stuart monarchy and sought to limit its powers. In France, Louis XIV, with the support of Roman Catholics, crushed the Protestant dissident movement to create religious unity.

- Government: The English system of a **parliamentary monarchy** remained ingrained in the political culture, even if it was not the strong institution it would become by the end of the seventeenth century. The parliamentary government in England involved nobility and large landowners trying to limit the power of the monarch to interfere on a local level. The French nobility preferred to support Louis XIV's **political absolutism** and to benefit from his patronage. In France, the Estates General was not an institutional base for political reform.

AP ® KEY CONCEPTS

1.2 The struggle for sovereignty within and among states resulted in varying degrees of political centralization.

    II. The competitive state system led to new patterns of diplomacy and new forms of warfare.

    III. The competition for power between monarchs and corporate groups produced different distributions of governmental authority in European states.

2.1 Different models of political sovereignty affected the relationship among states and between states and individuals.

    II. Challenges to absolutism resulted in alternative political systems.

CONSTITUTIONAL CRISIS AND SETTLEMENT IN STUART ENGLAND

- King James I was an outsider, a Scot who advocated the divine right of kings. James angered many of his subjects by his decision to maintain and augment Anglican episcopacy. He enforced a series of levies on his subjects—new custom duties known as *impositions* that were unpopular with Parliament. In 1620, Puritan separatists left England and founded the Plymouth Colony in Cape Cod Bay in North America. Another group left a few years later and founded the Massachusetts Bay Colony.
- Charles I forced more unpopular levies and taxes on the English people, and stationed troops en route to war with Spain in private homes. Parliament forced Charles to agree to the Petition of Right, a document that required the monarch to gain consent of Parliament before levying taxes or quartering soldiers in private homes. In 1629, Parliament declared that Charles's levying of taxes without consent was an act of treason.
- In 1641, Parliament presented Charles with the Grand Remonstrance, a summary of grievances. Charles invaded Parliament with his soldiers, and Parliament began to raise an army of its own, bringing about the civil war (1642–1646) of England. Oliver Cromwell (1599–1658) led the reorganized parliamentary army, known as the New Model Army into victory against Charles I's forces. England became a Puritan republic from 1649 until 1660, led by the military dictator Cromwell, who ruled as "Lord Protector" until his death in 1658. By then, the exiled Charles II was permitted to return and to bring peaceful rule back to England.
- Charles II's rule is known as the Stuart Restoration because it brought England back to the conditions of the 1640s, when an Anglican Church was at the fore of religion, and the monarch had little or no responsibility to call Parliament.
- James II renewed fears of a Catholic England by openly appointing Catholics to high positions in the court and in the army. In 1689, after James fled to France in the face of William of Orange's superior army, William and Mary were declared the new monarchs of England. This bloodless accession was known as the **Glorious Revolution**, and the subsequent Bill of Rights, which William and Mary recognized, limited the powers of the monarchy, prohibited Roman Catholics from occupying the throne, and guaranteed the role

of Parliament in government.

1.2 The struggle for sovereignty within and among states resulted in varying degrees of political centralization.

　II. The competitive state system led to new patterns of diplomacy and new forms of warfare.

　III. The competition for power between monarchs and corporate groups produced different distributions of governmental authority in European states.

2.1 Different models of political sovereignty affected the relationship among states and between states and individuals.

　I. In much of Europe, absolute monarchy was established over the course of the seventeenth and eighteenth centuries.

　II. Challenges to absolutism resulted in alternative political systems.

　III. After 1648, dynastic and state interests, along with Europe's expanding colonial empires, influenced the diplomacy of European states and frequently led to war.

RISE OF ABSOLUTE MONARCHY IN FRANCE

- Louis XIV ("The Sun King") successfully suppressed discontent among the nobility and landowners through absolute monarchy and strict Catholic rule. His motto was "one king, one law, one faith," and he sought glory for France in an aggressive series of foreign wars. Louis XIV was helped early in his reign by Cardinal Mazarin, who continued Richelieu's policy of centralization of government.

- Louis XIV was a master of propaganda and the cultivation of his public image. He believed himself to have a divine right to his royal authority and was contented to be unbound by the rules of princes and parliaments. He is famous for his alleged outburst, "L'état c'est moi" ("I am the state").

- Louis XIV's palace court and permanent residence at Versailles were symbolic of his majesty. Louis supported religious conformity and helped to suppress the rise of the **Jansenists**, a group of Catholics opposed to the influence of Jesuits on Catholic theology.

- During Louis XIV's reign, France was superior to other European countries in its administrative bureaucracy, military, and national unity. Jean-Baptiste Colbert, controller general of finances, helped Louis XIV consolidate France's wealth and create an economic base for funding wars. Colbert's close government control of the economy (known as mercantilism) aimed to maximize exports and internal stores of bullion.

- In 1685, Louis revoked the Edict of Nantes, which resulted in the immediate closure of Protestant churches and schools, the expulsion of Protestant ministers, the forced conversion of the laity, and the voluntary emigration of more than a quarter million French people, who joined resistance to France throughout the world.

AP® KEY CONCEPTS

2.1 Different models of political sovereignty affected the relationship among states and between states and individuals.

> I. In much of Europe, absolute monarchy was established over the course of the seventeenth and eighteenth centuries.
>
> II. Challenges to absolutism resulted in alternative political systems.
>
> III. After 1648, dynastic and state interests, along with Europe's expanding colonial empires, influenced the diplomacy of European states and frequently led to war.

2.2 The expansion of European commerce accelerated the growth of a worldwide economic network.

> III. Commercial rivalries influenced diplomacy and warfare among European states in the early modern era.

2.3 The popularization and dissemination of the scientific revolution and the application of its methods to political, social, and ethical issues led to an increased, although not unchallenged, emphasis on reason in European culture.

> I. Rational and empirical thought challenged traditional values and ideas.

CENTRAL AND EASTERN EUROPE

Central and eastern Europe were less economically advanced than their western European rivals, and their economies were more agrarian than maritime in nature.

- Charles XII of Sweden came to the throne and led a strong campaign against the Russians in the Great Northern War (1700–1721), but he was ultimately defeated. He exhausted Swedish military and economic resources and lost a section of the Baltic coast.

- The Ottoman Empire was overextended by the end of the seventeenth century, and its economy was dependent on the loyalty of local rulers in far-flung provinces. Russia began to extend its territory into the Ottoman Empire, and the Turks made a treaty with the Habsburgs and surrendered their control of revenues from Hungary, Transylvania, Croatia, and Slavonia.

- King John Sobieski (r. 1674–1696) struggled against a nobility that refused to submit to authority. Poland couldn't collect taxes or build an army without unity in the legislative body, the ***Sejm***.

- The Austrian Habsburgs consolidated their political power in the modern Czech Republic, Slovakia, Moravia, Silesia, Hungary, Croatia, and Transylvania. In the early eighteenth century, the Habsburgs received the former Spanish Netherlands, Lombardy, and the kingdom of Naples. These inherited territories faced problems of Magyar resistance in Hungary.

- The Hohenzollerns of Brandenburg-Prussia acquired a collection of land holdings and transformed them into a single unit. Frederick William (r. 1640–1688) forged these disparate areas by breaking up nobles' estates and organizing a royal bureaucracy. Known as the Great Elector, Frederick imposed taxes to build up a strong military, members of which took an oath of loyalty to him. Frederick I (the Great Elector's son) built palaces, patronized the arts, and eventually was rewarded for putting his army at the disposal of the Habsburg Holy Roman Emperor with the title of King of Prussia. Frederick I's son, Frederick William I, was a disciple of military discipline, and he built up the size of his army to more than 80,000 in 1740. The army became a great symbol of Prussian power.

2.1 Different models of political sovereignty affected the relationship among states and between states and individuals.

    I. In much of Europe, absolute monarchy was established over the course of the seventeenth and eighteenth centuries.

    II. Challenges to absolutism resulted in alternative political systems.

    III. After 1648, dynastic and state interests, along with Europe's expanding colonial empires, influenced the diplomacy of European states and frequently led to war.

RUSSIA ENTERS THE EUROPEAN POLITICAL ARENA

- The reign of Ivan the Terrible ended with a period of anarchy known as the Time of Troubles.
- In 1613, Michael Romanov was elected tsar by Russian nobles. This dynasty would rule Russia until 1917.
- In 1682, Peter the Great ascended the Russian throne as co-ruler with his half-brother, Ivan V. They rose to power under the *streltsy,* the guards of the Moscow garrison. Peter ruled personally, navigating between the jealousy of the *boyars* (nobles) and the greed of the *streltsy.* Peter's determination to Westernize Russia had five main goals: controlling the *boyars* and *streltsy,* gaining secular control of the church, reorganizing governmental administration, growing the economy, and building a major army and navy.

2.1 Different models of political sovereignty affected the relationship among states and between states and individuals.

    I. In much of Europe, absolute monarchy was established over the course of the seventeenth and eighteenth centuries.

Multiple-Choice Questions

Questions 1–2 refer to the following excerpt.

King James I Defends Popular Recreation Against the Puritans

With our own ears we heard the general complaint of our people, that they were barred from all lawful recreation and exercise upon the Sunday's afternoon, after the ending of all divine service, which cannot but produce two evils: the one the hindering of the conversion of many [Roman Catholic subjects], whom their priests will take occasion hereby to vex, persuading them that no honest mirth or recreation is lawful or tolerable in our religion, which cannot but breed a great discontentment in our people's hearts, especially as such as are peradventure upon the point of turning [to the Church of England]: the other inconvenience is, that this prohibition barreth the common and meaner sort of people from using such exercises as may make their bodies more able for war, when we or our successors shall have occasion to use them; and in place thereof sets up filthy tipplings and drunkenness, and breeds a number of idle and discontented speeches in their ale-houses. For when shall the common people have leave to exercise, if not upon the Sundays and holy days, seeing they must apply their labor and win their living in all working days? . . . [A]s for our good people's lawful recreation, our pleasure likewise is, that after the end of divine service our good people be not disturbed, . . . or discouraged from any lawful recreation, such as dancing, either men or women; archery for men, leaping, vaulting, or any other such harmless recreation, or from having of Hay-games, Whitsun-ales, and Morris-dances; and the setting up of May-poles and other sports therewith used; . . . but withal we do here account still as prohibited all unlawful games to be used upon Sundays only, as bear and bull-baitings . . . and at all times in the meaner sort of people by law prohibited, bowling.

And likewise we bar from this benefit and liberty all such known as recusants [Roman Catholics], either men or women, as will abstain from coming to church or divine service, being therefore unworthy of any lawful recreation after the said service, that will not first come to the church and serve God; prohibiting in like sort the said recreations to any that, though [they] conform in religion [i.e., members of the Church of England], are not present in the church at the service of God, before their going to the said recreations.

1. Which of these best characterizes James' religious stance, in the context of his time?
   A. moderate
   B. radical
   C. reactionary
   D. Puritanical

2. To what groups is James most tolerant in this decree?
   A. Catholics
   B. Puritans
   C. Anglicans
   D. Jews

Questions 3–5 refer to the following excerpt.

The Great Elector of Brandenburg-Prussia Welcomes Protestant Refugees from France

    We, Friedrich Wilhelm, by Grace of God Margrave of Brandenburg. . . . Do hereby proclaim and make known to all and sundry that since the cruel persecutions and rigorous ill-treatment in which Our co-religionists of the Evangelical-Reformed faith have for some time past been subjected in the Kingdom of France, have caused many families to remove themselves and to betake themselves out of the said Kingdom into other lands, We now . . . have been moved graciously to offer them through this Edict . . . a secure and free refuge in all Our Lands and Provinces. . . .

    Since Our Lands are not only well and amply endowed with all things necessary to support life, but also very well-suited to the reestablishment of all kinds of manufactures and trade and traffic by land and water, We permit, indeed, to those settling therein free choice to establish themselves where it is most convenient for their profession and way of living. . . .

    The personal property which they bring with them, including merchandise and other wares, is to be totally exempt from any taxes, customs dues, licenses, or other imposts of any description, and not detained in any way. . . .

    As soon as these Our French co-religionists of the Evangelical-Reformed faith have settled in any town or village, they shall be admitted to the domiciliary rights and craft freedoms customary there, gratis and without payments of any fee; and shall be entitled to the benefits, rights, and privileges enjoyed by Our other, native, subjects, residing there. . . .

    Not only are those who wish to establish manufacture of cloth, stuffs, hats, or other objects in which they are skilled to enjoy all necessary freedoms, privileges and facilities, but also provision is to be made for them to be assisted and helped as far as possible with money and anything else which they need to realize their intention. . . .

    Those who settle in the country and wish to maintain themselves by agriculture are to be given a certain plot of land to bring under cultivation and provided with whatever they need to establish themselves initially. . . .

3. What was probably a secondary motive for issuing this welcome, besides the stated reason of religious toleration?
   A. support for Catholicism
   B. encouraging settlers
   C. hostility towards Protestants
   D. war with Spain

4. This welcome is primarily directed at
    A. Dutch Calvinists.
    B. French Protestants.
    C. German Catholics.
    D. Prussian Calvinists.

5. Which of these best characterizes conditions offered for those welcomed into the Great Elector's territories?
    A. generous
    B. harsh
    C. miserable
    D. lavish, but only for Catholics

Questions 6–7 refer to the following map.

The First Three Wars of Louis XIV

6. Most of France's territorial gains were at the expense of
    A. Spain.   C. the Holy Roman Empire.
    B. Italy.   D. the Netherlands.

7. In terms of viable, strategic territorial gains, these wars appear to have been
   A. failures.
   B. enormously successful.
   C. inconclusive.
   D. moderately successful.

Questions 8–10 refer to the following excerpt.

Bishop Bossuet Defends the Divine Right of Kings

The royal power is absolute. . . . The prince need render account of his acts to no one. "I counsel thee to keep the king's commandment, and that in regard of the oath of God. Be not hasty to go out of his sight; stand not on an evil thing for he doeth whatsoever pleaseth him. Where the word of a king is, there is power; and who may say unto him, What doest thou? Whoso keepeth the commandment shall feel no evil thing" [Eccles. 8:2–5]. Without this absolute authority the king could neither do good nor repress evil. It is necessary that his power be such that no one can hope to escape him, and finally, the only protection of individuals against the public authority should be their innocence. This confirms the teaching of St. Paul: "Wilt thou then not be afraid of the power? Do that which is good" [Rom. 13:3].

God is infinite, God is all. The prince, as prince, is not regarded as a private person: he is a public personage, all the state is in him; the will of all the people is included in his. As all perfection and all strength are united in God, so all the power of individuals is united in the person of the prince. What grandeur that a single man should embody so much! . . .

Behold an immense people united in a single person; behold this holy power, paternal and absolute; behold the secret cause which governs the whole body of the state, contained in a single head: you see the image of God in the king, and you have the idea of royal majesty. God is holiness itself, goodness itself, and power itself. In these things lies the majesty of God. In the image of these things lies the majesty of the prince.

8. Relative to Louis XIV's statement "L'état, c'est moi," this excerpt by Bossuet
   A. is a complete rejection.
   B. agrees completely.
   C. has little relevance.
   D. is indecisive.

9. In this excerpt, the only limitation on the king's actions is the
   A. requirement that he do good.
   B. power of the church.
   C. law of the land.
   D. country's traditions.

Questions 10–12 refer to the following excerpt.

John Locke Denounces the Idea of Absolute Monarchy

Man being born . . . with a title to perfect freedom, and an uncontrolled enjoyment of all the rights and privileges of the law of nature, equally with any other man, or number of men in the world, hath by nature a power, not only to preserve his property, that is, his life, liberty and estate, against the injuries and attempts of other men; but to judge of, and punish the breaches of that law in others, as he is persuaded the offence deserve. . . . [T]here and there only is political society, where every one of the members hath quitted this natural power, resigned it up into the hands of the community in all cases that excludes him not from appealing for protection to the law established by it. And thus all private judgment of every particular member being excluded, the community comes to be umpire, by settled standing rules, indifferent, and the same to all parties; and by men having authority from the community, for the execution of those rules, decides all the differences that may happen between any members of that society concerning any matter of right . . .

Whenever therefore any number of men are so united into one society, as to quit every one his executive power of the law of nature, and to resign it to the public, there and there only is a political, or civil society. . . .

Hence it is evident, that absolute monarchy, which by some men is counted the only government in the world, is indeed inconsistent with civil society, and so can be no form of civil government at all; for the end of civil society, being to avoid, and remedy those inconveniencies of the state of nature, which necessarily follow from every man's being judge in his own case, by setting up a known authority, to which every one of that society may appeal upon any injury received, or controversy that may arise, and which every one of the society ought to obey; wherever any persons are, who have not such an authority to appeal to, for the decision of any difference between them, there those persons are still in the state of nature; and so is every absolute prince, in respect of those who are under his dominion.

For he being supposed to have all, both legislative and executive power in himself alone, there is no judge to be found, no appeal lies open to any one, who may fairly, and indifferently, and with authority decide, and from whose decision relief and redress may be expected of any injury or inconveniency, that may be suffered from the prince, or by his order: so that such a man, however entitled, czar, or grand seignior, or how you please, is as much in the state of nature, with all under his dominion, as he is with the rest of mankind: for wherever any two men are, who have no standing rule, and common judge to appeal to on earth, for the determination of controversies of right betwixt them, there they are still in the state of nature, and under all the inconveniencies of it. . . .

10. For Locke, the main purpose of government is to
    A. protect individual rights.
    B. limit the power of kings.
    C. promote equality.
    D. promote commerce.

11. According to Locke, civil society and the state of nature are
    A. at odds.
    B. the same thing.
    C. both products of absolute monarchy.
    D. forms of legal system.

12. For Locke, which of these are part of the state of nature?
    A. civil society
    B. property rights
    C. absolute monarchy
    D. legislatures

Questions 13–15 refer to the following excerpt.

Louis XIV Revokes the Edict of Nantes

Art. 1. Know that we . . . with our certain knowledge, full power and royal authority, have by this present, perpetual and irrevocable edict, suppressed and revoked the edict of the aforesaid king our grandfather, given at Nantes in the month of April, 1598, in all its extent . . . together with all the concessions made by [this] and other edicts, declarations, and decrees, to the people of the so-called Reformed religion, of whatever nature they be . . . and in consequence we desire . . . that all the temples of the people of the aforesaid so-called Reformed religion situated in our kingdom . . . should be demolished forthwith.

Art. 2. We forbid our subjects of the so-called Reformed religion to assemble any more for public worship of the above-mentioned religion. . . .

Art. 3. We likewise forbid all lords, of whatever rank they may be, to carry out heretical services in houses and fiefs . . . the penalty for . . . the said worship being confiscation of their body and possessions.

Art. 4. We order all ministers of the aforesaid so-called Reformed religion who do not wish to be converted and to embrace the Catholic, Apostolic, and Roman religion, to depart from our kingdom and the lands subject to us within fifteen days from the publication of our present edict . . . on pain of the galleys.

Art. 5. We desire that those among the said [Reformed] ministers who shall be converted [to the Catholic religion] shall continue to enjoy during their life, and their wives shall enjoy after their death as long as they remain widows, the same exemptions from taxation and billeting of soldiers, which they enjoyed while they fulfilled the function of ministers. . . .

Art. 8. With regard to children who shall be born to those of the aforesaid so-called Reformed religion, we desire that they be baptized by their parish priests. We command the fathers and mothers to send them to the churches for that purpose, on penalty of a fine of 500 livres or more if they fail to do so; and afterwards, the children shall be brought up in the Catholic, Apostolic, and Roman religion. . . .

Art. 10. All our subjects of the so-called Reformed religion, with their wives and children, are to be strongly and repeatedly prohibited from leaving our aforesaid kingdom . . . or of taking out . . . their possessions and effects. . . .

The members of the so-called Reformed religion, while awaiting God's pleasure to enlighten them like the others, can live in the towns and districts of our kingdom . . . and continue their occupation there, and enjoy their possessions . . . on condition . . . that they do not make public profession of [their religion].

13. The "temples" referred to in this passage are
    A. Catholic churches.
    B. Jewish synagogues.
    C. banks.
    D. Protestant churches.

14. Essentially, this statement forbids Protestants from
    A. remaining in France.
    B. practicing their faith in public.
    C. converting to Catholicism.
    D. private worship.

15. Article 10 appears to have the goal of
    A. prohibiting religious refugees from moving to and benefiting other countries.
    B. forcing children to convert to Catholicism.
    C. punishing Protestants who wish to remain in France.
    D. encouraging religious toleration.

Short-Answer Question

Absolute monarchy was rejected in England in the late seventeenth century.

    a. Choose ONE of the following and explain why your choice represents the key factor leading to this development.
- Catholics were often seen as supporting foreign influence in England.
- James I claimed to rule by divine right.
- Protestantism had popular support in England.

    b. Contrast your choice against ONE of the other options, demonstrating why that option is not as significant as your choice.

Long-Essay Question

Using the examples of France, England, and Russia, what were the principle challenges to royal absolutism in the seventeenth and eighteenth centuries?

ANSWERS AND EXPLANATIONS: AP® PRACTICE TEST

Multiple-Choice Questions

1. A   James's stance is fairly moderate, trying to accommodate Puritan demands, yet easing up on strict limits on people's actions.
2. C   James is extending more freedom on Sundays to those who attend Church of England (Anglican) services.
3. B   Brandenburg-Prussia was expanding in this period, and actively seeking settlers.
4. B   The welcome is extended to French Protestants who were left vulnerable in France after the revocation of the Edict of Nantes.
5. A   The Great Elector offers very generous terms, including tax incentives and free lands.
6. C   France gained Alsace, the Franche-Comté, and Lille, which were all formerly part of the Holy Roman Empire.
7. D   While some of the territory gained pushed France's boundaries outward, many of the gains were of little effect, such as acquiring Lille.
8. B   Bossuet was one of the most famous writers upholding the power of absolute monarchy. He clearly supports the idea of the king as the state.
9. A   Bossuet quotes St. Paul, who says "Do that which is good," and this is the only limit he mentions on divine power.
10. A   Locke indicates that the main purpose of government is to protect individual rights and to uphold the law.
11. A   For Locke, the purpose of civil society is to solve the problems occurring in humankind's natural state.
12. C   Locke condemns absolute monarchy as being part of the natural order of things, which civil society is supposed to remedy.
13. D   The king's reference to "temples of the people of the aforesaid so-called Reformed religion" is an attack on Protestant places of worship.
14. B   Protestants are allowed to remain in France, as long as they did not publicly declare their faith.
15. A   Other countries were encouraging religious refugees, but this decree seeks to stop that process, resulting in a drain of talent and resources.

Long-Essay Question

Using the examples of France, England, and Russia, what were the principle challenges to royal absolutism in the seventeenth and eighteenth centuries?

(Key topics to focus and elaborate on)
- Nobles
- Church authorities
- Legal traditions

New Directions in Thought and Culture in the Sixteenth and Seventeenth Centuries

This period saw a total transformation in the scientific understanding of the universe—a transformation that affected all aspects of daily life, including other branches of scientific thought, philosophy, and faith.

THE SCIENTIFIC REVOLUTION

- The **scientific revolution** was not a unified event, but rather a gradual movement that involved around a few hundred brilliant scientists laboring independently over many years in different countries. This new science, and especially the many significant discoveries in the field of astronomy, captured the public's imagination and enabled scientific discovery and knowledge to gain cultural authority.
- Nicholas Copernicus (1473–1543) is famous for questioning the geocentric view of the **Ptolemaic system** (in which the earth was believed to be at the center of the universe). In his work *On the Revolutions of Heavenly Spheres,* Copernicus argued on behalf of a heliocentric view of the universe.
- Tycho Brahe (1546–1601) spent much of his life advocating a geocentric view of the universe, but he made more extensive observations of the planets than any of his predecessors. Brahe's assistant, Johannes Kepler (1571–1630), used Brahe's research findings to advance a heliocentric view and demonstrate that planets orbited around the sun in an elliptical fashion in his book *The New Astronomy* (1609).
- Galileo Galilei (1564–1642) was one of the first astronomers to view the sky with the telescope. He popularized a Copernican interpretation of the heavens using the empirical, rational evidence that he found in his research.
- Isaac Newton (1642–1727), an English scientist, published his famous *Principia Mathematica* in 1687. In it he asserted—and proved mathematically—that planets and other physical objects moved through mutual attraction, or gravity.

AP® KEY CONCEPTS

1.1 The worldview of European intellectuals shifted from one based on ecclesiastical and classical authority to one based primarily on inquiry and observation of the natural world.

  IV. New ideas in science based on observation, experimentation, and mathematics challenged classical views of the cosmos, nature, and the human body, though folk traditions of knowledge and the universe persisted.

PHILOSOPHY RESPONDS TO CHANGING SCIENCE

The revolution in scientific thought extended to the philosophy of the era, which came to see the world in terms of its mechanical principles.

- The image of God as a divine watchmaker came into vogue at this time, and a new emphasis on mathematics and a mechanical understanding of nature pervaded all fields.
- Francis Bacon (1561–1626) urged his peers to continue their search for the truth in the natural world. In his *Novum Organum* and *The Advancement of Learning,* Bacon attacked the belief that everything had already been discovered, and he encouraged experiment.
- René Descartes (1596–1650) developed a scientific method that relied on deduction more than it did on empirical study and induction. In his 1637 *Discourse on Method,* Descartes endorsed the idea that all thought should be founded on a mathematical model, and he rejected outright any thought not postulated on reason.
- Thomas Hobbes (1588–1679) was supportive of the scientific movement and befriended Descartes and Galileo. Hobbes's *Leviathan* (1651) portrays human beings as materialistic, egotistical, and hedonistic. Hobbes believed human beings were constantly in a state of conflict. He felt that rulers should have no limits on their power.
- John Locke (1632–1704) was critical of Hobbes's views of absolutism and helped lay a foundation for European liberal political philosophy. In his *First Treatise of Government,* Locke rejected the idea of absolute government based on the concept of a patriarchal model of fathers ruling over a family. In his *Second Treatise of Government,* Locke argued for a government that was both accountable for and alert to the needs of the government. He believed that human beings were creatures of basically good will that entered into a social contract to preserve their existing liberties and rights.

AP® KEY CONCEPTS

1.1 The worldview of European intellectuals shifted from one based on ecclesiastical and classical authority to one based primarily on inquiry and observation of the natural world.

  IV. New ideas in science based on observation, experimentation, and mathematics challenged classical views of the cosmos, nature, and the human body, though folk traditions of knowledge and the universe persisted.

2.3 The popularization and dissemination of the scientific revolution and the application of its methods to political, social, and ethical issues led to an increased, although not unchallenged, emphasis on reason in European culture.

  I. Rational and empirical thought challenged traditional values and ideas.

  III. New political and economic theories challenged absolutism and mercantilism.

THE NEW SCIENCE AND RELIGIOUS FAITH

- Galileo angered the Catholic Church because he interpreted scripture in accord with the new science. For his disobedience, Galileo was put on trial and forced to live under house arrest.
- Blaise Pascal (1623–1662) was a French mathematician who saw religion as separate from reason and science; he believed that religion required a "leap of faith." He allied himself with the Jansenists. Pascal's famous wager with the skeptics was that it was better to believe that God exists and stake everything on his benevolence than not to do so.
- Faith in a rational God was an element in the English approach to the new science. Scientific advances came to be interpreted as a fulfillment of God's plan for mankind.

1.1 The worldview of European intellectuals shifted from one based on ecclesiastical and classical authority to one based primarily on inquiry and observation of the natural world.

IV. New ideas in science based on observation, experimentation, and mathematics challenged classical views of the cosmos, nature, and the human body, though folk traditions of knowledge and the universe persisted.

CONTINUING SUPERSTITION

- From 1400 to 1700, an estimated 70,000–100,000 people were sentenced to death for magic and witchcraft. Growing religious and political tensions of the age made use of theology that portrayed demons and the devil as powerful. Cunning folk were believed to possess special powers. Over time, these abilities came into conflict with the sacred rituals of the Christian church, like the sacraments, and the exorcism of demons. The church declared that only its priests could possess legitimate magical abilities and that those who practiced magic outside the church were infernally inspired.

AP ® KEY CONCEPTS

1.5 European society and the experiences of everyday life were increasingly shaped by commercial and agricultural capitalism, notwithstanding the persistence of medieval social and economic structures.

V. Popular culture, leisure activities, and rituals reflecting the persistence of folk ideas reinforced and sometimes challenged communal ties and norms.

2.3 The popularization and dissemination of the scientific revolution and the application of its methods to political, social, and ethical issues led to an increased, although not unchallenged, emphasis on reason in European culture.

V. The arts moved from the celebration of religious themes and royal power to an emphasis on private life and the public good.

Multiple-Choice Questions

Questions 1–2 refer to the following image.

Copernican Model of the Universe, 1543

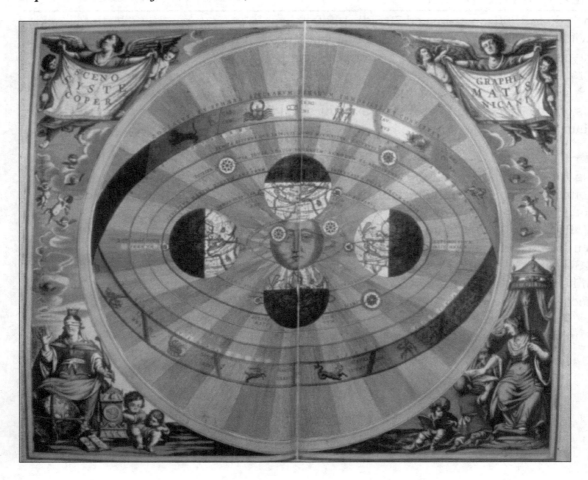

1. Unlike the most widely accepted model of its time, this model of the universe
    A. includes the concept of the zodiac.
    B. has the sun at its center.
    C. includes the earth.
    D. shows the revolution of one body around another.

2. What are represented by the figures of women in the lower corners of this image?
    A. motherhood
    B. the most powerful queens of the era
    C. biblical queens
    D. ideas

Questions 3–4 refer to the following image.

Title Page from Leviathan, *1651*

3. What provides authority to the figure in this image?
    A. law
    B. wisdom and experience
    C. the people
    D. military and religious power

4. Which of these ideas is represented by the large figure in this image?
    A. parliamentary monarchy
    B. the king supported by the law
    C. the harshness of royal rule
    D. the king embodying the will of the people

Questions 5–6 refer to the following excerpt.

Margaret Cavendish Questions the Fascination with Scientific Instruments, 1666

Art has intoxicated so many men's brains, and wholly imployed their thoughts and bodily actions about phaenomena, or the exterior figure of objects, as all better Arts and Studies are laid aside. . . . But though there be numerous Books written of the wonder of these [experimental optical] Glasses, yet I cannot perceive any such; at best, they are but superficial wonders, as I may call them. But could Experimental Philosophers find out more beneficial Arts then our Fore-fathers have done, either for the better increase of Vegetables and brute Animals to nourish our bodies, or better and commodious contrivances in the Art of Architecture to build us houses, or for the advancing of trade and traffick . . . it would not only be worth their labour, but of as much praise as could be given to them: But, as Boys that play with watry Bubbles . . . are worthy of reproof rather than praise, for wasting their time with useless sports; so those that addict themselves to unprofitable Arts, spend more time than they reap benefit thereby.

5. Which of these statements best summarizes the thesis of this excerpt?
    A. Science should be concerned primarily with knowledge for its own sake.
    B. Experimentation leads to false conclusions.
    C. Science should be concerned with practical applications.
    D. Optics is not a science but an art.

6. In this excerpt, "watry Bubbles" represent
    A. frivolous experimentation.
    B. ephemeral scientific findings.
    C. easily disproven findings.
    D. speculation on spiritual matters.

Questions 7–9 refer to the following excerpt.

René Descartes, from Discourse on Method, *1637*

My speculations were indeed truly pleasing to me; but I recognize that other men have theirs, which perhaps please them even more. As soon, however, as I had acquired some general notions regarding physics, and on beginning to make trial of them in various special difficulties had observed how far they can carry us and how much they differ from the principles hitherto employed, I believed that I could not keep them hidden without grievously sinning against the law which lays us under obligation to promote, as far as in us lies, the general good of all mankind. For they led me to see that it is possible to obtain knowledge highly useful in life, and that in place of the speculative philosophy taught in the Schools we can have a practical philosophy, by means of which, knowing the force and the actions of fire, water, air, and of the stars, of the heavens, and of all the bodies that surround us—knowing them as distinctly as we know the various crafts of the artisans—we may in the same fashion employ them in all the uses for which they are suited, thus rendering ourselves the masters and possessors of nature. This is to be desired, not only with a view to the invention of an infinity of arts by which we would be enabled to enjoy without heavy labor the fruits of the earth and all its conveniences, but above all for the preservation of health, which is, without doubt, of all blessings in this life, the first of all goods and the foundation on which the others rest. For the mind is so dependent on the temper and disposition of the bodily organisms that if any means can ever be found to render men wiser and more capable than they have hitherto been, I believe that it is in the science of medicine that the means must be sought. . . . With no wish to depreciate it, I am yet sure there is no one, even of those engaged in the profession, who does not admit that all we know is almost nothing in comparison with what remains to be discovered; and that we could be freed from innumerable maladies, both of body and of mind, and even perhaps from the infirmities of age, if we had sufficient knowledge of their causes and of the remedies provided by nature.

7. This passage illustrates the belief of scientists in this period in
    A. the Copernican model.
    B. the power of the human mind.
    C. the innate goodness of humans.
    D. God.

8. What are the Schools referred to by Descartes?
    A. universities
    B. monastic learning
    C. the new science
    D. Scholasticism

9. For Descartes, the primary goal of science is to
    A. know more.
    B. prove the existence of God.
    C. improve the human condition.
    D. exercise the mind.

Questions 10–12 refer to the following excerpt.

Jonathan Swift, from Gulliver's Travels, *1726*

Gulliver reports a conversation he encountered while visiting Lagardo:
"The Sum of his Discourse was to this Effect. That about Forty Years ago, certain Persons went up to Laputa, either upon Business or Diversion; and after five Months Continuance, came back with a very little Smattering in Mathematics, but full of Volatile Spirits acquired in that Airy Region. That these Persons upon their Return, began to dislike the Management of every Thing below; and fell into Schemes of putting all Arts, Sciences, Languages, and Mechanics upon a new Foot. To this End they procured a Royal Patent for erecting an Academy of Projectors in Lagado; And the Humour prevailed so strongly among the People, that there is not a Town of any Consequence in the Kingdom without such an Academy. In these Colleges, the Professors contrive new Rules and Methods of Agriculture and Building, and new Instruments and Tools for all Trades and Manufactures, whereby, as they undertake, one Man shall do the Work of Ten; a Palace may be built in a Week, of Materials so durable as to last for ever without repairing. All the Fruits of the Earth shall come to Maturity at whatever Season we think fit to chuse; and increase an Hundred Fold more than they do at present; with innumerable other happy

Proposals. The only Inconvenience is, that none of these Projects are yet brought to Perfection; and in the mean time, the whole Country lies miserably waste, the Houses in Ruins, and the People without Food or Cloaths. By all which, instead of being discouraged they are Fifty Times more violently bent upon prosecuting their Schemes, driven equally on by Hope and Despair. . . ."

Gulliver then reports what he found occurring in the rooms of an academy in Lagardo:

"The first Man I saw . . . had been Eight Years upon a Project for extracting Sun-Beams out of Cucumbers, which were to be put into Vials hermetically sealed, and let out to warm the Air in raw inclement Summers. . . .

"I saw another at work to calcine ice into Gunpowder . . .

"There was another most ingenius Architect who had contrived a new Method for building Houses, by beginning at the Roof, and working downwards to the Foundation. . . .

In another Apartment I was highly pleased with a Projector, who had found a Device of plowing the Ground with Hogs, to save the Charges of Plows, Cattle, and Labour. The Method is this: In an Acre of Ground you bury at six Inches Distance, and eight deep, a quantity of Acorns, Dates, Chesnuts, and other Masts or Vegetables whereof these Animals are fondest; then you drive six Hundred or more of them into the Field, where in a few Days they will root up the whole Ground in search of their Food, and make it fit for sowing, at the same time manuring it with their Dung. It is true, upon Experiment they found the Charge and Trouble very great, and they had little or no Crop. However, it is not doubted that this Invention may be capable of great Improvement."

10. This is best characterized as a(n)
    A. tribute.
    B. explanation.
    C. satire.
    D. play.

11. The method of plowing here is used to illustrate
    A. the scientific method.
    B. pointless innovation.
    C. the promise of science.
    D. poorly implemented theories.

12. The "Airy Region" in this passage is
    A. the world of scientists.
    B. experimentation.
    C. medieval learning.
    D. the heavens.

Questions 13–15 refer to the following excerpt.

Galileo, from Letter to the Grand Duchess Christina, 1615

The reason produced for condemning the opinion that the Earth moves and the sun stands still is that in many places in the Bible one may read that the sun moves and the Earth stands still. . . .

With regard to this argument, I think in the first place that it is very pious to say and prudent to affirm that the holy Bible can never speak untruth—whenever its true meaning is understood. But I believe nobody will deny that it is often very abstruse, and may say things which are quite different from what its bare words signify. . . . This being granted, I think that in discussions of physical problems we ought to begin not from the authority of scriptural passages, but from sense experiences and necessary demonstrations; for the holy Bible and the phenomena of nature proceed alike from the divine Word, the former as the dictate of the Holy Ghost and the latter as the observant executrix of God's commands. It is necessary for the Bible, in order to be accommodated to the understanding of every man, to speak many things which appear to differ from the absolute truth so far as the bare meaning of the words is concerned. But Nature, on the other hand, is inexorable and immutable; she never transgresses the laws imposed upon her, or cares a whit whether her abstruse reasons and methods of operation are understandable to men. For that reason it appears that nothing physical which sense-experience sets before our eyes, or which necessary demonstrations prove to us, ought to be called in question (much less condemned) upon the testimony of biblical passages which may have some different meaning beneath their words. For the Bible is not chained in every expression to conditions as strict as those which govern all physical effects; nor is God any less excellently revealed in Nature's actions than in the sacred statements of the Bible. . . . From this I do not mean to infer that we need not have an extraordinary esteem for the passages of holy Scripture. On the contrary, having arrived at any certainties in physics, we ought to utilize these as the most appropriate aids in the true exposition of the Bible and in the investigation of those meanings which are necessarily contained therein for these must be concordant with demonstrated truths. I should judge the authority of the Bible was designed to persuade men of those articles and propositions which, surpassing all human reasoning, could not be made credible by science, or by any other means than through the very mouth of the Holy Spirit. . . . But I do not feel obliged to believe that the same God who has endowed us with senses, reason, and intellect has intended to forgo their use and by some other means to give us knowledge which we can attain by them.

13. For Galileo, what is the most important authority for understanding the physical world?
    A. the Bible
    B. the Catholic Church
    C. one's sense
    D. the telescope

14. Which of these best summarizes Galileo's ideas about the Bible and science?
    A. Science holds more truth than the Bible.
    B. If one must choose between the two authorities, science is preferable.
    C. The Bible is a source of inspiration, not truth.
    D. Science can clarify biblical truths.

15. For Galileo, like the Bible, nature is
    A. a faulty representation of spiritual truth.
    B. to be read as God's creation.
    C. only for scientists to read.
    D. best interpreted through faith.

Short-Answer Question

The scientific revolution challenged the authority of the Catholic Church.

a. Choose ONE of the following and explain why your choice represents the key factor leading to this development.

- The Reformation splintered Christianity.
- New methods of scientific inquiry spread during this period.
- New institutions emerged in this period to foster the sharing of scientific knowledge.

b. Contrast your choice against ONE of the other options, demonstrating why that option is not as significant as your choice.

Long-Essay Question

Compare and contrast the political views of John Locke and Thomas Hobbes.

Multiple-Choice Questions

1. B   This is a heliocentric—as opposed to geocentric—model of the universe, which shows the earth revolving around the sun.
2. C   Ideas such as justice or faith were traditionally depicted as women.
3. D   In the king's hand are a sword and a crozier, representing military and spiritual authority. In the lower elements these ideas are repeated.
4. D   The king rules everything, but his body is composed of the people, implying that the king represents all of his subjects.
5. C   Cavendish argues that science should focus on innovations that confer benefits, not science for its own sake.
6. A   This phrase refers to childish pursuits, arguing that many scientists are merely wasting their time.
7. B   Optimism concerning the power of the human mind to solve humanity's problems was a leading characteristic of the scientific revolution.
8. D   Descartes is arguing against key principles of the Scholastics.
9. C   In referring to "practical philosophy," Descartes argues that science should be used to improve the human condition, through medicine and other scientific pursuits.
10. C   Swift mocks the activities of scientists in this work.
11. B   This new method is much more expensive than the traditional method of plowing, and is innovation for its own sake.
12. A   Swift mocks this region as being invigorating but not improving.
13. C   Galileo does not reject the Bible, but argues that the senses are the best source of knowledge about the world.
14. D   Galileo is careful in arguing that all that is in the Bible is true, but often needs clarifying, and may not always be the literal truth.
15. B   For Galileo, nature and the Bible are equally important as sources for understanding God.

Long-Essay Question

Compare and contrast the political views of John Locke and Thomas Hobbes.

(Key topics to focus and elaborate on)
- Both believe in legislature and monarchy
- Differ in ideas about human nature
- Idea of political contract

CHAPTER 7

Society and Economy under the Old Regime in the Eighteenth Century

The period known as the *ancien régime,* or the **Old Regime**, usually refers to the various political and social relationships and situation prior to the French Revolution of 1789. During this time both nobles and peasants called for the return to traditional rights, and society was fairly hierarchical.

MAJOR FEATURES OF LIFE IN THE OLD REGIME

- Tradition remained the most important factor shaping the lives of Europeans in this period. The peasants, above all, were committed to maintaining the status quo, and they were opposed to change.
- Likewise, a hierarchical society remained the accepted model. Each layer of the hierarchy had its own rights, duties, and privileges.

AP® KEY CONCEPTS

1.5 III. Population shifts and growing commerce caused the expansion of cities, which often found their traditional political and social structures stressed by the growth.

   I. Economic change produced new social patterns, while traditions of hierarchy and status persisted.

THE ARISTOCRACY

- Aristocrats represented a mere 5 percent of the population but controlled the majority of land, as well as social, economic, and political power. As monarchs' powers expanded, European aristocrats used existing governmental institutions to limit the power of the monarchy.
- In England, game laws gave aristocratic landowners the exclusive legal rights from 1671 to 1831 to hunt. The English aristocracy owned one-fourth of all arable land and consisted of about 400 families, many of whom controlled the House of Lords and the House of Commons.
- In France, the nobility consisted of military officers, bureaucrats, or other individuals who paid for it. French nobles fell into two groups: those who held court at Versailles, and those who did not.

- In eastern Europe, the nobility had more rights over peasants. Polish aristocrats exerted total control over serfs. In Austria and Hungary, nobles were exempt from taxation. In countries like Hungary and Poland, nobles were the only ones with political representation. In Prussia, nobles had authority over serfs. In Russia, nobles became determined to resist compulsory state service. In the 1785 Charter of the Nobility, Catherine the Great defined the legal rights of nobles and their families in exchange for the nobility's voluntary service of state.

AP® KEY CONCEPTS

2.1 Different models of political sovereignty affected the relationship among states and between states and individuals.

I. In much of Europe, absolute monarchy was established over the course of the seventeenth and eighteenth centuries.

THE LAND AND ITS TILLERS

- Over three-quarters of all Europeans lived in the country in the eighteenth century; many of them were peasants who were quite poor and lived through subsistence agriculture.
- In Great Britain, farmers had legal rights of English citizens, but the courts were run by landowners. French peasants had to pay feudal dues and were responsible for a certain amount of forced labor, known as *corvée*.
- In Prussia and Austria, landlords exercised almost complete control over serfs. The condition of serfs in Russia was worst; serfs had no legal rights and were effectively slaves. Russia experienced numerous peasant revolts between 1762 and 1769, a period culminating in Pugachev's Rebellion between 1773 and 1775. Southeastern European peasants were free, but only because of a scarcity of labor. Balkan peasants eventually became dependent on their Ottoman Empire landlords because they sought their protection from bandits and rebels.

AP® KEY CONCEPTS

2.1 Different models of political sovereignty affected the relationship among states and between states and individuals.

I. In much of Europe, absolute monarchy was established over the course of the seventeenth and eighteenth centuries.

FAMILY STRUCTURES AND FAMILY ECONOMY

- The **family economy** continued to prevail across most of Europe. Households in northwestern Europe often consisted of a married couple, children through their teens, and servants (people who were hired under contract to work for the head of the household in exchange for room, board, and wages). Households were small, usually no more than five or six people. Mortality was high, and no more than two generations lived together under one roof. Most children eventually married and formed their own household—a phenomenon known as *neolocalism*. The marriage age was in the mid-twenties for men and women.
- In eastern Europe, the marriage age was much earlier, usually before the age of twenty. Wives were often older than their husbands. Russian households often consisted of as many as three or four generations living together in one house.

1.5 European society and the experiences of everyday life were increasingly shaped by commercial and agricultural capitalism, notwithstanding the persistence of medieval social and economic structures.

 IV. The family remained the primary social and economic institution of early modern Europe and took several forms, including the nuclear family.

THE REVOLUTION IN AGRICULTURE

◼ The **agricultural revolution** began in the Netherlands, where farmers built dikes, expanded land, and experimented with new crops. English landlords popularized these Dutch innovations. Jethro Tull financed the experiments of others and conducted his own, including permitting land to be cultivated for longer periods without having to be left fallow. Robert Bakewell pioneered new methods of animal breeding. Charles Townsend learned how to use fertilizer and instituted crop rotation. By the second half of the seventeenth century, **enclosures** replaced the open-field method of farming. Enclosures commercialized agriculture, maximizing the profits of the landowner.

2.2 The expansion of European commerce accelerated the growth of a worldwide economic network.

 I. Early modern Europe developed a market economy that provided the foundation for its global role.

2.4 The experiences of everyday life were shaped by demographic, environmental, medical, and technological changes.

 I. In the seventeenth century, small landholdings, low-productivity agricultural practices, poor transportation, and adverse weather limited and disrupted the food supply, causing periodic famines. By the eighteenth century, Europeans began to escape from the Malthusian imbalance between population and the food supply, resulting in steady population growth.

THE INDUSTRIAL REVOLUTION OF THE EIGHTEENTH CENTURY

◼ The second half of the eighteenth century witnessed the industrialization of the European economy, which made possible the production of more goods and services than ever before: the **consumer revolution**. New machinery was invented that enabled this industrialization, including the **spinning jenny**, the **water frame**, and the steam engine. Iron production during this era was essential to the manufacturing of machinery. The **Industrial Revolution** forced women into cottage industries and resulted in the workplaces of men and women becoming more separate.

2.2 The expansion of European commerce accelerated the growth of a worldwide economic network.

 II. The European-dominated worldwide economic network contributed to the agricultural, industrial, and consumer revolutions in Europe.

2.4 The experiences of everyday life were shaped by demographic, environmental, medical, and technological changes.

II. The consumer revolution of the eighteenth century was shaped by a new concern for privacy, encouraged the purchase of new goods for homes, and created new venues for leisure activities.

III. By the eighteenth century, family and private life reflected new demographic patterns and the effects of the Commercial Revolution.

THE GROWTH OF CITIES

- Between 1650 and 1700, cities that grew most in population were capitals and ports; the urban Industrial Revolution, overseas trade, and governmental bureaucracy came to control European economies. New cities began to emerge in the middle of the eighteenth century; improved agricultural production enabled the growth of nearby urban centers that gave farmers access to consumer goods. Social divisions were marked between the upper classes, middle class, artisans, and peasants.

AP® KEY CONCEPTS

2.4 The experiences of everyday life were shaped by demographic, environmental, medical, and technological changes.

II. The consumer revolution of the eighteenth century was shaped by a new concern for privacy, encouraged the purchase of new goods for homes, and created new venues for leisure activities.

IV. Cities offered economic opportunities, which attracted increasing migration from rural areas, transforming urban life and creating challenges for the new urbanites and their families.

THE JEWISH POPULATION: THE AGE OF THE GHETTO

- The majority of Jews lived in Eastern Europe, with the Netherlands being a notable exception. The Jewish population was concentrated in Lithuania, Poland, and the Ukraine.
- Catherine the Great was intolerant of the Jewish population in Russia and discouraged their settlement there. Jews were often victims of intolerance in the countries where they settled.

AP® KEY CONCEPTS

2.3 The popularization and dissemination of the scientific revolution and the application of its methods to political, social, and ethical issues led to an increased, although not unchallenged, emphasis on reason in European culture.

IV. During the Enlightenment, the rational analysis of religious practices led to natural religion and the demand for religious toleration.

Multiple-Choice Questions

Questions 1–3 refer to the following excerpt.

Turgot Decries French Landholding

The real and fundamental distinction between the areas of large-scale cultivation and those where farming is done only on a small scale is that in the former, the landowners make deals with *fermiers* or tenant farmers who promise them a fixed payment for their land in exchange for the right to cultivate it during a certain number of years. These tenant farmers are responsible for all the expenses of cultivation, ploughing, seeds, and for stocking the farm with cattle, other animals, and tools. These tenant farmers are true agricultural entrepreneurs; like all other entrepreneurs, they have their own capital, which they use to make a profit by cultivating land . . . [The demand for land that makes it valuable is a result of] this indispensable kind of men who have not only their own labor, but capital to consecrate to agriculture, and who have no other occupation except to work the land, not to earn their living by the sweat of their brow as workers do, but to use their capital in a profitable way, like the ship owners of Nantes and Bordeaux who use theirs in overseas commerce. . . . [The sharecropping system]: The regions of small scale agriculture, which is to say at least four-sevenths of the land in the kingdom, are areas where there are no agricultural entrepreneurs, where a landowner who wants to profit from his land can only find unfortunate peasants who have no resources except their own labor, where he has to use his own money for all the expenses of growing crops, livestock, tools, seeds, and even to lend his métayer (sharecropper) enough to feed himself until the first harvest. In this situation, a landowner who has no resources other than his land, would have to leave it unplanted . . . After having deducted the cost of seed and of any interest payments due on the land, the landowner and the sharecropper divide what is left of the profits, according to the agreement they have made. The landowner, who has advanced all the money, runs all the risks of loss due to harvest failures and the loss of animals; he is the only real agricultural entrepreneur. The sharecropper is just a workman, a farmhand whom he pays with a share of the profits instead of wages. But this kind of landowner doesn't have the same advantages as the entrepreneurial farmer, who directs everything himself with attention and intelligence. The landowner has to trust all the money he advances to a man who may be negligent or dishonest, and who can't be held responsible for anything. This kind of sharecropper, accustomed to most meager existence and without any hope or even any desire of improving his condition, farms badly and doesn't even try to use the land for products that can be sold for the best profit. He prefers to grow things that take less work and that he can consume himself, such as buckwheat and especially chestnuts, which only have to be collected. He doesn't even worry about not having enough to eat; he knows that, if the harvest fails, his master will have to feed him to avoid having to abandon his land.

1. In this analysis, what motivates the *fermiers* to be good farmers?
   A. They will avoid heavy taxes.
   B. They can buy the land they farm.
   C. They can increase their profits.
   D. They can end their servitude.

2. What do sharecroppers contribute to production?
   A. seeds and the land
   B. labor and monetary investment
   C. land and monetary investment
   D. labor

3. In this analysis, the key difference between sharecroppers and *fermiers* is that sharecroppers
   A. are more lazy.
   B. own their own tools.
   C. have little incentive to work harder.
   D. work harder.

Questions 4–5 refer to the following excerpt.

David Hume Praises Luxury and the Refinement of the Arts

In times when industry and the arts flourish, men are kept in perpetual occupation, and enjoy, as their reward, the occupation itself, as well as those pleasures which are the fruit of their labour. The mind acquires new vigour; enlarges its powers and faculties; and by an assiduity in honest industry, both satisfies its natural appetites, and prevents the growth of unnatural ones, which commonly spring up, when nourished by ease and idleness. . . . Another advantage of industry and of refinements in the mechanical arts, is, that they commonly produce some refinements in the liberal; nor can one be carried to perfection, without being accompanied, in some degree, with the other. . . . The more these refined arts advance, the more sociable men become. . . . They flock into cities; love to receive and communicate knowledge; to show their wit or their breeding; their taste in conversation or living, in clothes or furniture. Curiosity allures the wise; vanity the foolish, and pleasure both. Particular clubs and societies are everywhere formed: Both sexes meet in an easy and sociable manner: and the tempers of men, as well as their behaviour, refine apace. So that, beside the improvements which they receive from knowledge and the liberal arts, it is impossible but they must feel an encrease of humanity, from the very habit of conversing together, and contributing to each other's pleasure and entertainment. Thus industry, knowledge, and humanity, are linked together by an indissoluble chain, and are found, from experience as well as reason, to be peculiar to the more polished, and, what are commonly denominated, the more luxurious ages. . . . But industry, knowledge, and humanity are not advantageous in private life alone: They diffuse their beneficial influence on the public, and render the government as great and flourishing as they make individuals happy and prosperous. The encrease and consumption of all the commodities . . . are advantageous to society; because . . . they are a kind of storehouse of labour, which, in the exigencies of state, may be turned to the public service. In a nation, where there is no demand for such superfluities, men sink into indolence, lose all enjoyment of life, and are useless to the public, which cannot maintain or support its fleets and armies, from the industry of such slothful members.

4. For Hume, the foundation of improvements in society is
   A. education.   C. faith.
   B. a strong economy.   D. refinement.

5. Hume appears to envisage the benefits he described being enjoyed by
   A. all of society.
   B. nobles only.
   C. merchants only.
   D. town dwellers only.

Questions 6–7 refer to the following image.

A Shop of the 1700s

6. This image best illustrates which of these developments of the 1700s?
   A. the Industrial Revolution
   B. the Scientific Revolution
   C. the Consumer Revolution
   D. social upheaval

7. This image is intended to portray
   A. moment in time.
   B. the harsh conditions of retail work.
   C. a typical day.
   D. an entire range of activities.

Questions 8–10 refer to the following excerpt.

Manchester's Calico Printers Protest the Use of New Machinery

Mr. Taylor, If you don't discharge James Hobson from the House of Correction we will burn your House about your Ears for we have sworn to stand by one another and you must immediately give over any more Mashen Work for we are determined there shall be no more of them made use of in the Trade and it will be madness for you to contend with the Trade as we are combined by Oath to fix Prices we can afford to pay him a Guinea Week and not hurt the fund if you was to keep him there till Dumsday therefore mind you comply with the above or by God we will keep our Words with you we will make some rare Bunfires in this Countey and at your Peril to call any more Meetings mind that we will make the Mosney Pepel shake in their Shoes we are determined to destroy all Sorts of Masheens for Printing in the Kingdom for there is more hands then is work for so no more from the ingerd Gurnemen Rember we are a great number sworn nor you must not advertise the Men that you say run away from you when your il Usage was the Cause of their going we will punish you for that our Meetings are legal for we want nothing but what is honest and to work for selvs and familers and you want to starve us but it is better for you and a few more which we have marked to die then such a Numbe

8. For these workers, more machines mean
   A. loss of pride.
   B. starvation.
   C. losing their homes.
   D. emigration.

9. What appears to be the main advantage of these workers?
   A. They own the machines.
   B. They are united.
   C. They hold a monopoly on printing expertise.
   D. They have great collective wealth.

10. The main demand of the petitioners is to
    A. continue working.
    B. make more money.
    C. gain the right to meet.
    D. work the new machines.

Questions 11–13 refer to the following excerpt.

Priscilla Wakefield Demands More Occupations for Women, 1798

Another heavy discouragement to the industry of women is the inequality of the reward of their labor, compared with that of men; an injustice which pervades every species of employment performed by both sexes. In employments which depend on bodily strength, the distinction is just; for it cannot be pretended that the generality of women can earn as much as men, when the produce of their labor is the result of corporeal exertion; but it is a subject of great regret, that this inequality should prevail even where an equal share of skill and application is exerted. Male stay-makers, mantua-makers, and hair-dressers, are better paid than female artists of the same professions; but surely it will never be urged as an apology for this disproportion, that women are not as capable of making stays, gowns, dressing hair, and similar arts, as men; if they are not superior to them, it can only be accounted for upon this principle, that the prices they receive for their labor are not sufficient to repay them for the expense of qualifying themselves for their business; and that they sink under the mortification of being regarded as artisans of inferior estimation. . . . Besides these employments which are commonly performed by women, and those already shown to be suitable for such persons as are above the condition of hard labor, there are some professions and trades customarily in the hands of men, which might be conveniently exercised by either sex. Watchmaking requiring more ingenuity than strength, seems peculiarly adapted to women; as do many parts of the business of stationer, particularly, ruling account books or making pens. The compounding of medicines in an apothecary's shop, requires no other talents than care and exactness; and if opening a vein occasionally be an indispensable requisite, a woman may acquire the capacity of doing it, for those of her own sex at least, without any reasonable objection. . . . Pastry and confectionery appear particularly consonant to the habits of women, though generally performed by men; perhaps the heat of the ovens, and the strength requisite to fill and empty them, may render male assistants necessary; but certain women are most eligible to mix up the ingredients, and prepare the various kinds of cakes for baking. Light turnery and toy-making depend more upon dexterity and invention than force, and are therefore suitable work for women and children. . . . Farming, as far as respects the theory, is commensurate with the powers of the female mind: nor is the practice of inspecting agricultural processes incompatible with the delicacy of their frames if their constitution be good.

11. In the context of her own society, Wakefield's ideas about women's work would have been considered
    A. reactionary.
    B. typical.
    C. progressive.
    D. radical.
12. In criticizing the inequality of pay she finds in men's and women's work, Wakefield
    A. agrees with traditional arguments.
    B. concludes that the pay inequalities do not actually exist.
    C. argues that there is no reason for these inequalities.
    D. urges women to protest these conditions.

13. In this period, it was generally thought that men and women should inhabit separate spheres. Wakefield
    A. agrees completely.
    B. disagrees.
    C. feels the spheres should be reversed.
    D. believes that women should find more employment opportunities, but in their own domestic spheres.

Questions 14–15 refer to the following excerpt.

Belorussian Jews Petition Catherine the Great

According to an ancient custom, when the squires built a new village, they summoned the Jews to reside there and gave them certain privileges for several years and then permanent liberty to distill spirits, brew beer and mead, and sell these drinks. On this basis, the Jews built houses and distillation plants at considerable expense. . . . A new decree of Her Imperial Majesty . . . reserved [this right] to the squires. . . . But a decree of the governor-general of Belorussia has now forbidden the squires to farm out distillation in their villages to Jews, even if the squires want to do this. As a result, the poor Jews who built houses in small villages and promoted both this trade and distillation have been deprived of these and left completely impoverished. But until all the Jewish people are totally ruined, the Jewish merchants suffer restraints equally with the poor rural Jews, since their law obliges them to assist all who share their religious faith. They therefore request an imperial decree authorizing the squire, if he wishes, to farm out distillation to Jews in rural areas.

   Although, with Her Imperial Majesty's permission, Jews may be elected as officials . . . , Jews are allotted fewer votes than other people and hence no Jew can ever attain office. Consequently, Jews have no one to defend them in courts and find themselves in a desperate situation—given their fear and ignorance of Russian—in case of misfortune, even if innocent. To consummate all the good already bestowed, Jews dare to petition that an equal number of electors be required from Jews as from others (or, at least, that in matters involving Jews and non-Jews, a representative from the Jewish community hold equal rights with non-Jews, be present to accompany Jews in court, and attend the interrogation of Jews). But cases involving only Jews (except for promissory notes and debts) should be handled solely in Jewish courts, because Jews assume obligations among themselves, make agreements and conclude all kinds of deals in the Jewish language and in accordance with Jewish rites and laws (which are not known to others). Moreover, those who transgress their laws and order should be judged in Jewish courts. [Similarly, preserve intact all their customs and holidays in the spirit of their faith, as is mercifully assured in the imperial manifesto.]

14. According to this petition, Jews should be judged in Jewish courts
    A. only when both parties are Jewish.
    B. whenever Jews are involved.
    C. only for criminal matters.
    D. when Jews break Christian laws.

15. Which of these is a key demand of these petitioners?
    A. the right to vote
    B. the right to emigrate
    C. religious freedom
    D. equal representation

Short-Answer Question

The Industrial Revolution first emerged in Great Britain.

a. Choose ONE of the following and explain why your choice represents the key factor leading to this development.

- All of Britain was a single trading zone.
- The textile industry was the first type of work to be fully mechanized.
- Britain had clear advantages in the area of natural resources.

b. Contrast your choice against ONE of the other options, demonstrating why that option is not as significant as your choice.

Long-Essay Question

How did the Industrial Revolution transform the lives of Europeans between 1750 and 1850?

Multiple-Choice Questions

1. C The *fermiers* are tenant farmers, who can make more money if they are better farmers.
2. D Sharecroppers own nothing, but contribute their labor.
3. C Sharecroppers are not motivated by the hope of increased profits, nor by fear of starvation.
4. B Hume thought that commerce and industrial production would make a strong economy, which would in turn improve society.
5. A Hume doesn't make any distinctions, and implies that the benefits he describes would be realized by the entire society.
6. C Shops such as this one were the product of the Commercial Revolution of the 1700s, in which consumer goods were produced on a much larger scale than before.
7. D This kind of image is intended to show the viewer all of the activities that might take place in this scene.
8. B For these workers, being replaced by machines is equated with starvation.
9. B The printers have sworn an oath to stand together, until "Dumsday."
10. A Although the petitioners make more than one demand, their main goal appears simply to be allowed to keep working.
11. C At this time, women had begun to work in new mechanized industries, as well as filling more traditional roles alongside their husbands. Her demands were, therefore, ahead of their time, but they would not have been considered outrageous.
12. C Wakefield argues that men and women perform the same tasks with equal skill and should be paid the same.
13. B Wakefield does mention that women are accustomed to certain areas of work, but then she argues that they could work well in very different fields.
14. A The petitioners ask that they be tried in Jewish courts whenever both parties are Jewish or when Jewish law is broken.
15. D The petitioners argue that they do not have the same number of votes as other groups, so that their representation in the government is less than they deserve.

Long-Essay Question

How did the Industrial Revolution transform the lives of Europeans between 1750 and 1850?

(Key topics to focus and elaborate on)
- Work life
- Family life
- Urbanization
- Commercialization

The Transatlantic Economy, Trade Wars, and Colonial Rebellion

PERIODS OF EUROPEAN OVERSEAS EMPIRES

- First era: the period of discovery, exploration, conquest, settlement. Completed by 1600.
- Second era: the era of mercantile empires. Marked by increased contact with Africa, and the development and peak of the slave trade. This period saw the emancipation of Europe's American colonies.
- Third era: the period of increasing colonization in Africa and Asia.
- Fourth era: decolonization of the mid-twentieth century.

AP® KEY CONCEPTS

2.1 Different models of political sovereignty affected the relationship among states and between states and individuals.

> III. After 1648, dynastic and state interests, along with Europe's expanding colonial empires, influenced the diplomacy of European states and frequently led to war.

2.2 The expansion of European commerce accelerated the growth of a worldwide economic network.

> II. The European-dominated worldwide economic network contributed to the agricultural, industrial, and consumer revolutions in Europe.
>
> III. Commercial rivalries influenced diplomacy and warfare among European states in the early modern era.

MERCANTILE EMPIRES

- The Treaty of Utrecht (1713) established the boundaries of empire until the 1750s.
- **Mercantilism** was the economic theory behind the system of acquiring colonies, and it entailed governments heavily regulating trade and commerce in hope of increasing national wealth. During this period, the economic well being of the home country was the primary concern; colonies provided markets and resources for the industries of the home country, which would help administer and defend the colony. Home countries and colonies had navigation laws, tariffs, and bounties to encourage production and to prohibit trade with other neighboring countries or colonies controlled by other empires.
- The West Indies and the Indian subcontinent were great sources of rivalry among European powers because they had resources that appealed to many of these powers.

2.2 The expansion of European commerce accelerated the growth of a worldwide economic network.

> II. The European-dominated worldwide economic network contributed to the agricultural, industrial, and consumer revolutions in Europe.
>
> III. Commercial rivalries influenced diplomacy and warfare among European states in the early modern era.

THE SPANISH COLONIAL SYSTEM

- Spanish control of the Americas was subject to few limitations. Colonial political structures existed to buoy Spanish commercial interests. Spain used the *flota* system to control supplies and bullion that went to and from its colonies. Trade outside the *flota* was forbidden.
- The Spanish throne saw that the Spanish Habsburgs were replaced by the French Bourbons, which led to some increased royal involvement and administrative changes in the Spanish colonies. Charles III (r. 1759–1788) abolished some of the Spanish monopolies, opened more South American ports to trade and commerce, and attempted to increase tax collection and end corruption. He introduced the *intendent* into the Spanish empire. These reforms stimulated the Spanish economy and brought the empire more fully under Spanish control.

1.4 Europeans explored and settled overseas territories, encountering and interacting with indigenous populations.

> III. Europeans established overseas empires and trade networks through coercion and negotiation.

2.2 The expansion of European commerce accelerated the growth of a worldwide economic network.

> II. The European-dominated worldwide economic network contributed to the agricultural, industrial, and consumer revolutions in Europe.

BLACK AFRICAN SLAVERY, THE PLANTATION SYSTEM, AND THE ATLANTIC ECONOMY

- Slave labor became a fundamental aspect of empire building. Labor shortages led Europeans settling in the New World to exploit Native Americans; however, disease killed many of them, so Europeans turned to the labor of imported African slaves. Slave markets in central West Africa, Sierra Leone, the Gold Coast, and other areas were sources for slaves.
- Slavery exploded in Brazil and in the Caribbean, thanks to the cultivation of sugar on plantations and the growing consumer demand for the product. High rates of mortality led to the constant need for a fresh influx of slaves.

1.4 Europeans explored and settled overseas territories, encountering and interacting with indigenous populations.

> IV. Europe's colonial expansion led to a global exchange of goods, flora, fauna, cultural practices, and diseases, resulting in the destruction of some indigenous civilizations, a shift toward European dominance, and the expansion of the slave trade.

2.2 The expansion of European commerce accelerated the growth of a worldwide economic network.

    II. The European-dominated worldwide economic network contributed to the agricultural, industrial, and consumer revolutions in Europe.

MID–EIGHTEENTH-CENTURY WARS

- Spain and England disagreed over British rights to the Spanish market in the West Indies, and during a 1731 coastal patrol of an English vessel, Spaniards cut off the ear of an English captain named Robert Jenkins. The War of Jenkins's Ear began in 1739, when Robert Walpole responded to pressure to stop Spanish intervention in trade.
- In December of 1740, Frederick II of Prussia seized Silesia, an Austrian province belonging to the Habsburg Dynasty. Cardinal Fleury, minister to Louis XV, supported the Prussian aggression against Austria. This move threatened Britain, which wanted the Low Countries to remain in possession of Austria rather than France. In 1744, the British-French conflict expanded beyond Europe as France supported Spain against Britain in the Americas. The War of the Austrian Succession ended in a stalemate in 1748.
- The Diplomatic Revolution of 1756 involved a series of alliances that set the stage for a larger European conflict. Britain and Prussia signed the Convention of Westminster, an alliance aimed at preventing the entry of foreign troops into Germany. Britain aligned itself with the enemy of its former ally, Austria. Austria and France allied, with the goal of crushing Prussia.
- The Seven Years' War (1756–1763) began with Frederick II's invasion of Saxony, which led to France, Austria, Sweden, Russia, and smaller German states agreeing to destroy Prussia. Prussia and Russia made peace, and Frederick II held off Austria and France. William Pitt used the continental wars to leverage England's position in America. Pitt used an unprecedented number of soldiers in the American colonies, India, and Canada to dominate against the French in every theater of battle and to gain English possessions.
- In the Treaty of Paris of 1763, Britain received all of Canada, the Ohio River Valley, and the eastern half of the Mississippi River Valley. Britain returned Pondicherry and Chandernagore in India and the West Indian islands of Guadeloupe and Martinique to the French. Great Britain emerged a world power as a result of its international efforts. A quest to pay the war debt had consequences in the British colonies of North America.

AP® KEY CONCEPTS

2.2 The expansion of European commerce accelerated the growth of a worldwide economic network.

    III. Commercial rivalries influenced diplomacy and warfare among European states in the early modern era.

THE AMERICAN REVOLUTION AND EUROPE

- The revolt of British colonies in North America was a reaction to perceived unfairness in revenue collection. The British wanted the colonies to pay for their protection and administration. The 1764 Sugar Act and the Stamp Act of 1765 were rejected as unfair by the American colonists, who argued that they were not represented in the Parliament.
- In March 1770, the Boston Massacre occurred, further inflaming colonists against Britain. The famous Boston Tea Party episode of 1773 escalated the conflict. By April 1775, battles

between colonials and British regiments had begun at Lexington and Concord.

- A colonial army and navy were established, and in 1776, the Continental Congress opened American ports to trade with all nations. On July 4, 1776, the Continental Congress adopted the Declaration of American Independence. The American Revolutionary War continued until 1781, when George Washington defeated Lord Cornwallis at Yorktown.
- France and Spain came to the aid of the colonies. The 1783 Treaty of Paris concluded the conflict, and the American colonies established their independence. The American Revolution had a broad impact on Continental views of government and established the idea of a government based on popular consent rather than on divine law or monarchy.

AP® KEY CONCEPTS

2.1 Different models of political sovereignty affected the relationship among states and between states and individuals.

III. After 1648, dynastic and state interests, along with Europe's expanding colonial empires, influenced the diplomacy of European states and frequently led to war.

Multiple-Choice Questions

Questions 1–2 refer to the following map.

Viceroyalties in Latin America in 1780

1. Which of these modern regions made up much of New Spain?
   A. Brazil
   B. Canada
   C. Argentina
   D. the American Southwest

2. According to this map, which region of Latin America was the least explored and settled?
   A. Mexico
   B. New Granada
   C. Brazil
   D. La Plata

Questions 3–4 refer to the following excerpt.

Buccaneers Prowl the High Seas

When a buccaneer is going to sea he sends word to all who wish to sail with him. When all are ready, they go on board, each bringing what he needs in the way of weapons, powder, and shot.

On the ship, they first discuss where to go and get food supplies. . . . The meat is either [salted] pork or turtle. . . . Sometimes they go and plunder the Spaniards' corrales, which are pens where they keep perhaps a thousand head of tame hogs. The rovers . . . find the house of the farmer . . . [whom] unless he gives them as many hogs as they demand, they hang . . . without mercy. . . .

When a ship has been captured, the men decide whether the captain should keep it or not: if the prize is better than their own vessel, they take it and set fire to the other. When a ship is robbed, nobody must plunder and keep the loot to himself. Everything taken . . . must be shared . . ., without any man enjoying a penny more than his fair share. To prevent deceit, before the booty is distributed everyone has to swear an oath on the Bible that he has not kept for himself so much as the value of a sixpence. . . . And should any man be found to have made a false oath, he would be banished from the rovers, and never be allowed in their company. . . .

When they have captured a ship, the buccaneers set the prisoners on shore as soon as possible, apart from two or three whom they keep to do the cooking and other work they themselves do not care for, releasing these men after two or three years.

The rovers frequently put in for fresh supplies at some island or other, often . . . lying off the south coast of Cuba. . . . Everyone goes ashore and sets up his tent, and they take turns to go on marauding expeditions in their canoes. They take prisoner . . . poor men who catch and set turtles for a living, to provide for their wives and children. Once captured, these men have to catch turtle for the rovers as long as they remain on the island. Should the rovers intend to cruise along a coast where turtle abound, they take the fishermen along with them. The poor fellows may be compelled to stay away from their wives and families four or five years, with no news whether they are alive or dead.

3. What appears to be the main goal of buccaneers?
   A. exploration
   B. slave trading
   C. plundering
   D. territorial expansion

4. According to this account, defenses against piracy appear to be
   A. extensive.
   B. nonexistent.
   C. weak.
   D. primarily successful.

Questions 5–6 refer to the following map.

The Slave Trade, 1400-1860

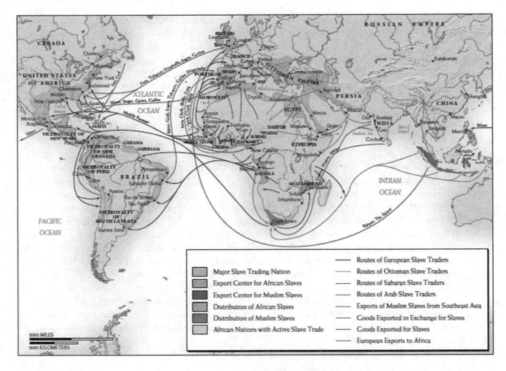

5. Which of these regions was least involved in the international slave trade?
   A. East Asia
   B. Africa
   C. the Americas
   D. Europe

6. From this map, the transatlantic slave trade was controlled by
   A. Ottomans
   B. Arabs
   C. Europeans
   D. Africans

Questions 7–8 refer to the following excerpt.

A Slave Trader Describes the Atlantic Passage

Having bought my complement of 700 slaves, 480 men and 220 women, and finish'd all my business at Whidaw [on the Gold Coast of Africa], I took my leave of the old king and his cappasheirs [attendants], and parted, with many affectionate expressions on both sides, being forced to promise him that I would return again the next year, with several things he desired me to bring from England. . . . I set sail the 27th of July in the morning, accompany'd with the East-India Merchant, who had bought 650 slaves, for the Island of St. Thomas . . . from which we took our departure on August 25th and set sail for Barbadoes.

We spent in our passage from St. Thomas to Barbadoes two months eleven days, from the 25th of August to the 4th of November following: in which time there happened such sickness and mortality among my poor men and Negroes. Of the first we buried 14, and of the last 320, which was a great detriment to our voyage, the Royal African Company losing ten pounds by every slave that died, and the owners of the ship ten pounds ten shillings, being the freight agreed on to be paid by the charter-party for every Negro delivered alive ashore to the African Company's agents at Barbadoes. . . . The loss in all amounted to near 6500 pounds sterling.

The distemper which my men as well as the blacks mostly died of was the white flux, which was so violent and inveterate that no medicine would in the least check it, so that when any of our men were seized with it, we esteemed him a dead man, as he generally proved. . . .

The Negroes are so incident to [subject to] the smallpox that few ships that carry them escape without it, and sometimes it makes vast havoc and destruction among them. But tho' we had 100 at a time sick of it, and that it went thro' the ship, yet we lost not above a dozen by it. All the assistance we gave the diseased was only as much water as they desir'd to drink, and some palm-oil to annoint their sores, and they would generally recover without any other helps but what kind nature gave them. . . .

But what the smallpox spar'd, the flux swept off, to our great regret, after all our pains and care to give them their messes in due order and season, keeping their lodgings as clean and sweet as possible, and enduring so much misery and stench so long among a parcel of creatures nastier than swine, and after all our expectations to be defeated by their mortality. . . .

No gold-finders can endure so much noisome slavery as they do who carry Negroes; for those have some respite and satisfaction, but we endure twice the misery; and yet by their mortality our voyages are ruin'd, and we pine and fret ourselves to death, and take so much pains to so little purpose.

7. From this description, the attitude of the African king that slave trader dealt with was
   A. hostile to Europeans.
   B. reluctance.
   C. willing participation.
   D. mixed.

8. This author thinks of these enslaved Africans as
    A. useless.
    B. to be pitied.
    C. a nuisance.
    D. valuable.

Questions 7–8 refer to the following map.

North America in 1763

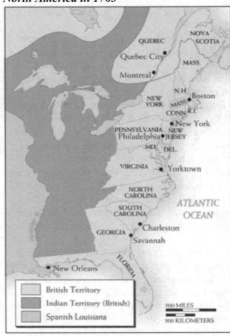

9. By 1763, the British controlled
    A. most of North America.
    B. about half of North America.
    C. mostly what is today Canada.
    D. the Atlantic coast of North America.

10. Which of these is reflected in this map?
    A. the British victory over France in the Seven Years' War
    B. the rapid expansion of the Spanish Empire
    C. the initial British colonization of North America
    D. the steadily shrinking Spanish Empire

Questions 11–13 refer to the following excerpt.

Thomas Paine's "Common Sense," 1776

The Sun never shined on a cause of greater worth. 'Tis not the affair of a City, a County, a Province, or a Kingdom; but of a Continent—of at least one-eighth part of the habitable Globe. 'Tis not the concern of a day, a year, or an age; posterity are virtually involved in the contest, and will be more or less affected even to the end of time, by the proceedings now. Now is the seed-time of Continental union, faith and honour. . . .

I have heard it asserted by some, that as America has flourished under her former connection with Great Britain, the same connection is necessary towards her future happiness, and will always have the same effect. Nothing can be more fallacious than this kind of argument. We may as well assert that because a child has thrived upon milk, that it is never to have meat . . .

America would have flourished as much, and probably much more, had no European power taken any notice of her. The commerce by which she hath enriched herself are the necessaries of life, and will always have a market while eating is the custom of Europe. . . . Our corn will fetch its price in any market in Europe. . . .

But the injuries and disadvantages which we sustain by that connection, are without number; and our duty to mankind at large, as well as to ourselves, instruct us to renounce the alliance: because, any submission to, or dependence on, Great Britain, tends directly to involve this Continent in European wars and quarrels, and set us at variance with nations who would otherwise seek our friendship, and against whom we have neither anger nor complaint. As Europe is our market for trade, we ought to form no partial connection with any part of it. It is the true interest of America to steer clear of European contentions, which she never can do, while, by her dependence on Britain, she is made the makeweight in the scale of British politics.

Europe is too thickly planted with Kingdoms to be long at peace, and whenever a war breaks out between England and any foreign power, the trade of America goes to ruin, BECAUSE OF HER CONNECTION WITH BRITAIN. . . .

There is something very absurd, in supposing a continent to be perpetually governed by an island.

11. For Thomas Paine, a close and exclusive connection between the American colonies and Britain is
    A. generally beneficial for both sides.
    B. disastrous for the colonies.
    C. more important for the colonies than for Britain.
    D. disastrous for both sides.

12. According to Thomas Paine, he speaks for
    A. British interests.
    B. all of North America.
    C. all British colonists.
    D. all European colonists.

13. According to this analysis, the great strength of the colonies lies in their
    A. mineral resources.
    B. military strength.
    C. friendship with Spain.
    D. grain exports.

Questions 14–15 refer to the following image.

"The Horse America Throwing His Master", 1779

14. In this image, the rider represents
    A. the American colonies.
    B. rebels.
    C. the English king.
    D. freedom.

15. According to this cartoon, the rider has treated the horse
    A. harshly.
    B. fairly.
    C. tolerantly.
    D. with great kindness.

Short-Answer Question

Thirteen of the British North American colonies revolted against British rule in 1776.

    a. Choose ONE of the following and explain why your choice represents the key factor leading to this development.

- the conflict that culminated in the Seven Years' War
- the Enlightenment
- the growth of Austrian power

    b. Contrast your choice against ONE of the other options, demonstrating why that option is not as significant as your choice.

Long-Essay Question

To what extent is it correct to typify the Seven Years' War as a world war?

Multiple-Choice Questions

1. D   The American Southwest and Mexico made up most of New Spain.
2. C   Brazil remained mostly unexplored into the late nineteenth and early twentieth centuries.
3. C   The buccaneers live off of their plunder.
4. B   No mention is made of any defenses of any kind.
5. A   Although India was marginally involved, most of Asia did not take part in this trade.
6. B   Looking at the different colored lines, and the areas fed by different traders, it appears that the transatlantic slave trade was controlled by Europeans.
7. C   Some African kingdoms rose to power as participants in the slave trade.
8. C   Although he attempts to keep some alive, he has no pity for the slaves, nor any real concern.
9. D   The British controlled colonies along the entire Atlantic coast but not far into the interior.
10. A   After the Seven Years' War ended, Britain held extensive territories that had formerly belonged to France.
11. B   Paine argues that trade with all of Europe would be better than trading exclusively with Britain.
12. B   Paine equates the colonies with the entire continent. At this point in history, this claim is a gross exaggeration.
13. D   According to Paine, grain exports make the colonies economically independent.
14. C   The rider is clearly the king, with the horse representing the colonies.
15. A   The whip being held by the rider indicates that Britain has treated the colonies with great harshness.

Long-Essay Question

To what extent is it correct to typify the Seven Years' War as a world war?

(Key topics to focus and elaborate on)
- international connections—political and commercial
- area of world concerned
- knock-on impact of conflict between two powers

The Age of Enlightenment: Eighteenth-Century Thought

The eighteenth-century sentiment that economic and political reforms were possible was a novel conviction that was fostered by people and ideas of the Enlightenment. The intellectuals, writers, and critics who championed this reform in the emerging print culture were known as philosophes. The philosophes were interested in greater freedoms and liberties, and they sought rational improvement on many levels of society.

FORMATIVE INFLUENCES ON THE ENLIGHTENMENT

- Isaac Newton's determining the role of gravitation in the relationship between objects enabled other Europeans to realize that much remained to be discovered. His use of empirical support for general laws became an important feature of Enlightenment thought.
- John Locke's view of psychology—that all humans begin life as a *tabula rasa,* or blank page—gave Enlightenment thinkers grounds for arguing that the human condition could be improved by modifying the surrounding social and political environment.
- Britain's domestic stability, religious toleration, freedom of the press, small army, unregulated domestic life, and the political sovereignty of Parliament all suggested to Enlightenment thinkers that absolutist monarchy might not be the best path.
- Louis XIV's heavy taxation, absolute monarchy, religious persecution, and large standing army were perceived by philosophes as obstacles to reform. Voltaire suggested reforms in his book, *Letters on the English,* that he believed could improve French life, modeling his theories on the English system. In *Candide* he attacked war and religious persecution.
- The emergence of a print culture during the Enlightenment helped spread the ideas of philosophes like Voltaire. The public became more literate during this era, a process that enabled these printed materials to be more influential in shifting public opinion.

AP® KEY CONCEPTS

2.3 The popularization and dissemination of the scientific revolution and the application of its methods to political, social, and ethical issues led to an increased, although not unchallenged, emphasis on reason in European culture.

    I. Rational and empirical thought challenged traditional values and ideas.

    II. New public venues and print media popularized Enlightenment ideas.

THE PHILOSOPHES

- Those thinkers who help to mold the Enlightenment are known as philosophes. Generally, they were independent scholars, writers, usually working towards reform.
- Philosophes depended on patrons, often royal. Sometimes there existed close personal, intellectual relations between philosophes and their patrons.

2.3 The popularization and dissemination of the scientific revolution and the application of its methods to political, social, and ethical issues led to an increased, although not unchallenged, emphasis on reason in European culture.

I. Rational and empirical thought challenged traditional values and ideas.

THE ENLIGHTENMENT AND RELIGION

- Many philosophes were critical of Christianity. Voltaire's famous slogan "Crush the Infamous Thing," summed up their general attitude. Philosophes felt that Christianity focused attention on the world to come to the detriment of the present condition. Philosophes also objected to the power structure of the old regime, which gave special rights to clergy.
- **Deism**, or the belief that religion and reason could be combined, was popular among some of the philosophes, who believed that God must be rational and religion should be so as well. Deists believed that God existed and could be empirically justified in the study of nature.
- Toleration and appreciation of other religions grew in this period. Gotthold Lessing's *Nathan the Wise* is perhaps the best example, arguing for greater toleration of Judaism. This toleration was by no means universal, and Christian views and values remained dominant in Europe.
- In the same period, Jewish scholars such as Baruch Spinoza applied a similar critique of their own religion that Voltaire had applied to Christianity.

2.3 The popularization and dissemination of the scientific revolution and the application of its methods to political, social, and ethical issues led to an increased, although not unchallenged, emphasis on reason in European culture.

IV. During the Enlightenment, the rational analysis of religious practices led to natural religion and the demand for religious toleration.

THE ENLIGHTENMENT AND SOCIETY

- Assembled by Denis Diderot and Jean le Rond d'Alembert, the *Encyclopedia* was a major undertaking by Enlightenment thinkers. The book was the product of writing by more than 100 authors, and it survived many attempts at censorship. It included the most advanced ideas of the day, secularized learning, and was, in part, a plea for freedom of expression.
- The philosophes were concerned with the application of laws of reason to the social condition. The Italian philosophe, Cesare Beccaria (1738–1794), attacked torture and capital punishment in his work *On Crimes and Punishments*, and he used critical analysis to address the problem of making punishments just and effective.
- Many philosophes believed that economic policy could be reformed in a way that was consistent with the operation of natural laws. These reformers, known as physiocrats, believed that mercantilist policies hampered the expansion of trade. Their leaders included François Quesnay and Pierre Dupont de Nemours.
- The English economist Adam Smith believed that economic liberty was the foundation for a natural economic system, and he urged that the mercantilist system of England be abolished. Smith believed that individuals should be able to pursue their own economic interests, and he is widely credited as being the founder of *laissez-faire* economic thought and policy. Smith's

four-stage theory of human social and economic development enabled Europeans to see themselves dwelling at the highest level of achievement, which served as a major justification for their economic and imperial domination of the world.

AP® KEY CONCEPTS

2.3 The popularization and dissemination of the scientific revolution and the application of its methods to political, social, and ethical issues led to an increased, although not unchallenged, emphasis on reason in European culture.

    II. New public venues and print media popularized Enlightenment ideas.

    III. New political and economic theories challenged absolutism and mercantilism.

POLITICAL THOUGHT OF THE PHILOSOPHES

- In his 1748 book, *Spirit of the Laws*, Baron de Montesquieu held up the British constitution as an example of the wisest model for regulating the power of government. A political conservative, Montesquieu championed the aristocracy as being an important part of improving the French political regime.

- In *The Social Contract* (1762), Jean-Jacques Rousseau envisioned a society in which each individual could maintain personal freedom while participating as a loyal member in a larger community. He saw human beings as enmeshed in social relationships, and he believed that loyalty to the community should be encouraged.

AP® KEY CONCEPTS

2.3 The popularization and dissemination of the scientific revolution and the application of its methods to political, social, and ethical issues led to an increased, although not unchallenged, emphasis on reason in European culture.

    I. Rational and empirical thought challenged traditional values and ideas.

    III. New political and economic theories challenged absolutism and mercantilism.

WOMEN IN THE THOUGHT AND PRACTICE OF THE ENLIGHTENMENT

- Women helped promote the careers of philosophes by giving them access to their social and political contacts and providing a forum for them to circulate their ideas. Louis XV's mistress, the marquise de Pompadour, helped the *Encyclopedia* overcome censorship efforts. Madame de Tencin promoted Montesquieu's *Spirit of the Laws* by purchasing it and circulating it among friends. The philosophes were by no means ardent feminists; Mary Wollstonecraft addressed their shortcomings and critiqued Rousseau in *A Vindication of the Rights of Woman*, in 1792.

AP ® KEY CONCEPTS

2.3 The popularization and dissemination of the scientific revolution and the application of its methods to political, social, and ethical issues led to an increased, although not unchallenged, emphasis on reason in European culture.

    I. Rational and empirical thought challenged traditional values and ideas.

ROCOCO AND NEOCLASSICAL STYLES IN EIGHTEENTH-CENTURY ART

- The **Rococo** style can be seen as a development and culmination of the Baroque style. It is marked by lavish decoration in architecture, and scenes of rural frivolity in painting.
- By contrast, the **Neoclassical** style was marked by greater restraint, drawing its inspiration from the classical Greek and Roman past and from Enlightenment thought. Painters tended to draw their subjects from Roman history.

AP® KEY CONCEPTS

2.3 The popularization and dissemination of the scientific revolution and the application of its methods to political, social, and ethical issues led to an increased, although not unchallenged, emphasis on reason in European culture.

    I. Rational and empirical thought challenged traditional values and ideas.

    V. The arts moved from the celebration of religious themes and royal power to an emphasis on private life and the public good.

ENLIGHTENED ABSOLUTISM 339–351

- The phrase, "enlightened absolutism," refers to the phenomenon (observed during the last third of the eighteenth century) of several European rulers' embrace of the reforms set out by the philosophes. Monarchs most closely associated with this phenomenon included Frederick II of Prussia, Joseph II of Austria, and Catherine II of Russia. These monarchs pushed for innovations that would increase their revenue.

AP® KEY CONCEPTS

2.1 Different models of political sovereignty affected the relationship among states and between states and individuals.

    I. In much of Europe, absolute monarchy was established over the course of the seventeenth and eighteenth centuries.

CHAPTER 9: AP® PRACTICE TEST

Multiple-Choice Questions

Questions 1–2 refer to the following excerpt.

Emilie Du Châtelet from "Discourse on Happiness."

One must begin by saying to oneself, and by convincing oneself, that we have nothing to do in the world but to obtain for ourselves some agreeable sensations and feelings. The moralists who say to men, curb your passions and master your desires if you want to be happy, do not know the route to happiness. One is only happy because of satisfied tastes and passions . . .

My goal is not to write for all sorts of social orders and all sorts of people; all ranks are not susceptible to the same kind of happiness. I write only for those who are called people of quality, that is to say, for those who are born with a fortune already made, more or less distinguished, more or less opulent, but such that they can maintain their station without being ashamed, and they are perhaps not the easiest to make happy. . . .

I say that one cannot be happy and immoral, and the demonstration of this axiom lies in the depths of the hearts of all men. I put it to them, even to the most villainous, that there is not one of them to whom the reproaches of his conscience—that is to say, of his innermost feeling, the scorn that he feels he deserves and that he experiences, as soon as he is aware of it—there is not one to whom these are not a kind of torture. By villains I do not mean thieves, assassins, poisoners; they do not belong in the category of those for whom I write. Villains are the false and perfidious, the slanderers, the informers, the ungrateful. In a word, all those who have vices the laws do not curb, but against which custom and society have brought formal judgments. These formal judgments are all the more terrible, as they are always carried out.

Undeniably, the love of study is much less necessary to the happiness of men than it is to that of women. Men have infinite resources for their happiness that women lack. They have many means to attain glory. . . . But women are excluded, by definition, from every kind of glory, and when, by chance, one is born with a rather superior soul, only study remains to console her for all the exclusions and dependencies to which she finds herself condemned by her place in society.

1. According to Du Châtelet, study is important to women because
   A. they are smarter than men.
   B. women have to work harder to achieve as much as men.
   C. study is one of the few opportunities available to men.
   D. study leads to better knowledge of the Bible.

2. Which of these principles of the Enlightenment is illustrated here?
   A. Women are the equals of men.
   B. The pursuit of knowledge is supreme amongst human activities.
   C. True knowledge is obtainable only through faith.
   D. A natural hierarchy exists, separating nobles from peasants.

Questions 3–4 refer to the following excerpt.

Adam Smith, from **The Wealth of Nations,** *1776*

In the progress of the division of labour, the employment of the far greater part of those who live by labour, that is, of the great body of the people, comes to be confined to a few very simple operations, frequently to one or two. But the understandings of the greater part of men are necessarily formed by their ordinary employments. The man whose whole life is spent in performing a few simple operations, of which the effects too are, perhaps, always the same, or very nearly the same, has no occasion to exert his understanding, or to exercise his invention in finding out expedients for removing difficulties which never occur. He naturally loses, therefore, the habit of such exertion, and generally becomes as stupid and ignorant as it is possible for a human creature to become. The torpor of his mind renders him not only incapable of relishing or bearing a part in any rational conversation, but of conceiving any generous, noble, or tender sentiment, and consequently of forming any just judgment concerning many even of the ordinary duties of private life. Of the great and extensive interest of his country he is altogether incapable of judging; and unless very particular pains have been taken to render him otherwise, he is equally incapable of defending his country in war. The uniformity of his stationary life naturally corrupts the courage of his mind, and makes him regard with abhorrence the irregular, uncertain, and adventurous life of a soldier. It corrupts even the activity of his body, and renders him incapable of exerting his strength with vigour and perseverance, in any other employment than that to which he has been bred. His dexterity at his own particular trade seems, in this manner, to be acquired at the expence of his intellectual, social, and martial virtues. But in every improved and civilized society this is the state into which the labouring poor, that is, the great body of the people, must necessarily fall, unless government takes some pains to prevent it. . . .

The common people . . . have little time to spare for education. Their parents can scarce afford to maintain them even in infancy. As soon as they are able to work, they must apply to some trade by which they can earn their subsistence. . . . But though the common people cannot . . . be so well instructed as people of some rank and fortune, the most essential parts of education, however, to read, write, and account, can be acquired at so early a period of life, that the greater part even of those who are to be bred to the lowest occupations, have time to acquire them before they can be employed in those occupations. For a very small expence the public can facilitate, can encourage, and can even impose upon almost the whole body of the people, the necessity of acquiring those most essential parts of education.

3.   For Smith, workers are incapable of "conceiving any generous, noble, or tender sentiment" because
   A. of their repetitive work.
   B. they are natural stupid.
   C. their family life is depressing.
   D. they are poor.

4. According to Smith, education should be undertaken for the common people by
   A. their parents.
   B. themselves.
   C. their employers.
   D. the government.

Questions 5–6 refer to the following image.

Image from Voltaire's **Mahomet,** *1793*

5. In this image, the black man and white man are represented as
   A. inferior and superior.
   B. superior and inferior.
   C. distinct but equals.
   D. inferior to women.

6. Which of these Enlightenment beliefs is illustrated here?
   A. toleration
   B. Deism
   C. the supremacy of reason
   D. imperialism

Questions 7–8 refer to the following excerpt.

Denis Diderot from **History of the Two Indies,** *after 1772*

Let the European nations make their own judgment and give themselves the name they deserve. . . . Their explorers arrive in a region of the New World unoccupied by anyone from the Old World, and immediately bury a small strip of metal on which they have engraved these words: This country belongs to us. . . why does it belong to you?

. . . You have no right to the natural products of the country where you land, and you claim a right over your fellow-men. Instead of recognizing this man as a brother you only see him as a slave, a beast of burden. Oh my fellow citizens! You think like that and you behave like that; and you have ideas of justice, a morality, a holy religion . . . in common with whose whom you treat so tyrannically.
* * *
Beyond the Equator a man is neither English, Dutch, French, Spanish, nor Portuguese. He retains only those principles and prejudices of his native country which justify or excuse his conduct. He crawls when he is weak; he is violent when strong; he is in a hurry to acquire, in a hurry to enjoy, and capable of every crime which will lead him most quickly to his goals. He is a domestic tiger returning to the forest; the thirst for blood takes hold of him once more. This is how all the Europeans, every one of them, indistinctly, have appeared in the countries of the New World. There they have assumed a common frenzy—the thirst for gold.

* * *
The Spaniard, the first to be thrown up by the waves onto the shores of the New World, thought he had no duty to people who did not share his color, customs, or religion. He saw in them only tools for his greed, and he clapped them in irons. These weak men, not used to work, soon died in the foul air of the mines, or in other occupations which were virtually as lethal. Then people called for slaves from Africa. Their number has gone up as more land has been cultivated. The Portuguese, Dutch, English, French, Danes, all the nations, free or subjected, have without remorse sought to increase their fortune in the sweat, blood and despair of these unfortunates. What a horrible system!

7.   In this essay, Diderot attacks
    A. imperialism.
    B. devotion to reason.
    C. faith.
    D. learning.

8.   Which of these common European assumptions is refuted here?
    A. Exploration is good in itself.
    B. Non-Europeans are inferior to Europeans.
    C. Education is improving.
    D. The Portuguese are the most chauvinistic people.

Questions 9–10 refer to the following excerpt.

Rousseau, from Émile, *1762*

There is no parity between the two sexes in regard to the consequences of sex. The male is male only at certain moments. The female is female her whole life or at least during her whole youth. Everything constantly recalls her sex to her; and, to fulfill its functions well, she needs a constitution which corresponds to it. She needs care during her pregnancy; she needs rest at the time of childbirth; she needs a soft and sedentary life to suckle her children; she needs patience and gentleness, a zeal and an affection that nothing can rebuff in order to raise her children. She serves as the link between them and their father; she alone makes him love them and gives him the confidence to call them his own. How much tenderness and care is required to maintain the union of the whole family! And, finally, all this must come not from virtues but from tastes, or else the human species would soon be extinguished.

The strictness of the relative duties of the two sexes is not and cannot be the same. When woman complains on this score about unjust man-made inequality, she is wrong. This inequality is not a human institution—or, at least, it is the work not of prejudice but of reason. It is up to the sex that nature has charged with the bearing of children to be responsible for them to the other sex. Doubtless it is not permitted to anyone to violate his faith, and every unfaithful husband who deprives his wife of the only reward of the austere duties of her sex is an unjust and barbarous man. But the unfaithful woman does more; she dissolves the family and breaks all the bonds of nature. . . .

Once it is demonstrated that man and woman are not and ought not be constituted in the same way in either character or temperament, it follows that they ought not to have the same education. In following nature's directions, man and woman ought to act in concert, but they ought not to do the same things. The goal of their labors is common, but their labors themselves are different, and consequently so are the tastes directing them. . . .

The good constitution of children initially depends on that of their mothers. The first education of men depends on the care of women. Men's morals, their passions, their tastes, their pleasures, their very happiness also depend on women. Thus the whole education of women ought to relate to men. To please men, to be useful to them, to make herself loved and honored by them, to raise them when young, to care for them when grown, to counsel them, to console them, to make their lives agreeable and sweet—these are the duties of women at all times, and they ought to be taught from childhood. So long as one does not return to this principle, one will deviate from the goal, and all the precepts taught to women will be of no use for their happiness or for ours.

9. For Rousseau, women are defined primarily as
   A. essentially equal to men.
   B. good wives.
   C. teachers.
   D. servants to men.

10. According to Rousseau, equality is impossible between women and men because of
   A. legal traditions.
   B. cultural norms.
   C. natural differences.
   D. male dominance.

Questions 11–12 refer to the following excerpt.

Mary Wollstonecraft, from **A Vindication of the Rights of Women,** *1792*

[T]he most perfect education . . . is such an exercise of the understanding as is best calculated to strengthen the body and form the heart. Or, in other words, to enable the individual to attain such habits of virtue as will render it independent. In fact, it is a farce to call any being virtuous whose virtues do not result from the exercise of its own reason. This was Rousseau's opinion respecting men: I extend it to women. . . .

I may be accused of arrogance; still I must declare what I firmly believe, that all the writers who have written on the subject of female education and manners from Rousseau to Dr. Gregory [a Scottish physician], have contributed to render women more artificial, weak characters, than they would otherwise have been; and, consequently, more useless members of society. . . .

Strengthen the female mind by enlarging it, and there will be an end to blind obedience; but, as blind obedience is ever fought for by power, tyrants and sensualists are in the right when they endeavour to keep women in the dark, because the former only wants slaves, and the latter a plaything. The sensualist, indeed, has been the most dangerous of tyrants, and women have been duped by their lovers, as princes by their ministers, whilst dreaming that they reigned over them.

Rousseau declares that a woman should never, for a moment, feel herself independent, that she should be governed by fear to exercise her natural cunning, and made a coquettish slave in order to render her a more alluring object of desire, a sweeter companion to man, whenever he chooses to relax himself. He carries the arguments, which he pretends to draw from the indications of nature, still further, and insinuates that truth and fortitude, the cornerstones of all human virtue, should be cultivated with certain restrictions, because, with respect to the female character, obedience is the grand lesson which ought to be impressed with unrelenting rigour.

What nonsense! When will a great man arise with sufficient strength of mind to puff away the fumes which pride and sensuality have thus spread over the subject! If women are by nature inferior to men, their virtues must be the same in quality, if not in degree, or virtue is a relative idea; consequently, their conduct should be founded on the same principles, and have the same aim.

Connected with man as daughters, wives, and mothers, their moral character may be estimated by their manner of fulfilling those simple duties; but the end, the grand end of their exertions should be to unfold their own faculties and acquire the dignity of conscious virtue. . . .

But avoiding . . . any direct comparison of the two sexes collectively, or frankly acknowledging the inferiority of women according to the present appearance of things, I shall only insist that men have increased that inferiority till women are almost sunk below the standard of rational creatures. Let their faculties have room to unfold, and their virtues to gain strength, and then determine where the whole sex must stand in the intellectual scale. . . .

I . . . will venture to assert, that till women are more rationally educated, the progress of human virtue and improvement in knowledge must receive continual checks. . . .

The mother, who wishes to give true dignity of character to her daughter, must, regardless of the sneers of ignorance, proceed on a plan diametrically opposite to that which Rousseau has recommended with all the deluding charms of eloquence and philosophical sophistry: for his eloquence renders absurdities plausible, and his dogmatic conclusions puzzle, without convincing, those who have not ability to refute them.

11. Which of these best encapsulates Wollstonecraft's idea of the highest achievement of women?
   A. fully developing their intellectual capacity
   B. raising children
   C. assisting their husbands' work
   D. protecting the home's virtue

12. As with many Enlightenment thinkers, Wollstonecraft placed great faith in
   A. education.
   B. gender divisions.
   C. social norms.
   D. traditional family roles.

Questions 13–15 refer to the following map.

Expansion of Russia, 1689–1796

13. In the 1700s, the general direction of Russian expansion was to the
    A. south.
    B. west.
    C. east.
    D. north.

14. Expansion under Peter the Great most threatened which nation?
    A. Sweden
    B. Russia
    C. Poland
    D. Hungary

15. Compared to expansion under Peter the Great, expansion under Catherine the Great was
    A. minimal.
    B. more important strategically.
    C. much more extensive.
    D. about the same.

Short-Answer Question

The Enlightenment became the dominant intellectual trend across Europe in the 1700s and into the 1800s.

a. Choose ONE of the following and explain why your choice represents the key factor leading to this development.

- the development of print culture
- the impact of the Reformation
- the impact of the scientific revolution

b. Contrast your choice against ONE of the other options, demonstrating why that option is not as significant as your choice.

Long-Essay Question

How did the *Encyclopedia* embody the main currents of Enlightenment thought?

Answers and Explanations: AP® Practice Test

Multiple-Choice Questions

1. C   The author argues that study is much more valued by women than by men, because men have so many more ways of distinguishing themselves.
2. B   Du Châtelet implicitly places the "love of study" as humankind's most valuable pursuit.
3. A   Smith argues that doing the same work over and over has a negative impact on one's ability to think.
4. D   Smith implies that public education should be undertaken by the government for the young.
5. C   In this image, Europeans and others are represented as culturally different, but sharing the same dignity.
6. A   A growing—although by no means universal—toleration of non-European cultures emerged in the Enlightenment.
7. A   Diderot ridicules the notion of landing in a country and claiming all of its resources.
8. B   Diderot also argues against the idea that other peoples are inferior and do not deserve decent treatment.
9. D   Whether as wives or mothers, women are defined by their duties to men.
10. C   For Rousseau, women are limited by nature, and no equality between the sexes is possible.
11. A   Wollstonecraft argues that women should aspire to "unfold their own faculties and acquire the dignity of conscious virtue."
12. A   The author argues that education would help women fulfill their innate abilities.
13. B   Russia expanded primarily westward, into eastern Europe.
14. A   Peter expanded at the expense of Sweden, which had dominated the Baltic prior to Russian expansion.
15. C   Although Peter's expansion was arguably more critical, Catherine added much more territory.

Long-Essay Question

How did the *Encyclopedia* embody the main currents of Enlightenment thought?

(Key topics to focus and elaborate on)
- Knowledge
- Optimism that all can be known
- Sharing of knowledge

The French Revolution

THE CRISIS OF THE FRENCH MONARCHY

- The French monarchy emerged from the Seven Years' War defeated and in debt; support of the American Revolution further endangered its financial stability. Louis XV and Louis XVI were unable to solve taxation disputes with the *parlements*.
- Jacques Necker issued a report blaming the aristocratic government for France's financial troubles. In 1786, Charles Alexandre de Calonne proposed new taxes, like the *gabelle* on salt and a new tax on landowners, regardless of status. An Assembly of Notables met with Calonne and claimed they had no authority to consent to new taxes; only the Estates General had that right. In 1788, Louis XVI agreed to convene the Estates General in 1789.

AP® KEY CONCEPTS
2.1 Different models of political sovereignty affected the relationship among states and between states and individuals.

    IV. The French Revolution posed a fundamental challenge to Europe's existing political and social order.

THE REVOLUTION OF 1789

- The Estates General consisted of the First Estate (the clergy), the Second Estate (the nobility), and the **Third Estate** (wealthy members of the professional middle class). The organization of the Estates General was a source of initial debate. After the calling of the Estates General, new conflicts between aristocrats and the bourgeoisie emerged.
- The Cahiers de Doléances were lists of grievances presented to the monarch. The Third Estate petitioned the king for equality of rights among the king's subjects. After a standoff, the Third Estate invited the clergy and nobles to join them in creating a new legislative body. On June 17, the body declared itself the National Assembly. Members pledged their loyalty in the Tennis Court Oath and renamed their group the National Constituent Assembly.
- On July 14, more than 800 Parisians stormed the Bastille in search of weapons for the citizen militia they had formed in response to the presence of royal troops in the city and their frustrations with Louis XVI. The crowd stormed the fortress, released prisoners, and killed troops as well as the governor.
- The "Great Fear" that swept the countryside was driven by peasants who felt that they were reclaiming what was rightfully theirs but what had been lost to aristocrats over time.
- In August of 1789, the Assembly set forth the Declaration of the Rights of Man and Citizen, a document that claimed that all men were "born and remain free and equal in rights." Louis XVI was forced by a group of women to return from Versailles to Paris.

AP® KEY CONCEPTS
2.1 Different models of political sovereignty affected the relationship among states and between states and individuals.

IV. The French Revolution posed a fundamental challenge to Europe's existing political and social order.

THE RECONSTRUCTION OF FRANCE

- The National Constituent Assembly declared that only "active citizens"—men paying annual taxes equal to three days of local labor were allowed to vote for electors, who, in turn, voted for members of the legislature. Women could not vote or hold office. This law transferred power from aristocratic wealth to anyone with accumulated land or property.
- In local and judicial administration, eighty-three *départements* replaced ancient provinces.
- The National Constituent Assembly suppressed guilds, liberated the grain trade, and established the metric system.
- The Roman Catholic Church was reconstructed by the Assembly into a branch of the secular state by the issuance of the Civil Constitution of the Clergy.
- Disgruntled aristocrats known as émigrés left France and resettled in areas near the French border where they plotted counterrevolution.

AP® KEY CONCEPTS

2.1 Different models of political sovereignty affected the relationship among states and between states and individuals.

    IV. The French Revolution posed a fundamental challenge to Europe's existing political and social order.

THE END OF THE MONARCHY: A SECOND REVOLUTION

- A group of deputies from the Third Estate, called **Jacobins**, pressed for more radical reform. In the Legislative Assembly, a group of Jacobins known as Girondists ordered the émigrés to return or suffer loss of property and demanded that clergy who had refused to take the oath to support the Civil Constitution do so or lose their state pensions. Louis XVI vetoed both acts.
- In August of 1792, a Parisian crowd invaded the Tuileries Palace and forced Louis XVI and Marie Antoinette to take refuge in the Legislative Assembly. Louis effectively lost his power, which was now in the hands of the Paris Commune, a committee of representatives from wards of Paris. During the **September Massacres**, the Paris Commune murdered about 1,200 people in jails, many of whom were aristocrats or priests. Following these acts, the **Convention**, a new assembly, declared France a republic. In December of 1792, Louis XVI was executed; one month later, France was at war with England, Holland, Spain, and Prussia.

AP® KEY CONCEPTS

2.1 Different models of political sovereignty affected the relationship among states and between states and individuals.

    IV. The French Revolution posed a fundamental challenge to Europe's existing political and social order.

EUROPE AT WAR WITH THE REVOLUTION

- Edmund Burke, a British statesman and Irish-born writer, condemned the Revolution for its extreme measures in *Reflections on the Revolution in France* (1790). Other European leaders, like William Pitt in England, and rulers in Prussia, Russia, discouraged popular uprisings.

AP® KEY CONCEPTS

2.1 Different models of political sovereignty affected the relationship among states and between states and individuals.

    I. In much of Europe, absolute monarchy was established over the course of the seventeenth and eighteenth centuries.

    IV. The French Revolution posed a fundamental challenge to Europe's existing political and social order.

THE REIGN OF TERROR

- War brought new challenges for the Republic of France. The revolutionary government established a series of committees to protect its new creation. The Committee of General Security and the Committee of Public Safety were created to carry out executive duties of the government. A *levée en masse,* or military conscription, for all males in the population was mobilized to defend the country. This citizen army led to the **Reign of Terror**, a period marked by quasi-judicial executions from autumn 1793 to mid-summer 1794. The Christian calendar, with its religious holidays, was replaced by a secular calendar, and other places of worship were "de-Christianized."

- Executions were increasingly arbitrary, with ***sans-culottes*** revolutionaries serving as victims as well as persecutors. Marie Antoinette and other members of the royal family were the first victims. Maximilien Robespierre, a powerful member of the Committee for Public Safety, who established the "Cult of the Supreme Being," a civic religion modeled after the views of Rousseau, had encouraged the execution of key republican political figures, including his Committee colleague Jacques Danton. Robespierre also became a victim of the terror he had helped create and was executed. The Reign of Terror claimed more than 25,000 victims.

AP® KEY CONCEPTS

2.1 Different models of political sovereignty affected the relationship among states and between states and individuals.

    IV. The French Revolution posed a fundamental challenge to Europe's existing political and social order.

THE THERMIDORIAN REACTION 385–390

- The **Thermidorian Reaction** involved political reconstruction, and abandoned the Constitution of 1793. In its place, the Convention issued the Constitution of the Year III, which provided for a legislature of two houses. The upper body, or Council of Elders, consisted of men over forty who were husbands or widowers. The lower Council of Five Hundred consisted of men of at least thirty years old who were either married or single. The executive body was a five-person Directory, chosen by the Elders from a list submitted by the Council of Five Hundred.

AP® KEY CONCEPTS

2.1 Different models of political sovereignty affected the relationship among states and between states and individuals.

    IV. The French Revolution posed a fundamental challenge to Europe's existing political and social order.

CHAPTER 10: AP® PRACTICE TEST

Multiple-Choice Questions

Questions 1–3 refer to the following excerpt.

From a Cahiers de Doléances, *1789*

The order of the third estate of the City . . . of Dourdan . . . supplicates [the king] to accept the grievances, complaints, and remonstrances which it is permitted to bring to the foot of the throne, and to see therein only the expression of its zeal and the homage of its obedience.

It wishes:

1. That his subjects of the third estate, equal by such status to all other citizens, present themselves before the common father without other distinction which might degrade them.

2. That all the orders, already united by duty and common desire contribute equally to the needs of the State, also deliberate in common concerning its needs.

3. That no citizen lose his liberty except according to law: that, consequently, no one be arrested by virtue of special orders, or, if imperative circumstances necessitate such orders that the prisoner be handed over to regular courts of justice within forty-eight hours at the latest.

12. That every tax, direct or indirect, be granted only for a limited time, and that every collection beyond such term be regarded as peculation, and punished as such.

15. That every personal tax be abolished; that thus the capitation [a poll tax] and the taille [tax from which nobility and clergy were exempt] and its accessories be merged with the vingtièmes [an income tax] in a tax on land and real or nominal property.

16. That such tax be borne equally, without distinction, by all classes of citizens and by all kinds of property, even feudal . . . rights.

17. That the tax substituted for the corvée be borne by all classes of citizens equally and without distinction. That said tax, at present beyond the capacity of those who pay it and the needs to which it is destined, be reduced by at least one-half.

1. Which of these would have been most likely to be among those signing this petition?
   A. lawyers
   B. nobles
   C. royalty
   D. priests

2. The most common theme of this petition is the desire for
   A. voting rights.
   B. an end to class privilege.
   C. an end of the monarchy.
   D. a single royal court.

3. Which of these best describes these petitioners?
   A. They are in open rebellion.
   B. They are threatening the king with rebellion.
   C. Their demands are reactionary, rather than revolutionary.
   D. Their demands threaten the existing social and political order.

Questions 4–6 refer to the following excerpt.

The National Assembly Decrees Civic Equality in France

The National Assembly completely abolishes the feudal regime. It decrees that, among the rights and dues . . . all those originating in real or personal serfdom, personal servitude, and those which represent them, are abolished without indemnification; all other are declared redeemable, and that the price and mode of redemption shall be fixed by the National Assembly. . . .

2. The exclusive right to maintain pigeon-houses and dove-cotes is abolished. . . .

3. The exclusive right to hunt and to maintain unenclosed warrens is likewise abolished. . . .

4. All manorial courts are suppressed without indemnification.

5. Tithes of every description and the dues which have been substituted for [them] . . . are abolished on condition, however, that some other method be devised to provide for the expenses of divine worship, the support of the officiating clergy, the relief of the poor, repairs and rebuilding of churches and parsonages, and for all establishments, seminaries, schools, academies, asylums, communities, and other institutions, for the maintenance of which they are actually devoted. . . .

6. The sale of judicial and municipal offices shall be suppressed forthwith. . . .

7. Pecuniary privileges, personal or real, in the payment of taxes are abolished forever. . .

8. All citizens, without distinction of birth, are eligible to any office or dignity, whether ecclesiastical, civil or military. . . .

4. For the citizens of Dourdan, concerning their petition above, this decree would have been
   A. an insult.
   B. a triumph.
   C. generally disappointing.
   D. irrelevant.

5. According to this decree, education would be
   A. placed under civic authority.
   B. carried out by the Church, but with public funds.
   C. carried out as before the French Revolution.
   D. undertaken by families.

6. The changes embodied in this document are
   A. primarily social.
   B. social and economic.
   C. political, social, legal, and economic.
   D. only legal.

Questions 7–9 refer to the following excerpt.

Julian Raymond Petitions the French National Assembly, 1791

Remaining to this day under the oppression of the white colonists, we dare hope that we do not ask the National Assembly in vain for the rights, which it has declared, belong to every man.

In our just protests, if the troubles, the calumnies that you have witnessed until today under the legislation of white colonists, and finally, if the truths which we had the honor of presenting yesterday to the bar of the Assembly do not overcome the unjust pretensions of the white colonial legislators who want to [proceed] without our participation, we beg the Assembly not to jeopardize the little remaining liberty we have, that of being able to abandon the ground soaked with the blood of our brothers and of permitting us to flee the sharp knife of the laws they will prepare against us.

If the Assembly has decided to pass a law which lets our fate depend on twenty-nine whites [in the colonial Assembly], our decided enemies, we demand to add an amendment to the decree which would be rendered in this situation, that free men of color can emigrate with their fortunes so that they can be neither disturbed nor hindered by the whites.

Mr. President, this is the last recourse which remains for us to escape the vengeance of the white colonists who menace us for not having given up our claims to the rights which the National Assembly has declared belong to every man.

7. Which of these probably spurred the writing of this petition?
   A. the Seven Years' War
   B. the outbreak of the French Revolution
   C. the Reign of Terror
   D. the Napoleonic Wars

8. Unlike the petition of the citizens of Dourdan, this petitioner
   A. was not a French citizen.
   B. was a slave.
   C. demanded an end to traditional privileges.
   D. addressed the French premier.

9. Like the Third Estate in France, a key complaint of this petitioner is the
   A. racial basis of injustice.
   B. power of the church.
   C. small minority that controls the country.
   D. high taxes imposed on the lower classes.

Questions 10–12 refer to the following excerpt.

Edmund Burke, from **Reflections on the Revolution in France,** *1790*

A government of the nature of that set up at our very door has never been hitherto seen, or ever imagined in Europe. . . . France, since her revolution, is under the sway of a sect, whose leaders have deliberately, at one stroke, demolished the whole body of that jurisprudence which France had pretty nearly in common with other civilized countries. . . .

Its foundation is laid in regicide, in Jacobinism, and in atheism, and it has joined to those principles a body of systematic manners, which secures their operation. . . .

I call a commonwealth regicide, which lays it down as a fixed law of nature, and a fundamental right of man, that all government, not being a democracy, is an usurpation. That all kings, as such, are usurpers; and for being kings may and ought to be put to death, with their wives, families, and adherents. That commonwealth which acts uniformly upon those principles . . . —this I call regicide by establishment.

Jacobinism is the revolt of the enterprising talents of a country against its property. When private men form themselves into associations for the purpose of destroying the pre-existing laws and institutions of their country; when they secure to themselves an army, by dividing amongst the people of no property the estates of the ancient and lawful proprietors, when a state recognizes those acts; when it does not make confiscations for crimes, but makes crimes for confiscations; when it has its principal strength, and all its resources, in such a violation of property . . . —I call this Jacobinism by establishment.

I call it atheism by establishment, when any state, as such, shall not acknowledge the existence of God as a moral governor of the world; . . . — when it shall abolish the Christian religion by a regular decree;—when it shall persecute with a cold, unrelenting, steady cruelty, by every mode of confiscation, imprisonment, exile, and death, all its ministers;—when it shall generally shut up or pull down churches; when the few buildings which remain of this kind shall be opened only for the purpose of making a profane apotheosis of monsters, whose vices and crimes have no parallel amongst men. . . . When, in the place of that religion of social benevolence, and of individual self-denial, in mockery of all religion, they institute impious, blasphemous, indecent theatric rites, in honour of their vitiated, perverted reason, and erect altars to the personification of their own corrupted and bloody republic; . . . when wearied out with incessant martyrdom, and the cries of a people hungering and thirsting for religion, they permit it, only as a tolerated evil—I call this atheism by establishment.

When to these establishments of regicide, of Jacobinism, and of atheism, you add the correspondent system of manners, no doubt can be left on the mind of a thinking man concerning their determined hostility to the human race.

10. In 1796, the government of England, unlike France, was
    A. a republic.   C. a monarchy.
    B. under threat by rebels.   D. a democracy.

11. Burke argues in support of the rights of what group in France?
    A. the Third Estate   C. the nobles
    B. the clergy   D. the military

12. Which of these best explains why Burke defines regicide so narrowly?
    A. to vilify the failure of the French nobles to support their king
    B. to label only the Jacobins as regicides
    C. to tie the French Jacobins with tyranny
    D. to distinguish between the English and French acts of killing their kings

Questions 13–15 refer to the following excerpt.

Paris Jacobin Club Circular, 1793

Friends, we are betrayed! To arms! To arms! The terrible hour is at hand when the defenders of the Patrie must vanquish or bury themselves under the bloody ruins of the Republic. Frenchmen, never was your liberty in such great peril! At last our enemies have put the finishing touch to their foul perfidy, and to complete it their accomplice Dumouriez is marching on Paris. . . .

But Brothers, not all your dangers are to be found there! . . . You must be convinced of a grievous truth! Your greatest enemies are in your midst, they direct your operations. O Vengeance !!! . . .

Yes, brothers and friends, yes, it is in the Senate that parricidal hands tear at your vitals! Yes, the counterrevolution is in the Government . . . , in the National Convention. It is there, at the center of your security and your hope, that criminal delegates hold the threads of the web that they have woven with the horde of despots who come to butcher us! . . . It is there that a sacrilegious cabal is directed by the English court . . . and others. . . .

Let us rise! Yes, let us rise! Let us arrest all the enemies of our revolution, and all suspected persons. Let us exterminate, without pity, all conspirators, unless we wish to be exterminated ourselves. . . .

Let the departments, the districts, the municipalities, and all the popular societies unite and concur in protesting to the Convention, by dispatching thereto a veritable rain of petitions manifesting the formal wish for the immediate recall of all unfaithful members who have betrayed their duty by not wishing the death of the tyrant, and, above all, against those who have led astray so many of their colleagues. Such delegates are traitors, royalists, or fatuous men. The Republic condemns the friends of kings! . . .

Let us all unite equally to demand that the thunder or indictments be loosed against generals who are traitors to the Republic, against prevaricating ministers, against postal administrators, and against all unfaithful agents of the government. Therein lies our most salutary means of defence; but let us repel the traitors and tyrants.

The center of their conspiracy is here: it is in Paris that our perfidious enemies wish to consummate their crime. Paris, the cradle, the bulwark of liberty, is, without doubt, the place where they have sworn to annihilate the holy cause of humanity under the corpses of patriots.

13. This document underlines which of these characteristics of revolutions?
    A. extreme violence
    B. loss of revolutionary fervor
    C. economic upheaval
    D. factionalism

14. Which of these issues appears to be dividing groups referred to in this appeal?
    A. whether or not to go to war with England
    B. who would be the next king of France
    C. support or opposition to regicide
    D. whether or not to include the Third Estate in the National Assembly

15. The authors of this appeal would have viewed the creation of the National Assembly in 1789 as
    A. only a first step.
    B. the culmination of the Revolution.
    C. a disaster.
    D. a betrayal.

Short-Answer Question

In August, 1789, the nobles of France voluntarily abandoned their traditional titles and privileges.

   a. Choose ONE of the following and explain why your choice represents the key factor leading to this development.

   - The Great Fear led to peasant attacks on rural estates.
   - The Fall of the Bastille took place in July 1789.
   - Louis XVI wavered between opposition to and qualified support for the Revolution.

   b. Contrast your choice against ONE of the other options, demonstrating why that option is not as significant as your choice.

Long-Essay Question

Were the Reign of Terror and the Directory predictable events in the unfolding of the French Revolution?

Multiple-Choice Questions

1. A   The third estate included everyone who was not a member of the clergy or of the nobility; the group included professionals such as doctors and lawyers.
2. C   The common thread throughout these demands is that all citizens be treated equally, ending centuries of special privileges for the clergy and nobility.
3. D   While these petitioners appeal respectfully to the king, their demands are progressive, if not radical for their day.
4. B   This decree would have satisfied the petitioners both in the spirit and in the letter of their demands.
5. B   At this point, the plan was to have education provided by the clergy, but new taxes would be imposed to fund education.
6. C   This decree enacts profound changes ending the entire socio-political system, including legal and economic traditions based on class privilege.
7. B   This petition came in the middle of the French Revolution, just two years after it began.
8. A   There are numerous parallels between this petition and the cahier of the citizens of Dourdon.
9. C   As in the French petition, this Haitian petitioner hopes to end the monopoly of power by a tiny privileged class; in this case the class is defined primarily by race.
10. C   Both of the governments were republics, but the French government was a democracy, while the English government was a monarchy.
11. C   Burke was horrified by the French revolutionaries' abolition of class privilege and by the seizure of noble and royal property.
12. D   Both countries had killed their kings, but Burke is careful to point out that the French had replaced monarchy with a democracy.
13. D   This call to arms illustrates both the factionalism and the volatility that characterize revolutions.
14. C   A key issue here is that the Jacobins called for the death of the king, while their political enemies opposed taking that step.
15. A   For these Jacobins, the initial revolution did not go far enough in ending all traces of noble privilege and in ending the monarchy.

Long-Essay Question

Were the Reign of Terror and the Directory predictable events in the unfolding of the French Revolution?

(Key topics to focus and elaborate on)
- two different political directions
- radicalizing trend of the Revolution
- waves of radicalization and reaction
- every revolution arguably has radical and reactionary phases

CHAPTER 11

The Age of Napoleon and the Triumph of Romanticism

THE RISE OF NAPOLEON BONAPARTE

- Napoleon Bonaparte (1769–1821) rose to power in the aftermath of the Thermidorian Reaction by defending the new regime on October 5, 1795 against a rebellion.
- In November of 1799, Napoleon overthrew the Directory through a *coup d'état*, issued the Constitution of Year VIII, which effectively established him as ruler, and formed a new government: the Consulate.

AP® KEY CONCEPTS
2.1 Different models of political sovereignty affected the relationship among states and between states and individuals.
> V. Claiming to defend the ideals of the French Revolution, Napoleon Bonaparte imposed French control over much of the European continent that eventually provoked a nationalistic reaction.

THE CONSULATE IN FRANCE (1799–1804)

- The **Consulate** was composed of three Consuls, but Napoleon retained all of the power as First Consul. His constitution was overwhelmingly approved in a plebiscite.
- Bonaparte quickly made peace with France's enemies, restored peace and order at home, requiring loyalty from those he employed from every political faction. He was also ruthless and efficient in suppressing opposition. Napoleon made peace with the Catholic Church in the Concordat of 1801. In 1802, a plebiscite raified Napoleon as consul for life, and Napoleon began the codification of French law by producing the Civil Code of 1804—also known as the Napoleonic Code.

AP® KEY CONCEPTS
2.1 Different models of political sovereignty affected the relationship among states and between states and individuals.
> V. Claiming to defend the ideals of the French Revolution, Napoleon Bonaparte imposed French control over much of the European continent that eventually provoked a nationalistic reaction.

THE HAITIAN REVOLUTION (1799–1804)

- Inspired by the events and principles of the French Revolution, Haiti divided between whites, free blacks, and black slaves.
- A revolution broke out in 1791, led by François-Dominique Toussaint L'Ouverture. Haitian slaves rose to join the free blacks.
- The uprising was suppressed by Napoleon who feared the loss of French colonies in the region.

- In 1803, Napoleon abandoned his American colonies, allowing Haiti to gain its freedom

2.1 Different models of political sovereignty affected the relationship among states and between states and individuals.

> V. Claiming to defend the ideals of the French Revolution, Napoleon Bonaparte imposed French control over much of the European continent that eventually provoked a nationalistic reaction.

NAPOLEON'S EMPIRE (1804–1814)

- In 1804, Napoleon crowned himself Napoleon I. He proceeded to conquer much of Europe in a series of military campaigns that transformed the map of the continent.
- Citizen loyalty and a *levée en masse* gave Napoleon virtually limitless resources of soldiers to wage war. Napoleon sent an army to restore the rebellious colony of Haiti to French rule.
- William Pitt the Younger formed the Third Coalition, persuading Austria and Russia to move against French aggression in Germany. In 1805, the British defeated Napoleon's navy at the Battle of Trafalgar, which ended to Napoleon's plans to invade the British Isles.
- In his greatest victory, Napoleon defeated Austrian and Russian forces at Austerlitz in 1805. The subsequent treaty with Austria gave Napoleon major concessions and recognized him as king of Italy. In 1806, Napoleon organized the Confederation of the Rhine, enabling the dissolution of the Holy Roman Empire.

2.1 Different models of political sovereignty affected the relationship among states and between states and individuals.

> V. Claiming to defend the ideals of the French Revolution, Napoleon Bonaparte imposed French control over much of the European continent that eventually provoked a nationalistic reaction.

EUROPEAN RESPONSE TO THE EMPIRE

- The Napoleonic Code was established in the territories that French forces had conquered, and Enlightenment attitudes of liberalism and nationalism spread to nations throughout Europe.
- When Napoleon deposed the Spanish Bourbons and put his brother on the throne, a rebellion arose, which began a guerilla war that was consummated when British and Spanish forces under the Duke of Wellington drove the French out.
- Napoleon resolved to invade Russia after Alexander I withdrew from the Continental System in 1812, which prohibited trade with Britain. Napoleon had superior manpower, but the Russians burned crops and villages, destroying all food and supplies as they retreated. Napoleon captured Moscow, but ordered his army to retreat; many of his soldiers perished during this ill-fated attempt at domination. Napoleon abdicated his throne in 1814 and was exiled to Elba, an island off the Italian coast.

2.1 Different models of political sovereignty affected the relationship among states and between states and individuals.

V. Claiming to defend the ideals of the French Revolution, Napoleon Bonaparte imposed French control over much of the European continent that eventually provoked a nationalistic reaction.

2.4 The experiences of everyday life were shaped by demographic, environmental, medical, and technological changes.

I. In the seventeenth century, small landholdings, low-productivity agricultural practices, poor transportation, and adverse weather limited and disrupted the food supply, causing periodic famines. By the eighteenth century, Europeans began to escape from the Malthusian imbalance between population and the food supply, resulting in steady population growth.

THE CONGRESS OF VIENNA AND THE EUROPEAN SETTLEMENT

- The Congress of Vienna took more than a year to conclude, and England, Prussia, Russia, and Austria dominated the discussions. All the powers agreed that France should not be allowed to dominate Europe again. However, to pacify France, the leaders restored the French Bourbon monarchy and worked out a boundary settlement that was not overly punitive.
- Napoleon returned from exile and was restored to power for 100 days before the Duke of Wellington defeated him at the Battle of Waterloo. Thereafter, Napoleon lived on Saint Helena. The Quadruple Alliance among England, Austria, Prussia, and Russia was renewed. The purpose of the alliance was to serve as a coalition for peace and to maintain the balance of power, while suppressing revolutionary ideas of nationalism.

AP ® KEY CONCEPTS

3.4 European states struggled to maintain international stability in an age of nationalism and revolutions.

I. The Concert of Europe (or Congress System) sought to maintain the status quo through collective action and adherence to conservatism.

THE ROMANTIC MOVEMENT

- **Romanticism** was a reaction against much of the thought of the Enlightenment. Romantic writers rejected the ideas of the philosophes and sought to interpret nature in terms of their experience with it and reaction to it, rather than through mechanical terms or categories.
- Romanticism elevated the role of the individual and the importance of individual cultures. A new spirit of nationalism developed across Europe, partly in reaction to the new importance placed on individual feeling and experience.

AP® KEY CONCEPTS

2.3 The popularization and dissemination of the scientific revolution and the application of its methods to political, social, and ethical issues led to an increased, although not unchallenged, emphasis on reason in European culture.

VI. While Enlightenment values dominated the world of European ideas, they were challenged by the revival of public sentiment and feeling.

3.6 European ideas and culture expressed a tension between objectivity and scientific realism on one hand, and subjectivity and individual expression on the other.

    I. Romanticism broke with neoclassical forms of artistic representation and with rationalism, placing more emphasis on intuition and emotion.

THE ROMANTIC QUESTIONING OF THE SUPREMACY OF REASON

- Some of the intellectuals affiliated with the Romantic movement were influenced by the work of Jean-Jacques Rousseau. Rousseau's *Émile* focuses on the importance of letting children grow and learn by trial and error. This concept of human development appealed to Romantics who believed that people should grow in accord with their individual natures.
- Immanuel Kant's works of philosophy endorsed his belief in human freedom, immortality, and existence in God. Many Romantics believed his work refuted the rational focus of the Enlightenment, which negated the importance of imagination and feeling.

AP® KEY CONCEPTS

2.3 The popularization and dissemination of the scientific revolution and the application of its methods to political, social, and ethical issues led to an increased, although not unchallenged, emphasis on reason in European culture.

    VI. While Enlightenment values dominated the world of European ideas, they were challenged by the revival of public sentiment and feeling.

3.6 European ideas and culture expressed a tension between objectivity and scientific realism on one hand, and subjectivity and individual expression on the other.

    I. Romanticism broke with neoclassical forms of artistic representation and with rationalism, placing more emphasis on intuition and emotion.

ROMANTIC LITERATURE

- Romantic authors wrote works that did not conform to classical rules and made use of the imagination. This kind of literature was represented by Victor Hugo in France and Goethe and Schlegel in Germany. English Romantics tended to be absorbed by the idea of the imagination, how it was affected by nature, and the mystical elements of experience. William Blake, Samuel Taylor Coleridge, William Wordsworth, and Lord Byron are some of the most important English Romantics.

AP® KEY CONCEPTS

2.3 The popularization and dissemination of the scientific revolution and the application of its methods to political, social, and ethical issues led to an increased, although not unchallenged, emphasis on reason in European culture.

    VI. While Enlightenment values dominated the world of European ideas, they were challenged by the revival of public sentiment and feeling.

3.6 European ideas and culture expressed a tension between objectivity and scientific realism on one hand, and subjectivity and individual expression on the other.

    I. Romanticism broke with neoclassical forms of artistic representation and with rationalism, placing more emphasis on intuition and emotion.

ROMANTIC ART

- As in literature, painters and architects were inspired by the culture of the Middle Ages. At the same time, the landscapes John Constable and Caspar David Friedrich focused on natural forces.

AP® KEY CONCEPTS

2.3 The popularization and dissemination of the scientific revolution and the application of its methods to political, social, and ethical issues led to an increased, although not unchallenged, emphasis on reason in European culture.

    VI. While Enlightenment values dominated the world of European ideas, they were challenged by the revival of public sentiment and feeling.

3.6 European ideas and culture expressed a tension between objectivity and scientific realism on one hand, and subjectivity and individual expression on the other.

    I. Romanticism broke with neoclassical forms of artistic representation and with rationalism, placing more emphasis on intuition and emotion.

RELIGION IN THE ROMANTIC PERIOD

- Many Romantics believed in the supremacy of the imagination for perceiving nature and the world, and they were drawn to the medieval Christianity and spiritual mysteries of all kinds, believing that religion and their beliefs were compatible. **Methodism**, a faith that stressed inward, heartfelt religion was founded by John Wesley in England.

AP® KEY CONCEPTS

2.3 The popularization and dissemination of the scientific revolution and the application of its methods to political, social, and ethical issues led to an increased, although not unchallenged, emphasis on reason in European culture.

    VI. While Enlightenment values dominated the world of European ideas, they were challenged by the revival of public sentiment and feeling.

3.6 European ideas and culture expressed a tension between objectivity and scientific realism on one hand, and subjectivity and individual expression on the other.

    I. Romanticism broke with neoclassical forms of artistic representation and with rationalism, placing more emphasis on intuition and emotion.

ROMANTIC VIEWS OF NATIONALISM AND HISTORY

- Nationalism and Romanticism were essentially distinct movements but with important mutual influences.
- In Germany and Italy, nationalism assisted the formation of new nations.
- In viewing other cultures, Christian Europeans veered between a fondness for tales of Crusader victories over Muslims and romanticized views of Muslim leaders.
- The French Egyptian campaign and translations of Persian classics led to a new appreciation of Middle Eastern culture, especially the ancient past.

2.3 The popularization and dissemination of the scientific revolution and the application of its methods to political, social, and ethical issues led to an increased, although not unchallenged, emphasis on reason in European culture.

VI. While Enlightenment values dominated the world of European ideas, they were challenged by the revival of public sentiment and feeling.

3.6 European ideas and culture expressed a tension between objectivity and scientific realism on one hand, and subjectivity and individual expression on the other.

I. Romanticism broke with neoclassical forms of artistic representation and with rationalism, placing more emphasis on intuition and emotion.

Multiple-Choice Questions

Questions 1–2 refer to the following excerpt.

Napoleon Announces His Seizure of Power

On my return to Paris, I found a division reigning amongst all the constituted authorities. There was no agreement but on this single point—that the constitution was half destroyed, and could by no means effect the salvation of our liberties. All the parties came to me . . . and demanded my support. I refused to be a man of any party. A council of elders invited me, and I answered to their call. [Their] plan demanded a calm and liberal examination, free from every influence and every fear. The council of elders resolved, in consequence, that the sittings of the legislative body should be removed to St. Cloud, and charged me with the disposition of the force necessary to secure its independence, I owed it, my fellow-citizens, to the soldiers who are perishing in our armies, and the national glory, acquired at the price of their blood, to accept of this command. The councils being assembled at St. Cloud, the republican troops guaranteed their safety from without; but within, assassins had established the reign of terror. . . . The majority was disorganized, the most intrepid orators were disconcerted, and the inutility of every wise proposition was made evident. I bore my indignation and my grief to the council of elders, I demanded of them to ensure the execution of their generous designs. I represented to them the maladies of their country, from which those designs originated. . . . I then repaired to the council of five hundred without arms, and my head uncovered. . . . I wished to recall to the majority their wishes, and to assure them of their power. . . . Twenty assassins threw themselves upon me, and sought my breast. The grenadiers of the legislative body, whom I had left at the door of the hall, came up and placed themselves between me and my assassins. . . . They succeeded in bearing me away. I gave orders to rescue [the president, Napoleon's brother] from their power, and six grenadiers of the legislative body brought him out of the hall. . . . The factious were intimidated, and dispersed themselves. The majority, released from their blows, entered freely and peaceably into the hall of sitting, heard the propositions which were made to them for the public safety deliberated, and prepared the salutary resolution which is to become the new and provisional law of the republic. Frenchmen! you will recognize, without doubt, in this conduct, the zeal of a soldier of liberty, and of a citizen devoted to the republic. The ideas of preservation, protection, and freedom, immediately resumed their places on the dispersion of the faction who wished to oppress the councils, and who, in making themselves the most odious of men, never cease to be the most contemptible.

1. With respect to the French Revolution, Napoleon claims that he
   A. initiated it.
   B. ended it.
   C. rescued it.
   D. ignored it.

2. According to Napoleon, he came to power because
   A. the Assembly elected him.
   B. of a popular vote.
   C. he assassinated his opponents.
   D. he was invited to take charge.

Questions 3–4 refer to the following map.

The Continental System, 1806–1810

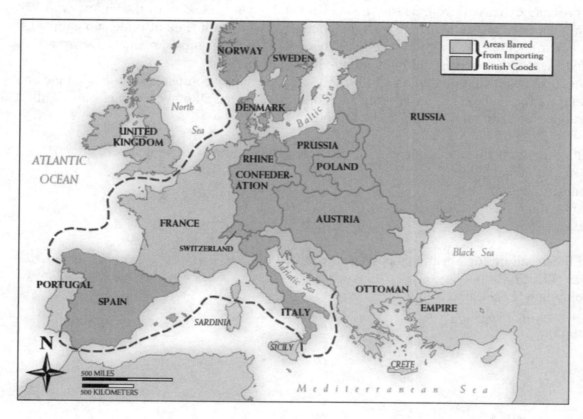

3. By this period, Napoleon controlled
   A. only France and Italy.
   B. most of western Europe.
   C. all of Europe.
   D. only eastern Europe.

4. Which of these was Britain's best hope for assistance in breaking the Continental System?
   A. Portugal
   B. France
   C. Italy
   D. Austria

Questions 5–6 refer to the following excerpt.

A German Writer Describes the War of Liberation

Fired with enthusiasm, the people rose, "with God for King and Fatherland." Among the Prussians there was only one voice, one feeling, one anger and one love, to save the Fatherland and to free Germany. . . . War, war, sounded the cry from the Carpathians to the Baltic, from the Niemen to the Elbe. War! cried the nobleman and landed proprietor who had become impoverished. War! that peasant who was driving his last horse to death. . . . War! the citizen who was growing exhausted from quartering soldiers and paying taxes. War! the widow who was sending her only son to the front. War! the young girl who, with tears of pride and pain, was leaving her betrothed. . . . Even young women, under all sorts of disguises, rushed to arms; all wanted to drill, arm themselves and fight and die for the Fatherland. . . .

The most beautiful thing about all this holy zeal and happy confusion was . . . that the one great feeling for the Fatherland, its freedom and honor, swallowed all other feelings, caused all other considerations and relationships to be forgotten.

5. Which of these notable consequences of Napoleon's conquests is illustrated here?
   A. the Continental System
   B. industrialization
   C. nationalism
   D. destruction

6. All of those calling for war in this passage are united by
   A. class identity.
   B. belonging to the same country.
   C. German identity.
   D. religion.

Questions 7–8 refer to the following map.

Europe in Late 1812

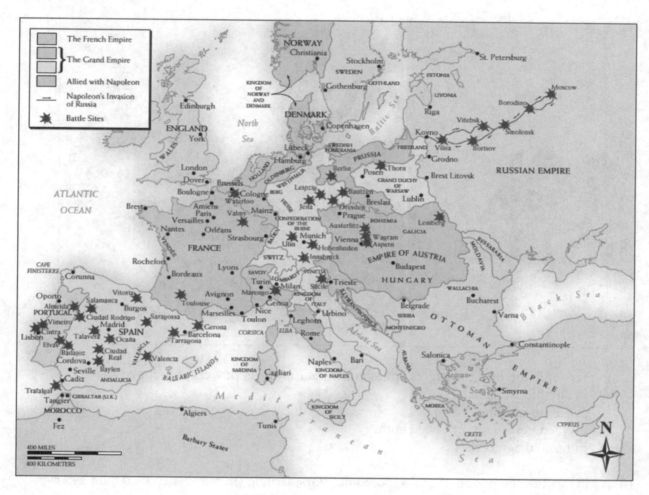

7. Which of these countries experienced the fewest battles, according to this map?
    A. Spain
    B. France
    C. Russia
    D. Portugal

8. By 1812, which of these was the only ally left available to England?
    A. Portugal
    B. Austria
    C. Spain
    D. Norway

Questions 9–11 refer to the following excerpt.

The Congress of Vienna

LE CONGRÈS.

9. In this depiction of the Congress of Vienna, the European powers are represented as
    A. in complete chaos.
    B. acting in unison.
    C. divided between north and south.
    D. in limited agreement.

10. As in most of the period of the Napoleonic Wars, Britain (in red) is depicted here as
    A. part of the Concert of Europe.
    B. hostile to the Holy Alliance.
    C. aloof.
    D. a French ally.

11. Which region of Europe appears most united in this cartoon?
    A. northern
    B. western
    C. eastern
    D. southern.

Questions 12–13 refer to the following excerpt.

Madame de Staël from Concerning Germany, *1813*

The word romantic has been lately introduced in Germany, to designate that kind of poetry which is derived from the songs of the Troubadours; that which owes its birth to the union of chivalry and Christianity. If we do not admit that the empire of literature has been divided between paganism and Christianity, the north and the south, antiquity and the middle ages, chivalry and the institutions of Greece and Rome, we shall never succeed in forming a philosophical judgment of ancient and of modern taste. Some French critics have asserted that German literature is still in its infancy; this opinion is entirely false: men who are best skilled in the knowledge of languages, and the works of the ancients, are certainly not ignorant of the defects and advantages attached to the species of literature which they either adopt or reject; but their character, their habits, and their modes of reasoning, have led them to prefer that which is founded on the recollection of chivalry, on the wonders of the middle ages, to that which has for its basis the mythology of the Greeks. The literature of romance is alone capable of further improvement, because, being rooted in our own soil, that alone can continue to grow and acquire fresh life: it expresses our religion; it recalls our history; its origin is ancient, although not of classical antiquity. Classic poetry, before it comes home to us, must pass through our recollections of paganism; that of the Germans is the Christian era of the fine arts; it employs our personal impressions to excite strong and vivid emotions; the genius by which it is inspired addresses itself immediately to our hearts; of all phantoms at once the most powerful and the most terrible. . . . The new school maintains the same system in the fine arts as in literature, and affirms that Christianity is the source of all modern genius; the writers of this school also characterize, in a new manner, all that in Gothic architecture agrees with the religious sentiments of Christians. . . . It is only of consequence to us, in the present silence of genius, to lay aside the contempt which has been thrown on all the conceptions of the middle ages.

12. In this passage, which of these historical influences are contrasted?
    A. classical and medieval
    B. European and American
    C. Greek and Roman
    D. Christian and Muslim

13. For Madame de Staël, Romanticism is tied to
    A. Greece, Rome, and paganism.
    B. Germany, the ancient past, and Gothic architecture.
    C. Greece, Rome, and ancient epics.
    D. Christianity, the Middle Ages, and Gothic architecture

Questions 14–15 refer to the following image.

Caspar David Friedrich's **The Polar Sea.**

14. As in most Romantic painting, this image gives pride of place to
    A. human activity.
    B. industry.
    C. disaster.
    D. nature

15. For this artist, as for most Romantic painters, natural forces are depicted as
    A. bloody.
    B. majestic.
    C. benign.
    D. insignificant.

Short-Answer Question

Romanticism was the dominant trend in European arts in the first half of the 1800s.

a. Choose ONE of the following and explain why your choice represents the key factor leading to this development.

- The Enlightenment had focused on rationality and on the classical past.
- The Industrial Revolution transformed Europe.
- The French Revolution changed the European political order.

b. Contrast your choice against ONE of the other options, demonstrating why that option is not as significant as your choice.

Long-Essay Question

How did the experience of the French Revolution and the creation of Napoleon's empire lead to the Concert of Europe?

ANSWERS AND EXPLANATIONS: AP® PRACTICE TEST

Multiple-Choice Questions

1. C   In this statement, Napoleon presents himself as the savior of France and of the Revolution.
2. D   In this description, Napoleon used force to gain control because he was invited to.
3. B   With the exception of Portugal and the British Isles, Napoleon controlled western Europe.
4. A   Portugal remained beyond French control, and ultimately gave Britain access to the continent.
5. C   This passage is an excellent illustration of the waves of nationalism that resulted across Europe after the French conquests.
6. B   Although the regions described were within different countries, they felt united by their German culture.
7. B   Because the war was one of conquest, France brought much more destruction to other states than to its own lands.
8. A   Most of Europe was either directly or indirectly controlled by Napoleon by 1812.
9. D   This depiction shows a dance, but only three of its members are in agreement: Austria, Russia, and Prussia.
10. C   In a theme that has lasted for centuries, Britain stands apart from its continental neighbors.
11. C   The three great powers of eastern Europe—Austria, Prussia, and Russia—dance in great harmony in this image.
12. A   While the Enlightenment favored the classical past—ancient Greece and Rome—the Romantics preferred the medieval past.
13. D   De Staël rightly associates German Romanticism with a love for the medieval past, inspired by Gothic architecture and the literature of the troubadours.
14. D   Although a wrecked ship is visible here, most of the painting is devoted to the power of nature.
15. B   Although the ship is destroyed, the focus is on the majesty and power of nature, rather than on the loss of human life.

Long-Essay Question

How did the experience of the French Revolution and the creation of Napoleon's empire lead to the Concert of Europe?

(Key topics to focus and elaborate on)
- liberalism versus conservatism
- reaction to revolution
- traditional political order

CHAPTER 12

The Conservative Order and the Challenges of Reform (1815–1832)

Nationalism was the most powerful political ideology of nineteenth- and twentieth-century European affairs.

THE CONSERVATIVE ORDER

- After the Congress of Vienna, the major European powers—the **Concert of Europe**—met informally to discuss their differences in what was known as the Concert of Europe. This system functioned well for the first few years, until 1820, when the Bourbon Ferdinand VII of Spain violated his promise to govern according to a written constitution. At this time, revolution occurred in Naples. Metternich was especially concerned about the events in Italy that threatened to spread to Austria. The other powers were divided on the proper course of action.
- Nineteenth-century **conservatism** was dominated by monarchies, landed aristocracies, and established churches that united over their resistant to any change of the social order. These groups cooperated to slow the progress of nationalism and liberalism.

AP® KEY CONCEPTS
3.4 European states struggled to maintain international stability in an age of nationalism and revolutions.

> I. The Concert of Europe (or Congress System) sought to maintain the status quo through collective action and adherence to conservatism.

THE EMERGENCE OF NATIONALISM AND LIBERALISM

- Early nineteenth-century nationalists opposed the Congress of Vienna because it did not allow for individual representation of ethnic groups, but rather upheld monarchies and dynasties in its redistribution of land. Many issues of nationalism arose during this era.
- Nineteenth-century European conservatives defined as *liberal* anything or anyone that challenged their own political, social, or religious values. Nineteenth-century liberals were influenced by Enlightenment writers and the French Revolution, and they sought to gain legal equality, religious toleration, and freedom of speech. Many liberals had economic goals of being able to enrich themselves without governmental interference. The economic ideas of Adam Smith were popular among economic liberals.
- Nationalism was sometimes associated with liberalism, but it could also occur alongside conservatism.

AP® KEY CONCEPTS
3.3 The problems of industrialization provoked a range of ideological, governmental, and collective responses.

I. Ideologies developed and took root throughout society as a response to industrial and political revolutions.

II. Governments responded to the problems created or exacerbated by industrialization by expanding their functions and creating modern bureaucratic states.

CONSERVATIVE RESTORATION IN EUROPE

- Austrian Prince Metternich embodied conservatism more than any other nineteenth-century statesman. Metternich feared that recognizing minority rights would destroy his empire.
- Frederick III of Prussia reneged on his pledge to create constitutional government, and he resisted aspirations by German nationalists to dissolve the conservative order.
- Students in the southern German states Baden, Bavaria, and Württemberg reacted against the lack of popular sovereignty and formed *Burschenschaften,* or student associations, to address their goal of a unified Germany.
- In England, the Tory ministry of Lord Liverpool focused on the issues of landowners and the elite rather than on the average citizens. Unruly meetings of reformers resulted in Parliament's passage of the Coercion Act of March 1817, which suspended the rights of *habeas corpus* and discouraged free speech. By 1819, a liberal crowd gathered in Manchester at Saint Peter's Fields, and when the militia moved into the audience, it set off a mass panic. Eleven people were killed, many more were injured; the event is known as the Peterloo Massacre. Parliament went on to pass laws called the Six Acts, which were designed at intimidating agitators and limiting their free speech.
- A Bourbon restoration in France brought Louis XVIII to the throne after Napoleon's abdication. He issued a constitution known as the Charter that gave the monarch greater control over government leaders, maintained the Declaration of the Rights of Man and Citizen, and did not challenge the property rights of lands confiscated from aristocrats and the church. Louis XVIII's moderate Charter angered royalists who carried out attacks against Napoleon's allies. In 1820, the assassination of the duke of Berri gave royalists an excuse to persecute liberal politicians. Louis XVIII responded with more repressive measures that gave royalists and conservatives greater power.
- Metternich sought the help of Prussia and Russia, and unofficial groups from Britain and France assisted in suppressing of Italian nationalism. They issued the Protocol of Troppau, which stated that stable governments could intervene in countries experiencing revolution to help restore order. All of the interventions that occurred through the congress system sought to maintain the international order achieved at the Congress of Vienna.

AP® KEY CONCEPTS

3.3 The problems of industrialization provoked a range of ideological, governmental, and collective responses.

    I. Ideologies developed and took root throughout society as a response to industrial and political revolutions.

    II. Governments responded to the problems created or exacerbated by industrialization by expanding their functions and creating modern bureaucratic states.

    III. Political movements and social organizations responded to the problems of industrialization.

3.4 European states struggled to maintain international stability in an age of nationalism and revolutions.

I. The Concert of Europe (or Congress System) sought to maintain the status quo through collective action and adherence to conservatism.

THE CONSERVATIVE ORDER SHAKEN IN EUROPE

- Other movements for independence—such as that of the Greek Revolution of 1821 and the 1830 fight for Serbian independence—demonstrated the growing issues of nationalism and liberalism coming into conflict with conservatism.

- Political discontent spread to Europe in the mid-1820s. In Russia, Russian officers who had fought Napoleon were exposed to ideas of the Enlightenment, and they developed reformist sympathies. Two secret societies, the Northern Society and the Southern Society united forces in 1825 to carry out a coup d'état in 1826. When the Russian army was required to swear its allegiance to the new Tsar Nicholas, the Moscow regiment refused, and Nicholas had the artillery attack them. This so-called Decembrist Revolt came to symbolize to Russian liberals the oppressive conditions of life under the tsars. Nicholas reasserted his conservative authority when Poland nationalists agitated for change.

- In France in 1830, Charles X was the new king, and he favored aristocrats and ultra-royalists. He restored the rule of primogeniture, supported the Catholic Church, and gave special rights to the descendants of émigrés. Liberals gained enough seats in the Chamber of Deputies in 1827 to override some of Charles's new laws. When this happened again after the elections of 1830, Charles attempted a royalist seizure of power of the Chamber of Deputies. Parisians responded by staging massive protests and Charles X turned troops against them before departing in August for exile. The July Monarchy, as Louis Philippe's ascension was called, focused on his role as a king of the French people.

- In Britain, the Great Reform Bill was passed in 1832. It represented a compromise between liberal and conservative factions. Catholic emancipation was a triumph for Irish nationalists, but it was passed as a means of avoiding unrest.

AP® KEY CONCEPTS

3.3 The problems of industrialization provoked a range of ideological, governmental, and collective responses.

I. The Concert of Europe (or Congress System) sought to maintain the status quo through collective action and adherence to conservatism.

II. The breakdown of the Concert of Europe opened the door for movements of national unification in Italy and Germany, as well as liberal reforms elsewhere.

THE WARS OF INDEPENDENCE IN LATIN AMERICA

- Wars of independence in Latin America included efforts by Haiti, Brazil, and the present-day lands of Venezuela, Mexico, Paraguay, Uruguay, and Argentina to shed their colonial ties to Europe and gain their sovereignty.

AP® KEY CONCEPTS

2.2 The expansion of European commerce accelerated the growth of a worldwide economic network.

II. The European-dominated worldwide economic network contributed to the agricultural, industrial, and consumer revolutions in Europe.

CHAPTER 12: AP® PRACTICE TEST

Multiple-Choice Questions

Questions 1–3 refer to the following excerpt.

Mazzini Defines Nationality

The essential characteristics of a nationality are common ideas, common principles and a common purpose. A nation is an association of those who are brought together by language, by given geographical conditions or by the role assigned them by history, who acknowledge the same principles and who march together to the conquest of a single definite goal under the rule of a uniform body of law.

The life of a nation consists in harmonious activity (that is, the employment of all individual abilities and energies comprised within the association) towards this single goal. . . .

But nationality means even more than this. Nationality also consists in the share of mankind's labors which God assigns to a people. This mission is the task which a people must perform to the end that the Divine Idea shall be realized in this world; it is the work which gives a people its rights as a member of Mankind; it is the baptismal rite which endows a people with its own character and its rank in the brotherhood of nations. . . .

Nationality depends for its very existence upon its sacredness within and beyond its borders.

If nationality is to be inviolable for all, friends and foes alike, it must be regarded inside a country as holy, like a religion, and outside a country as a grave mission. It is necessary too that the ideas arising within a country grow steadily, as part of the general law of Humanity which is the source of all nationality. It is necessary that these ideas be shown to other lands in their beauty and purity, free from any alien mixture, from any slavish fears, from any skeptical hesitancy, strong and active, embracing in their evolution every aspect and manifestation of the life of the nation. These ideas, a necessary component in the order of universal destiny, must retain their originality even as they enter harmoniously into mankind's general progress.

The people must be the basis of nationality; its logically derived and vigorously applied principles its means; the strength of all its strength; the improvement of the life of all and the happiness of the greatest possible number its results; and the accomplishment of the task assigned to it by God its goal. This is what we mean by nationality.

1. For Mazzini, "harmonious activity," means that Italians will all
   A. have similar origins.
   B. share a religion.
   C. get along with each other.
   D. have the same purpose.

2. For Mazzini, which of these groups would he reject in Italy?
   A. clergy
   B. the military
   C. foreigners
   D. artists

3. The kind of nation-state Mazzini envisions is best described as a
   A. democracy.
   B. single will.
   C. collection of regional states.
   D. atheist collective.

Questions 4–6 refer to the following excerpt.

Lord Acton Condemns Nationality

The greatest adversary of the rights of nationality is the modern theory of nationality. By making the State and the nation commensurate with each other in theory, it reduces practically to a subject condition all other nationalities that may be within the boundary. It cannot admit them to an equality with the ruling nation which constitutes the State, because the State would then cease to be national, which would be a contradiction of the principle of its existence. According, therefore, to the degree of humanity and civilization in that dominant body which claims all the rights of the community, the inferior races are exterminated, or reduced to servitude, or outlawed, or put in a condition of dependence.

If we take the establishment of liberty for the realization of moral duties to be the end of civil society, we must conclude that those states are substantially the most perfect which, like the British and Austrian Empires, include various distinct nationalities without oppressing them. Those in which no mixture of races has occurred are imperfect; and those in which its effects have disappeared are decrepit. A State which is incompetent to satisfy different races condemns itself; a State which labors to neutralize, to absorb, or to expel them, destroys its own vitality; a State which does not include them is destitute of the chief basis of self-government. The theory of nationality, therefore, is a retrograde step in history. . . .

[N]ationality does not aim either at liberty or prosperity, both of which it sacrifices to the imperative necessity of making the nation the mold and measure of the State. Its course will be marked with material as well as moral ruin, in order that a new invention may prevail over the works of God and the interests of mankind. There is no principle of change, no phrase of political speculation conceivable, more comprehensive, more subversive, or more arbitrary than this. It is a confutation of democracy, because it sets limits to the exercise of the popular will, and substitutes for it a higher principle.

4. Like Austria, Britain feared militant nationalism because in each case the country
   A. was a democracy.
   B. contained substantial minorities.
   C. had a weak economy.
   D. feared a dominating church.

5. Concerning the kind of nationalism envisaged by Mazzini, the "nationality" condemned by Lord Action is
   A. identical.
   B. the opposite.
   C. roughly similar.
   D. irrelevant.

6. For Lord Action, nationalism and democracy are
   A. the same thing.
   B. cause and effect.
   C. incompatible.
   D. the root causes of tyranny.

Questions 7–9 refer to the following excerpt.

From Letters of John Stuart Mill and Harriet Taylor

Mill:
   Women are so brought up, as not to be able to subsist in the mere physical sense, without a man to keep them: they are so brought up as not to be able to protect themselves against injury or insult, without some man on whom they have a special claim, to protect them, they are so brought up, as to have no vocation or useful office to fulfil in the world. . . .
   There is no natural inequality between the sexes; except perhaps in bodily strength; even that admits of doubt: and if bodily strength is to be the measure of superiority, mankind are no better than savages. . . .
   If nature has not made men and women unequal, still less ought the law to make them so. . . . A woman ought not to be dependent on a man, more than a man on a woman, except so far as their affections make them so. . . .
   But this perfect independence of each other for all save affection, cannot be, if there be dependence in pecuniary circumstances. . . .
   The first and indispensable step, therefore, towards the enfranchisement of woman, is that she be so educated, as not to be dependent either on her father or her husband for subsistence: a position which in nine cases out of ten, makes her either the plaything or the slave of the man who feeds her; and in the tenth case, only his humble friend. . . .
   It does not follow that a woman should actually support herself because she should be capable of doing so: in the natural course of events she will not. It is not desirable to burthen the labour market with a double number of competitors. . . .
   The great occupation of woman should be to beautify life: to cultivate, for her own sake and that of those who surround her, all her faculties of mind, soul, and body; all her powers of enjoyment, and powers of giving enjoyment; and to diffuse beauty, and elegance, and grace, everywhere.
Taylor:
   There is equality in nothing now—all the pleasures such as there are being men's, and all the disagreeables and pains being women's. . . . Women are educated for one single object, to gain their living by marrying. . . . To be married is the object of their existence and that object being gained they do really cease to exist as to anything worth calling life or any useful purpose.

. . . I have no doubt that when the whole community is really educated, tho' the present laws of marriage were to continue[,] they would be perfectly disregarded, because no one would marry. The widest and perhaps the quickest means to do away with its evils is to be found in promoting education—as it is the means of all good. . . .

At this present time, in this state of civilization, what evil could be caused by, first placing women on the most entire equality with men, as to all rights and privileges, civil and political, and then doing away with all laws whatever relating to marriage? Then if a woman had children she must take charge of them, women would not then have children without considering how to maintain them. Women would have no more reason to barter person for bread, or for anything else, than men have—public offices being open to them alike, all occupations would be divided between the sexes in their natural arrangement. Fathers would provide for their daughters in the same way as for their sons.

7. For Mill, what makes women dependent?
   A. men
   B. nature
   C. their upbringing
   D. God

8. Mill and Taylor would agree that women should
   A. have children.
   B. be legally independent.
   C. are men's inferiors.
   D. work.

9. Unlike Mill, Taylor believes that women
   A. are naturally men's equals.
   B. capable of independence.
   C. need to be better educated.
   D. should hold public office.

Questions 10–12 refer to the following excerpt.

The Carlsbad Decrees

Regarding University Life

There shall be appointed for each university a special representative of the ruler of each state, the said representatives to have appropriate instructions and extended powers, and they shall have their place of residence where the university is located. . . .

This representative shall enforce strictly the existing laws and disciplinary regulations; he shall observe with care the attitude shown by the university instructors in their public lectures and registered courses; and he shall, without directly interfering in scientific matters or in teaching methods, give a beneficial direction to the teaching, keeping in view the future attitude of the students. Finally, he shall give . . . attention to everything that may promote morality . . . among the students. . . .

2. The confederated governments mutually pledge themselves to eliminate from the

universities or any other public educational institutions all instructors who shall have obviously proved their unfitness for the important work entrusted to them by openly deviating from their duties, or by going beyond the boundaries of their functions, or by abusing their legitimate influence over young minds, or by presenting harmful ideas hostile to public order or subverting existing governmental instructions. . . .

Any instructor who has been removed in this manner becomes ineligible for a position in any other public institution of learning in another state of the Confederation.

3. The laws that have for some time been directed against secret and unauthorized societies in the universities shall be strictly enforced. . . . The special representatives of the government are enjoined to exert great care in watching these organizations.

The governments mutually agree that all individuals who shall be shown to have maintained their membership in secret or unauthorized associations, or shall have taken membership in such associations, shall not be eligible for any public office.

4. No student who shall have been expelled from any university by virtue of a decision of the university senate ratified or initiated by the special representative . . . , shall be admitted by any other university. . . .

Regarding the Press

1. As long as this edict remains in force, no publication which appears daily, or as a serial not exceeding twenty sheets of printed matter, shall be printed in any state of the Confederation without the prior knowledge and approval of the state officials. . . .

4. Each state of the Confederation is responsible, not only to the state against which the offense is directly committed but to the entire Confederation, for any publication printed within the limits of its jurisdiction, in which the honor or security of other states is impinged upon or their constitution or administration attacked. . . .

7. When a newspaper or periodical is suppressed by a decision of the Diet, the editor of such publication may not within five years edit a similar publication in any state of the Confederation.

10. According to these laws, nationalist student associations are
   A. seditious.
   B. patriotic.
   C. encouraged.
   D. too exclusive.

11. Reading between the lines, the professors targeted by these laws were
   A. too lenient towards their students.
   B. the cause of anti-foreign sentiment.
   C. engaging in anti-government speech.
   D. foreigners.

12. These laws have what impact on the power of the state?
   A. They weaken the state.
   B. They significantly increase the power of the state.
   C. They have little impact on the power of the state.
   D. They dramatically increase the power of the state.

Questions 13–15 refer to the following map.

Centers of Revolution, 1820–1831

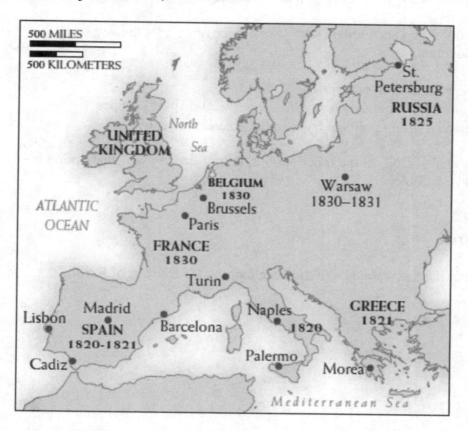

13. Which of these appear to have had the greatest influence in shaping revolution as reflected in this map?
    A. Napoleon's conquests
    B. the Reformation
    C. the Austrian Empire
    D. Peter the Great

14. The 1820–1831 uprisings can be typified as
    A. concentrated in eastern Europe.
    B. Europe-wide.
    C. strongest in monarchies.
    D. concentrated in German lands.

15. Where were the uprisings shown here most likely associated with nationalist sentiments?
    A. Spain
    B. France
    C. Russia
    D. Italy

Short-Answer Question

Uprisings occurred in Europe in 1820–1821 and again in 1830–1831.

a. Choose ONE of the following and explain why your choice represents the key factor leading to this development.

- The Enlightenment introduced new ideals.
- The French Revolution temporarily reshaped the political map of Europe.
- Nationalism became a strong political force in the nineteenth century.

b. Contrast your choice against ONE of the other options, demonstrating why that option is not as significant as your choice.

Long-Essay Question

What were the most important factors shaping and then challenging the Concert of Europe?

ANSWERS AND EXPLANATIONS: AP® PRACTICE TEST

Multiple-Choice Questions

1. **D** In this paragraph, Mazzini argues that nations not only have a common origin, but should also have a common goal.
2. **C** Like many fervent nationalists, Mazzini wants his country to be "free from any alien mixture."
3. **B** Mazzini's vision is of a homogenous body with a single purpose and a single culture.
4. **B** In both of these cases, the presence of distinct national groups led the central governments to fear the power of nationalism.
5. **A** The kind of nationalism in which nationality and the state are fused is very much the nationalism described by Mazzini.
6. **C** For the author, nationalism suppresses the popular will, and is the enemy of democracy.
7. **C** Mill argues that women are dependent because that is how they are raised, not how they are naturally.
8. **B** Both authors argue for the legal emancipation of women.
9. **D** Both argue that women should be better educated, that they can work, and are capable of being independent. However, Taylor envisages a much broader scope for women.
10. **A** The purpose of these laws was to ban student organizations that fomented nationalist sentiment.
11. **C** Not only the university, but also their professors, are feared for the ideas they spread.
12. **B** These laws increased state control of university teaching and university life and limited the power of the press.
13. **A** The area of uprisings corresponds closely to the areas conquered by Napoleon, with a few exceptions.
14. **B** The uprisings were not concentrated on any one region, but stretched across continental Europe.
15. **D** Only the Italian uprisings were motivated strongly by nationalism.

Long-Essay Question

What were the most important factors shaping and then challenging the Concert of Europe?

(Key topics to focus and elaborate on)
- French Revolution
- liberalism
- conservatism
- nationalism

CHAPTER 13

Economic Advance and Social Unrest (1830–1850)

TOWARD AN INDUSTRIAL SOCIETY

- Through its textile industry, Britain achieved economic stability that led to its dominance in the world in the nineteenth century.
- As industrialization spread, the population of Europe continued to grow, and more people chose to live in cities. Migration from the countryside put new pressures on urban infrastructure: Poor harvests from 1845 to 1847 caused massive emigration to cities.
- The explosion of railway building in the 1830s and 1840s and the improvement of canals and roads made transportation to urban centers easier and increased industrialization.

AP® KEY CONCEPTS

3.1 The Industrial Revolution spread from Great Britain to the continent, where the state played a greater role in promoting industry.

    II. Following the British example, industrialization took root in continental Europe, sometimes with state sponsorship.

3.2 The experiences of everyday life were shaped by industrialization, depending on the level of industrial development in a particular location.

    II. Europe experienced rapid population growth and urbanization, leading to social dislocations.

    V. Because of the persistence of primitive agricultural practices and landowning patterns, some areas of Europe lagged in industrialization, while facing famine, debt, and land shortages.

THE LABOR FORCE

- The nineteenth-century workforce was extremely varied; conditions differed from country to country and decade to decade.
- Artisans and factory workers alike underwent a process of proletarianization, whereby they entered into a wage economy and gradually lost significant ownership in the means of production. This process occurred rapidly wherever the factory system existed.
- The economic security of factory workers was often better than that of urban artisans. By the nineteenth century, it became more difficult for artisans to exercise control over their trades; European liberals disapproved of and banned labor and guild organizations.
- Some workshops began the practice known in France as *confection,* which involved the production of goods in standard sizes and styles rather than by special orders, in order to compete with larger establishments or machine production.
- In 1836, William Lovett and other radical London artisans formed the London Working Men's Association, and in 1838 they demanded six specific reforms in a charter: universal male suffrage, annual election of the House of Commons, the secret ballot, equal electoral districts, abolition of property qualifications for members of the House of Commons, and

payment of salaries to members of the House of Commons. **Chartism**, as this movement was called, failed as a national faction, but many of the six points were enacted into law.

FAMILY STRUCTURES AND THE INDUSTRIAL REVOLUTION

- Prior to the Industrial Revolution, home life and economic life occurred in the same place; thereafter, these worlds were increasingly distinct.
- Factory wages for skilled adult males enabled some families to rely solely on the male breadwinner's income. As machines became less complex and required fewer skilled operators, more women and children maintained them, earning reduced salaries compared to their adult male counterparts.
- The shift from the domestic system of production to the factory system brought with it profound shifts in family life. Often, adult males could earn enough to support their entire family.
- As child labor was gradually curtailed, and public education expanded, the role of parents in educating and training their children shrank.

WOMEN IN THE EARLY INDUSTRIAL REVOLUTION

- As more husbands were able to support their families on one salary, more wives came to be associated with domestic duties, such as housekeeping, food preparation, and cottage industries. By the 1820s, more unmarried women became employed in factories, tending machines that required little skilled labor. These women were usually young, single, or widowed.
- The largest groups of working women were found in domestic service or in agricultural work.
- The English Factory Act of 1833 prohibited the employment of children under the age of nine, limited the workday for children, and required that children receive two hours of daily education at the factory owner's expense. The wage economy meant that families were not spending as much time together as they had before.

3.2 The experiences of everyday life were shaped by industrialization, depending on the level of industrial development in a particular location.

> III. Over time, the Industrial Revolution altered the family structure and relations for bourgeois and working-class families.

PROBLEMS OF CRIME AND ORDER, AND POVERTY

- Cities became associated with crime as the Industrial Revolution continued.
- Propertied members of society strove to improve the crime situation during this time via prison reform and better systems of police. Professional police forces helped an orderly European society emerge.
- Prison reform was undertaken in France and in Britain in the 1840s. Isolation was a common feature of competing models. Transportation was abandoned by the British, but used by the French into the twentieth century.
- Most economists followed the *laissez-faire* thought of Adam Smith's *Wealth of Nations,* and encouraged most economic decisions being made through the mechanism of the marketplace. They emphasized thrift, competition, and personal industry, all of which appealed to the middle class.
- Thomas Malthus (1766–1834) published his *Essay on the Principle of Population,* in which he argued that population would eventually outstrip food supply. He encouraged chastity and discouraged the raising of families. David Ricardo (1772–1823) argued his theory of "the iron law of wages" based on Malthus's principles that if wages were raised, more children would be produced, which would cause wages to fall and working people to produce fewer children, which would then cause wages to rise, in a continuous cycle.

3.3 The problems of industrialization provoked a range of ideological, governmental, and collective responses.

> I. Ideologies developed and took root throughout society as a response to industrial and political revolutions.
> II. Governments responded to the problems created or exacerbated by industrialization by expanding their functions and creating modern bureaucratic states.

EARLY SOCIALISM

- Early socialists were in favor of the new productive capacity of industrialism. A group of writers known as the **utopian socialists** questioned the structures and values of the existing capitalistic framework.
- Other important forms of socialism, including Saint-Simonianism, Owenism, Fourierism, Anarchism, and Marxism developed during this period.

3.3 The problems of industrialization provoked a range of ideological, governmental, and collective responses.

I. Ideologies developed and took root throughout society as a response to industrial and political revolutions.

1848: YEAR OF REVOLUTIONS 486-496

■ A series of liberal and nationalist revolutions exploded across the Continent in 1848. Political liberals were the chief advocates of reforms. In France, a "Second Republic" emerged with Napoleon's nephew, Louis Napoleon Bonaparte, at the helm. In 1851, he seized power and became emperor in 1852, returning France to a dictatorship. The Habsburg lands saw unrest, and there were revolts in Hungary and Austria. Czech nationalists rebelled and the Pan-Slavic Congress—which consisted of Poles, Ruthenians, Czechs, Slovaks, Croats, Slovenes, and Serbs—called for national equality of Slavs and protested the repression of all Slavic peoples. Other revolts in Italy and Germany were suppressed, the liberal era ended, and the European middle class ceased to be revolutionary.

AP® KEY CONCEPTS

3.3 The problems of industrialization provoked a range of ideological, governmental, and collective responses.

I. Ideologies developed and took root throughout society as a response to industrial and political revolutions.

Multiple-Choice Questions

Questions 1–3 refer to the following map.

European Railroads in 1850

1. Which of these had the densest network of railroads?
   A. England
   B. France
   C. the German states
   D. the Austrian Empire

2. Which two countries were comparable concerning the extent of their railroads in 1850?
   A. Portugal and France
   B. England and the Austrian Empire
   C. Spain and Italy
   D. England and France

3. Which of these regions of Europe was best served by railroads in 1850?
   A. eastern
   B. northern
   C. southern
   D. western

Questions 4–6 refer to the following excerpt.

Women Factory Workers Write to the Editor of **The Examiner,** *1832*

Sir,

Living as we do, in the densely populated manufacturing districts of Lancashire, and most of us belonging to that class of females who earn their bread either directly or indirectly by manufactories, we have looked with no little anxiety for your opinion on the Factory Bill. . . . You are for doing away with our services in manufactories altogether. So much the better, if you had pointed out any other more eligible and practical employment for the surplus female labour, that will want other channels for a subsistence. If our competition were withdrawn, and short hours substituted, we have no doubt but the effects would be as you have stated, "not to lower wages, as the male branch of the family would be enabled to earn as much as the whole had done," but for the thousands of females who are employed in manufactories, who have no legitimate claim on any male relative for employment or support, and who have, through a variety of circumstance, been early thrown on their own resources for a livelihood, what is to become of them?

In this neighbourhood, hand-loom has been almost totally superseded by power-loom weaving, and no inconsiderable number of females, who must depend on their own exertions, or their parishes for support, have been forced, of necessity into the manufactories, from their total inability to earn a livelihood at home.

It is a lamentable fact that, in these parts of the country, there is scarcely any other mode of employment for female industry, if we except servitude and dressmaking. Of the former of these, there is no chance of employment for one-twentieth of the candidates that would rush into the field, to say nothing of lowering the wages of our sisters of the same craft; and of the latter, galling as some of the hardships of manufactories are (of which the indelicacy of mixing with the men is not the least), yet there are few women who have been so employed, that would change conditions with the ill-used genteel little slaves, who have to lose sleep and health, in catering to the whims and frivolities of the butterflies of fashion.

We see no way of escape from starvation, but to accept the very tempting offers of the newspapers, held out as baits to us, fairly to ship ourselves off to Van Dieman's Land [Tasmania] on the very delicate errand of husband hunting, and having safely arrived at the "Land of Goshen," jump ashore, with a "Who wants me?" . . .

The Female Operatives of Todmorden

4. According to these women, *The Examiner* article wrongly assumed that
   A. all women are dependents.
   B. all factory workers are skilled.
   C. no women were currently working in factories.
   D. men earn more than women.

5. Who are the "genteel little slaves" referred to in this letter?
   A. factory workers
   B. mothers
   C. domestic servants
   D. dressmakers

6. Which of these would make the best thesis for this letter?
   A. Women make the best factory workers.
   B. Factory conditions are degrading to women.
   C. Women have few attractive work options.
   D. The factory system has put domestic weavers out of work.

Questions 7–9 refer to the following excerpt.

Karl Marx and Friedrich Engels from* The Communist Manifesto, *1848

The history of all hitherto existing society is the history of class struggles. . . .

Our epoch, the epoch of the bourgeoisie, possesses, however, this distinctive feature: it has simplified the class antagonisms. Society as a whole is more and more splitting up into two great hostile camps, into two great classes directly facing each other: Bourgeoisie and Proletariat. . . .

Each step in the development of the bourgeoisie was accompanied by a corresponding political advance of that class. . . .

The bourgeoisie, wherever it has gotten the upper hand, has put an end to all feudal, patriarchal, idyllic relations. It has pitilessly torn asunder the motley feudal ties that bound man to his "natural superiors," and has left remaining no other nexus between man and man than naked self-interest, than callous "cash payment." . . .

The proletariat goes through various stages of development. With its birth begins its struggle with the bourgeoisie. . . .

But with the development of industry the proletariat not only increases in number; it becomes concentrated in greater masses, its strength grows, and it feels that strength more. The various interests and conditions of life within the ranks of the proletariat are more and more equalized, in proportion as machinery obliterates all distinctions of labour, and nearly everywhere reduces wages to the same low level. . . .

The bourgeoisie finds itself involved in a constant battle. . . .

Of all the classes that stand face to face with the bourgeoisie today, the proletariat alone is a really revolutionary class. . . .

All previous historical movements were movements of minorities, or in the interest of minorities. The proletarian movement is the self-conscious, independent movement of the immense majority, in the interest of the immense majority. . . .

The advance of industry, whose involuntary promoter is the bourgeoisie, replaces the isolation of the labourers, due to competition, by their revolutionary combination, due to association. The development of Modern Industry, therefore, cuts from under its feet the very foundation on which the bourgeoisie produces and appropriates products. What the bourgeoisie, therefore, produces, above all, is its own grave-diggers. Its fall and the victory of the proletariat are equally inevitable. . . .

The proletarians have nothing to lose but their chains. They have a world to win.

7. For these authors, the coming revolution differs from the French Revolution because it will be more
   A. bloody.
   B. broadly based.
   C. successful.
   D. peaceful.

8. According to this excerpt, the current class conflict was created by what two developments?
   A. the Protestant Reformation and European imperialism
   B. the scientific revolution and the creation of the nation-state
   C. the discovery of the Americas and the Enlightenment
   D. the French Revolution and the Industrial Revolution

9. For Marx and Engels, the central class conflict they describe is between what two groups?
   A. nobles and peasants
   B. workers and peasants
   C. bourgeoisie and proletariat
   D. proletariat and workers

Questions 10–12 refer to the following map.

Centers of Revolution, 1848–1849

10. Looking at this map, what was the apparent impact of the Industrial Revolution on these uprisings?
    A. crucial
    B. insignificant
    C. close
    D. negative

11. In most of the regions where uprisings occurred between 1848–1849, which of these was also present?
    A. growing nationalist unrest
    B. early industrialization
    C. religious conflict
    D. economic disaster

12. The uprisings shown here were all
    A. related to foreign commerce.
    B. rural.
    C. urban.
    D. German.

Questions 13–15 refer to the following excerpt.

František Palacky to the Frankfurt Parliament, 1848

I can neither accept your invitation, gentleman, on my own behalf nor by delegating another "reliable patriot." Allow me to explain, as briefly as possible, my reasons.

The declared goal of your assembly is to substitute a confederation of the German nation for the hitherto existing confederation of princes, to bring the German nation to real unity, to strengthen German national feeling, and to thus increase Germany's internal and external power. . . .

I am not a German, at least I don't feel myself to be one. . . . I am a Bohemian of Slavic origin, and I have dedicated myself, with all the little I possess and am capable of, completely and forever to the service of my nation. That nation is admittedly a small one, but has always been a separate one, existing for itself; its rulers have participated in the confederation of German princes for centuries, but it never considered itself to be part of the German nation, and was never, at any point over the course of centuries, considered part of the German nation by others. The entire bond tying Bohemia first to the Holy Roman Empire and then to the German Confederation was always a purely dynastic one, of which the Bohemian nation, the Bohemian estates hardly took any notice. . . .

The second reason that prohibits me from participating in your proceedings is the fact that you, of necessity, both wish to and will fatally weaken Austria as an independent empire; yes, you will even render its existence impossible. [Austria is] a state whose preservation, integrity, and strengthening are and must be a primary and important matter not only for my own nation, but for all of Europe— yes even for all of humanity and civilization itself.

You know what Power holds the entire Eastern portion of our continent. . . . Since I, for all my love of my own nation, have always set the interests of humanity and science above those

163

of nationality, there is no greater opponent and antagonist of even the mere possibility of a Russian universal monarchy than I—not because it would be Russian, but because it would be universal.

You know that the southeast of Europe, all along the border of the Russian Empire, is populated by many peoples who differ markedly in their origin, language, history, and culture— Slavs, Romanians, Hungarians, and Germans, not to mention Greeks, Turks, and Albanians— none of whom is, on its own, powerful enough to successfully resist their superior neighbor to the East for all time. That is something they can only do when united with one another by a firm bond. . . . Truly, if the Austrian state had not long since come into existence, one would have to create it as quickly as possible, in the interest of Europe, in the interest of humanity itself. . . .

Why, then, did we see this state in the critical moment . . . anchorless and well nigh helpless? Because [Austria], in unfortunate blindness, has for a long time failed to recognize and even denied the actual legal and moral foundation of its own existence: the basic principle of complete equality of rights and mutual regard for all the nationalities and religions united under its scepter. The law of nations is a true natural law. . . .

As soon as I direct my gaze beyond the borders of Bohemia, natural and historical considerations oblige me to look not towards Frankfurt but towards Vienna, and to seek there the center that is suited and destined to guarantee and protect the peace, freedom, and rights of my nation.

13. When Palacky speaks of "my nation," to what does he refer?
    A. all Austrians
    B. Russians
    C. his countrymen
    D. those that speak his language

14. What is the "Power (that) holds the entire Eastern portion of our continent"?
    A. the Austrian Empire
    B. Russia
    C. France
    D. the Holy Alliance

15. For Palacky, Austria is more attractive because it will
    A. protect Germans in Bohemia.
    B. favor Czechs over Hungarians.
    C. grant equality to all nationalities.
    D. be stronger than the Frankfurt government.

Short-Answer Question

A number of uprisings broke out across Europe between 1848–1849.

a. Choose ONE of the following and explain why your choice represents the key factor leading to this development.

- the power of the Holy Alliance
- the Enlightenment
- the growth of Austrian power

b. Contrast your choice against ONE of the other options, demonstrating why that option is not as significant as your choice.

Long-Essay Question

What were the most important influences leading to the emergence of socialism, and how did these influence shape the development of socialism?

ANSWERS AND EXPLANATIONS: AP® PRACTICE TEST

Multiple Choice Questions

1. A Because of its early start in the Industrial Revolution, Britain also had a big lead in building railroads.
2. C Both of these countries had a handful of railroads tied into major cities.
3. B Northern Europe—especially England, northern France, and the northern German states.
4. A A common source of conflict was the assumption that women didn't need the money they made.
5. D Work as dressmakers was a common, though unattractive, option for women.
6. C The authors of this petition summarize their options if they lose their factory work: as domestic servants or dressmakers.
7. B For Marx and Engels, all earlier revolutions were led by minorities, whereas the proletariat revolution would be a mass movement.
8. D The authors refer to the dominance of the bourgeoisie resulting from the French Revolution and the creation of the proletariat by the Industrial Revolution.
9. C The central theme of *The Communist Manifesto* was the climactic conflict between the workers and the factory owners.
10. B There is no correlation between the spread of industrialization and these uprisings.
11. A In the Germanic regions—including Austria—and in Italy nationalism played an important role in these years of unrest.
12. C All of these revolutions were based in cities, enflamed by nationalism and by economic disruption.
13. D In this context, "nation" refers to a group identified as sharing the same culture, with language a key component of that culture.
14. B Palacky refers to Russia, which was an expansionist country, and in particular it was threatening to engulf all Slavic lands.
15. C Austria had a long history as a kingdom of many different peoples, all granted at least limited rights.

Long-Essay Question

What were the most important influences leading to the emergence of socialism, and how did these influence shape the development of socialism?

(Key topics to focus and elaborate on)
- industrialization
- Enlightenment
- proletarianization

CHAPTER 14

The Age of Nation-States

THE CRIMEAN WAR (1853–1856)

- The Crimean War grew out of the rivalry between the Ottoman Empire and Russia. A war among the major European states ensued with France and Britain declaring war on Russia, and Austria and Prussia remaining neutral. Russia fell to the French and British, who settled the matter in 1856 at the Treaty of Paris.
- The Crimean War broke the Concert of Europe, marking a new era in European politics.

AP® KEY CONCEPTS

3.4 European states struggled to maintain international stability in an age of nationalism and revolutions.

   II. The breakdown of the Concert of Europe opened the door for movements of national unification in Italy and Germany, as well as liberal reforms elsewhere.

REFORMS IN THE OTTOMAN EMPIRE

- The *Tanzimat*, or "reorganization" of the empire, was inspired by European models. The reorganization widen the tolerance of other religions. A constitution was promulgated in 1876.
- Balkan wars weakened the Ottoman Empire.

AP® KEY CONCEPTS

3.4 European states struggled to maintain international stability in an age of nationalism and revolutions.

   II. The breakdown of the Concert of Europe opened the door for movements of national unification in Italy and Germany, as well as liberal reforms elsewhere.

3.5 A variety of motives and methods led to the intensification of European global control and increased tensions among the Great Powers.

   II. Industrial and technological developments (i.e., the Second Industrial Revolution) facilitated European control of global empires.

ITALIAN UNIFICATION

- Nationalists hoped for Italian unification, but Italian statesmen disagreed about how to accomplish it.
- Romantic republican nationalism was led by Giuseppe Mazzini (1805–1872), who founded the Young Italy Society to drive Austria from the peninsula. Mazzini and Giuseppe Garibaldi (1807–1882) led insurrections in the 1830s through the 1850s.
- Between 1852 and 1860, Italy was transformed into a nation-state governed by a constitutional monarchy. Full unification remained elusive.

3.4 European states struggled to maintain international stability in an age of nationalism and revolutions.

   II. The breakdown of the Concert of Europe opened the door for movements of national unification in Italy and Germany, as well as liberal reforms elsewhere.

   III. The unification of Italy and Germany transformed the European balance of power and led to efforts to construct a new diplomatic order.

GERMAN UNIFICATION

- The construction of a unified Germany was one of the most important political developments in Europe between 1848 and 1914 because it altered the international balance of power.
- In 1862, William I of Prussia turned to Otto von Bismarck (1815–1898), who moved against the liberal Parliament and sought support for unifying Germany through a war with Denmark.
- Bismarck supported the duchies of Schleswig and Holstein in their efforts to avoid getting incorporated into Denmark. Together, Prussia and Austria defeated Denmark in 1864, which elevated Bismarck's prestige and led to a conflict between the two countries in 1865.
- Bismarck then provoked war with Austria over the administration of Schleswig and Holstein. The Seven Weeks' War led to the defeat of Austria in 1866 and established Prussia as the only major power among the German states. In 1867, the North German Confederation formed, with Bismarck representing the King of Prussia as president. Germany had become a military monarchy, crushing Prussian liberalism.
- The Franco-Prussian War (1870–1871) enabled Bismarck to bring the states of southern Germany into the confederation. Bismarck orchestrated the war by provoking France against Prussia, and the southern German states joined Prussia against Napoleon III's armies. The Germans beat the French army, captured Napoleon III, besieged Paris, and proclaimed the German Empire.

AP® KEY CONCEPTS

3.4 European states struggled to maintain international stability in an age of nationalism and revolutions.

   II. The breakdown of the Concert of Europe opened the door for movements of national unification in Italy and Germany, as well as liberal reforms elsewhere.

   III. The unification of Italy and Germany transformed the European balance of power and led to efforts to construct a new diplomatic order.

FRANCE: FROM LIBERAL EMPIRE TO THE THIRD REPUBLIC

- The provinces and Paris differed on how to handle a settlement with the Prussians. The National Assembly was dominated by monarchists and led by Adolphe Thiers, who agreed in the Treaty of Frankfurt that France would pay an indemnity, and that Prussians would occupy France until it was paid. Alsace and part of Lorraine were granted to the Prussians.
- Parisians who had suffered under the Prussian siege rebelled against the Treaty of Frankfurt, and elected a new, short-lived municipal government on March 28, 1871, called the Paris Commune, that was created to administer Paris separately from the rest of France. On May 8, the National Assembly bombarded the city and broke through defenses on May 21.

Troops restored order to Paris, killing 20,000 Parisians in the process and ending the Commune.

- In 1875, the National Assembly adopted a new republican political system that provided for a chamber of deputies elected by universal male suffrage, a senate chosen indirectly, and a president elected by the two legislative houses. Following the 1879 resignation of President Marshal MacMahon, Republicans gained control of the national government. The Dreyfus Affair, a case involving the trumped-up case of a Jewish captain, was the major crisis.

AP® KEY CONCEPTS

3.4 European states struggled to maintain international stability in an age of nationalism and revolutions.

II. The breakdown of the Concert of Europe opened the door for movements of national unification in Italy and Germany, as well as liberal reforms elsewhere.

THE HABSBURG EMPIRE

- The Habsburg domains had remained primarily absolutist after the revolutions of 1848.
- In 1861, Francis Joseph issued the February Patent, which set up a bicameral imperial parliament or *Reichsrat,* with an upper chamber appointed by the emperor and an indirectly elected lower chamber. The Magyars refused to recognize this system, but the February Patent ruled the empire for six years. In 1867, Francis Joseph transformed the Habsburg Empire into Austria-Hungary to satisfy the desires of Magyars to maintain their lands separately from Austria while sharing the same monarch. The unrest of the many nationalities in the Habsburg Empire caused instability throughout Europe.

AP® KEY CONCEPTS

3.4 European states struggled to maintain international stability in an age of nationalism and revolutions.

II. The breakdown of the Concert of Europe opened the door for movements of national unification in Italy and Germany, as well as liberal reforms elsewhere.

III. The unification of Italy and Germany transformed the European balance of power and led to efforts to construct a new diplomatic order.

RUSSIA: EMANCIPATION AND REVOLUTIONARY STIRRINGS

- Alexander II restructured Russian society after Russia's defeat in the Crimean War, ushering in some of the much-needed reforms, including the abolition of serfdom in 1861. Alexander II became known as the Tsar Liberator, but he was never popular with his noble subjects, who resented his control over policy.
- In the 1870s, young Russians drew on the ideas of Alexander Herzen and formed a populism movement, which sought social revolution based on the communal life of the Russian peasants.

3.2 The experiences of everyday life were shaped by industrialization, depending on the level of industrial development in a particular location.

> V. Because of the persistence of primitive agricultural practices and landowning patterns, some areas of Europe lagged in industrialization, while facing famine, debt, and land shortages.

3.4 European states struggled to maintain international stability in an age of nationalism and revolutions.

> II. The breakdown of the Concert of Europe opened the door for movements of national unification in Italy and Germany, as well as liberal reforms elsewhere.

GREAT BRITAIN: TOWARD DEMOCRACY

- Britain took a step toward democracy in the reform bill sponsored by Benjamin Disraeli (1804–1881), a House of Commons leader, in 1867. By the time the measure had passed, the number of voters had been almost doubled from 1,430,000 to 2,470,000.
- William Gladstone ushered in many liberal reforms, including opening more institutions to the public and people from other classes and religious denominations. The Education Act of 1870 made the government responsible for administering elementary schools. Gladstone was forced to confront the Irish question during his administration.

AP® KEY CONCEPTS

3.3 The problems of industrialization provoked a range of ideological, governmental, and collective responses.

> II. Governments responded to the problems created or exacerbated by industrialization by expanding their functions and creating modern bureaucratic states.
>
> III. Political movements and social organizations responded to the problems of industrialization.

3.4 European states struggled to maintain international stability in an age of nationalism and revolutions.

> II. The breakdown of the Concert of Europe opened the door for movements of national unification in Italy and Germany, as well as liberal reforms elsewhere.

Multiple-Choice Questions

Questions 1–2 refer to the following excerpt.

The Unification of Italy

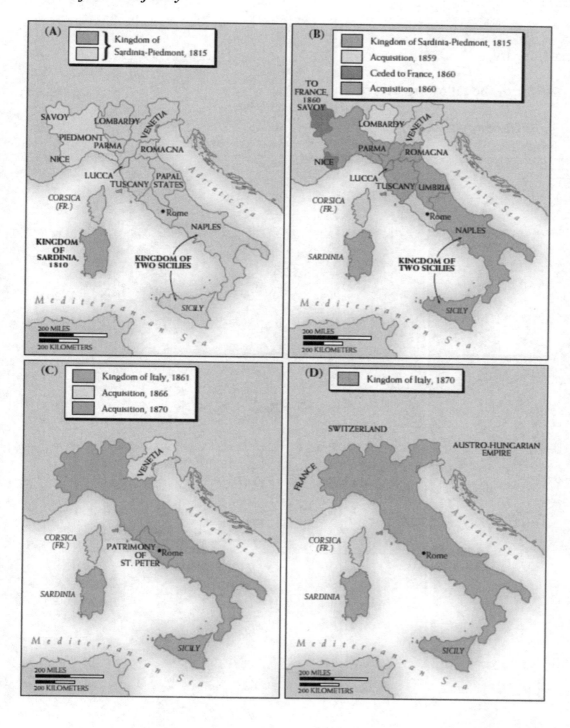

1. Which of these remained a barrier to unification the longest?
   A. Venetia
   B. Tuscany
   C. Sicily
   D. the Papal States

2. Which of these gained the most from the process of Italian unification?
   A. Switzerland
   B. Sicily
   C. France
   D. Austria-Hungary

Questions 3–5 refer to the following excerpt.

The Unification of Germany

172

3. Which of these led German unification?
   A. Bavaria
   B. Lorraine
   C. Prussia
   D. Hanover

4. What nation was likely the most threatened by German unification?
   A. Switzerland
   B. France
   C. Russia
   D. Belgium

5. As in the case of Italy, German unification
   A. involved small territorial losses for the new nation's neighbors.
   B. depended on the conquest of large territories.
   C. was more about imperialism than nationalism.
   D. lacked any territorial rationale.

Questions 6–7 refer to the following excerpt.

Garibaldi Calls Italians to Act to Unify Their Nation

Italians! The Sicilians are fighting against the enemies of Italy and for Italy. To help them with money, arms, and especially men, is the duty of every Italian.

Let the Marches, Umbria, Sabine, the Roman Campagna, and the Neapolitan territory rise, so as to divide the enemy's forces.

If the cities do not offer a sufficient basis for insurrection, let the more resolute throw themselves into the open country. A brave man can always find a weapon. In the name of Heaven, hearken not to the voice of those who cram themselves at well served tables. Let us arm. Let us fight for our brothers; tomorrow we can fight for ourselves.

A handful of brave men, who have followed me in battles for our country, are advancing with me to the rescue. Italy knows them; they always appear at the hour of danger. Brave and generous companions, they have devoted their lives to their country; they will shed their last drop of blood for it, seeking no other reward than that of a pure conscience.

"Italy and Victor Emmanuel!"—that was our battle cry when we crossed the Tincino; it will resound into the very depths of Aetna [the volcanic mountain]. As this prophetic battle-cry re-echoes from the hills of Italy to the Tarpeian Mount, the tottering thrones of tyranny will fall to pieces, and the whole country will rise like one man.

6. This address appeals primarily to Italian
   A. liberalism.
   B. nationalism.
   C. socialism.
   D. hatred of France.

7. Which of these longstanding barriers to unification does Garibaldi hope to overcome in this speech?
   A. apathy
   B. religious differences
   C. regionalism
   D. nationalism

Questions 8–10 refer to the following excerpt.

Heinrich von Treitschke Demands the Annexation of Alsace and Lorraine

The sense of justice to Germany demands the lessening of France. . . .
What is demanded by justice is, at the same time, absolutely necessary for our security. . .

.

Every State must seek the guarantees of its own security in itself alone. . . .
In view of our obligation to secure the peace of the world, who will venture to object that the people of Alsace and Lorraine do not want to belong to us? The doctrine of the right of all the branches of the German race to decide on their own destinies, the plausible solution of demagogues without a fatherland, shiver to pieces in presence of the sacred necessity of these great days. These territories are ours by the right of the sword, and we shall dispose of them in virtue of a higher right—the right of the German nation, which will not permit its lost children to remain strangers to the German Empire. We Germans, who know Germany and France, know better than these unfortunates themselves what is good for the people of Alsace. . . . Against their will we shall restore them to their true selves. We have seen with joyful wonder the undying power of the moral forces of history, manifested far too frequently in the immense changes these days, to place much confidence in the value of a mere popular disinclination. A generation which lives beside it, but of those who are before and behind it. We appeal from the mistaken wishes of the men who are there today to the wishes of those who were there before them. We appeal to all those strong German men who once stamped the seal of our German nature on the language and manners, the art and the social life of the Upper Rhine. Before the nineteenth century closes, the world will recognize that . . . we were only obeying the dictates of national honor when we made little account of the preferences of the people who live in Alsace today. . . .
At all times the subjection of a German race to France has been an unhealthy thing; today it is an offence against the reason of history—a vassalship of free men to half-educated barbarians. . . .
There is no perfect identity between the political and national frontier of any European country. Not one of the great Powers, and Germany no more than the rest of them, can ever subscribe to the principle that "language alone decides the formation of States." It would be impossible to carry that principle into effect. . . .
The German territory which we demand is ours by nature and by history. . . . In the tempests of the great Revolution the people of Alsace, like all the citizens of France, learned to forget their past. . . .
Most assuredly, the task of reuniting there the broken links between the ages is one of the heaviest that has ever been imposed upon the political forces of our nation. . . .
The people of Alsace are already beginning to doubt the invincibility of their nation, and at all events to divine the mighty growth of the German Empire. Perverse obstinacy, and a

thousand French intrigues creeping in the dark, will make every step on the newly conquered soil difficult for us: but our ultimate success is certain, for on our side fights what is stronger than the lying artifices of the stranger—nature herself and the voice of common blood.

8. Which of these best summarizes Von Treitschke's rationale for the annexation of Alsace?
   A. The people of Alsace wish to join Germany.
   B. Alsace has always been part of Germany.
   C. Alsace is naturally German.
   D. Nationality should dictate political boundaries.

9. Reading between the lines, why does the author argue against the principle "language alone decides the formation of States"?
   A. He rejects nationalism.
   B. He supports the right of Alsace to choose its allies.
   C. He hopes to create a nation-state.
   D. The Alsatians do not speak German.

10. The author's primary rationale for adding Alsace to Germany is
    A. based on language.
    B. historical.
    C. strategic.
    D. popular opinion.

Questions 11–12 refer to the following excerpt.

Manifesto of the People's Will

Although we are ready to submit wholly to the popular will, we regard it as none the less our duty, as a party, to appear before the people with our program. . . . It is as follows: 1. Perpetual popular representation . . . having full power to act in all national questions. 2. General local self-government, secured by the election of all officers, and the economic independence of the people. 3. The self-controlled village commune as the economic and administrative unit. 4. Ownership of the land by the people. 5. A system of measures having for their object the turning over to the laborers of all mining works and factories. 6. Complete freedom of conscience, speech, association, public meeting, and electioneering activity. 7. The substitution of a territorial militia for the army. . . . In view of the stated aim of the party its operations may be classified as follows: 1. Propaganda and agitation. Our propaganda has for its object the popularization, in all social classes, of the idea of a political and popular revolution as a means of social reform, as well as popularization of the party's own program. Its essential features are criticism of the existing order of things, and a statement and explanation of revolutionary methods. The aim of agitation should be to incite the people to protest as generally as possible against the present state of affairs, to demand such reforms as are in harmony with the party's purposes, and, especially, to demand the summoning of an Organizing Assembly. . . .
2. Destructive and terroristic activity. Terroristic activity consists in the destruction of the most harmful persons in the Government, the protection of the party from spies, and the punishment of official lawlessness and violence in all the more prominent and important cases in which such

lawlessness and violence are manifested. The aim of such activity is to break down the prestige of Governmental power, to furnish continuous proof of the possibility of carrying on a contest with the Government, to raise in that way the revolutionary spirit of the people and inspire belief in the practicability of revolution, and, finally, to form a body suited and accustomed to warfare.

11. Considering the goals of liberalism, the goals of the People's Will can be said to
    A. have considerable overlap.
    B. be identical.
    C. have nothing in common.
    D. the exact opposite.

12. Which is most likely reflected in the methods advocated by the People's Will?
    A. the emancipation of Russia's serfs
    B. the tsars' traditional autocracy
    C. the strong democratic tradition in Russia
    D. the outbreak of the Bolshevik revolution

Questions 13–15 refer to the following excerpt.

Emancipation Manifesto, 1861

By the Grace of God WE, Alexander II, Emperor and Autocrat of All Russia, King of Poland, Grand Duke of Finland, etc., make known to all OUR faithful subjects . . .

WE have left to the nobles themselves, in accordance with their own wishes, the task of preparing proposals for the new organization of peasant life—proposals that would limit their rights over the peasants, and the realization of which would inflict on them [the nobles] some material losses. OUR confidence was justified. Through members of the provincial committees, who were entrusted [with the task] by the corporate organizations of the nobility in each province, after collecting the necessary data, have formulated proposals on a new arrangement for serfs and their relationship with the nobles.

These proposals were diverse, because of the nature of the problem. They have been compared, collated, systematized, rectified and finalized in the Main Committee instituted for that purpose; and these new arrangements dealing with the peasants and household serfs of the nobility have been examined in the Council of State.

Having invoked Divine assistance, WE have resolved to execute this task.

On the basis of the above-mentioned new arrangements, the serfs will receive in time the full rights of free rural inhabitants.

The nobles, while retaining their property rights to all the lands belonging to them, grant the peasants perpetual use of their household plots in return for a specified obligation; and, to assure their livelihood as well as to guarantee fulfillment of their obligations toward time government, [the nobles] grant them a portion of arable land fixed by the said arrangements as well as other property.

While enjoying these land allotments, the peasants are obliged, in return, to fulfill obligations to the noblemen fixed by the same arrangements. In this status, which is temporary, the peasants are temporarily bound.

At the same time, they are granted the right to purchase their household plots, and, with the consent of the nobles, they may acquire in full ownership the arable lands and other properties which are allotted them for permanent use. Following such acquisition of full ownership of land, the peasants will be freed from their obligations to the nobles for the land thus purchased and will become free peasant landowners.

A special decree dealing with household serfs will establish a temporary status for them, adapted to their occupations and their needs. At the end of two years from the day of the promulgation of this decree, they shall receive full freedom and some temporary benefits.

In accordance with the fundamental principles of these arrangements, the future organization of peasants and household serfs will be determined, the order of general peasant administration will be established, and the rights given to the peasants and to the household serfs will be spelled out in detail, as will the obligations imposed on them toward the government and the nobles.

Although these arrangements, general as well as local, and the special supplementary rules affecting some particular localities, estates of petty nobles, and peasants working in factories and enterprises of the nobles, have been as far as possible adapted to economic necessities and local customs; nevertheless, to preserve the existing order where it presents reciprocal advantages, WE leave it to the nobles to reach a voluntary understanding with the peasants and to reach agreements on the extent of the land allotment and the obligations stemming from it, observing, at the same time, the established rules to guarantee the inviolability of such agreements . . .

The nobles will continue to keep order on their estates, with the right of jurisdiction and of police, until the organization of cantons and of cantonal courts.

Aware of the unavoidable difficulties of this reform, WE place OUR confidence above all in the graciousness of Divine Providence, which watches over Russia . . .

To facilitate the realization of these agreements between the nobles arid the peasants, by which the latter may acquire full ownership of their household plots and their houses, the government will lend assistance, under special regulations, by means of loans or transfer of debts encumbering an estate.

WE rely upon the common sense of OUR people. When the government advanced the idea of abolishing serfdom, there developed a partial misunderstanding among the unprepared peasants. Some were concerned about freedom and not concerned about obligations. But, generally, the common sense of the nation has not wavered, because it has realized that every individual who enjoys freely the benefits of society owes it in return certain positive obligations; according to Christian law every individual is subject to higher authority (Romans, chap. xiii, 1); everyone must fulfill his obligations, and, above all, render tribute, dues, respect, and honor (Ibid., chap. xiii, 7). What legally belongs to nobles cannot be taken away from them without adequate compensation, or through their voluntary concession; it would be contrary to all justice to use the land of the nobles without assuming corresponding obligations . . .

And now, Orthodox people, make the sign of the cross, and join with Us to invoke God's blessing upon your free labor, the sure pledge of your personal well being and the public prosperity.

Given at St. Petersburg, March 3, the year of Grace 1861, and the seventh of OUR reign.

13. According to this document, organization of the peasants' lives after emancipation was planned by the
    A. tsar.
    B. peasants.
    C. nobles.
    D. Orthodox Church.

14. Reading this document, what are the peasants likely to own after emancipation?
    A. their lands
    B. their tools
    C. their homes
    D. their clothes

15. According to this document, emancipation would lead the traditional social order in Russia to be
    A. overturned.
    B. minimally changed.
    C. reinforced.
    D. substantially changed.

Short-Answer Question

Britain's experience in the mid-nineteenth century followed a different course from the experience of continental European nations in the same period.

a. Choose ONE of the following and explain why your choice represents the key factor leading to this development.

- experience of the French Revolution
- industrialization
- liberal reform

b. Contrast your choice against ONE of the other options, demonstrating why that option is not as significant as your choice.

Long-Essay Question

Compare the experiences of Italian and German unification, considering the main barriers to and factors in favor of unification.

ANSWERS AND EXPLANATIONS: AP® PRACTICE TEST

Multiple-Choice Questions

1. D   For a variety of reasons, the popes were strongly opposed to joining in the new Italian nation.
2. C   France supported Italian unification, mostly to thwart Austria-Hungary, and gained territory into the bargain.
3. C   The role of Prussia is clear in the size of Prussian territory and in the fact that the Prussian capital became the German capital, Berlin.
4. B   Not only did France lose some territory, the newly united Germany was also large enough to threaten France.
5. A   In each case, formerly independent territories were brought together, with relatively small gains and losses for neighboring nations.
6. B   This is an appeal based primarily on nationalist sentiments.
7. C   Italian and German unification faced the challenge of extremely strong local, rather than national, loyalties.
8. C   In this article, von Treitschke argues that Alsace was historically German, and should return to Germany, even if its people resist.
9. D   It appears that the Alsatians do not identify themselves as German.
10. B   The author appeals to a past that even the Alsatians themselves have forgotten.
11. A   Many of the goals—though not the methods—of the People's Will are inspired by classic liberal goals.
12. B   The extreme measures advocated by the People's Will resulted largely from the fact that the Russian monarchy was deaf to calls for reform.
13. C   One of the weaknesses of this move was leaving the peasants under the control of the nobles.
14. D   Anything belonging to the nobles will remain with the nobles, presumably leaving the peasants only with their clothing.
15. B   The only difference appears to be that the serfs will be free peasants; otherwise the social order appears unchanged.

Long-Essay Question

Compare the experiences of Italian and German unification, considering the main barriers to and factors in favor of unification.

(Key topics to focus and elaborate on)
- militant versus more patriotic types of nationalism
- key opponents
- allies

CHAPTER 15

The Building of European Supremacy: Society and Politics to World War I

POPULATION TRENDS AND MIGRATION

- European population, with respect to world population, was at its all-time high in 1900—one-fifth of the world was European at that time. After that time, birth and death rates leveled off in Europe and grew in other areas, which led in turn to the divide between the developed and the undeveloped world (which is still characterized by food and resource crises).
- More than 50 million Europeans migrated away from their continent between 1846 and 1932. This outflow of people relieved social and population pressures on the Continent and spread European culture throughout the world. Combined with Europe's economic and technological superiority, the migration contributed to the dominant role Europe continues to play in the world.

AP® KEY CONCEPTS

3.1 The Industrial Revolution spread from Great Britain to the Continent, where the state played a greater role in promoting industry.

    III. During the Second Industrial Revolution (c. 1870–1914), more areas of Europe experienced industrial activity, and industrial processes increased in scale and complexity.

3.2 The experiences of everyday life were shaped by industrialization, depending on the level of industrial development in a particular location.

    II. Europe experienced rapid population growth and urbanization, leading to social dislocations.

THE SECOND INDUSTRIAL REVOLUTION

- Continental industries caught up to those of Britain toward the end of the nineteenth century, and the expansion of railroad systems on the Continent helped to spur economic growth and enable new industries to emerge. This phase of development, which concerned the production of steel, chemicals, electricity, and oil, is known as the Second Industrial Revolution.
- Several inventions were essential in this period: Henry Bessemer's process for manufacturing steel, the Solway process of alkali production enabled the recovery of more chemical by-products, the application of electrical energy to production and to homes and transportation, and the invention of the internal combustion engine (which eventually gave birth to the automobile) were the major developments during this period. Machines that required petroleum created a great need for oil.

AP® KEY CONCEPTS

3.1 The Industrial Revolution spread from Great Britain to the Continent, where the state played a greater role in promoting industry.

> III. During the Second Industrial Revolution (c. 1870–1914), more areas of Europe experienced industrial activity, and industrial processes increased in scale and complexity.

THE MIDDLE CLASSES IN ASCENDANCY

■ The middle class was at its height in the sixty years prior to World War I: They defined consumer taste and were no longer associated with the radical revolutions of the 1840s, but rather they were identified with a desire to protect their assets. The middle class grew more diverse as it came to encompass more people—some were magnates, others were entrepreneurs and professionals who had sufficient income for private homes and some basic domestic luxuries.

AP® KEY CONCEPTS

3.1 The Industrial Revolution spread from Great Britain to the Continent, where the state played a greater role in promoting industry.

> III. During the Second Industrial Revolution (c. 1870–1914), more areas of Europe experienced industrial activity, and industrial processes increased in scale and complexity.

3.2 The experiences of everyday life were shaped by industrialization, depending on the level of industrial development in a particular location.

> I. Industrialization promoted the development of new classes in the industrial regions of Europe.

LATE NINETEENTH-CENTURY URBAN LIFE

■ Europe became more urbanized as migration to the cities continued. From 1850 to 1911, urban dwellers grew from 25 percent to 44 percent of the population in France and from 30 percent to 60 percent of the population in Germany. Rural migrants frequently lived in bad social conditions and experienced widespread discrimination.

■ Cities were redesigned to accommodate the changes in urban living. While central urban areas had always been places for people of all social classes, urban planners transformed these areas into business and government centers, but not residential dwelling spaces.

■ Suburbs became popular for both middle and working classes, and improved transit eased this transformation. Sanitation improvements were made following concerns with health and housing after the cholera epidemics of the 1830s and 1840s. New water and sewer systems were constructed to improve conditions, which led to a reduction of the mortality rate.

AP® KEY CONCEPTS

3.2 The experiences of everyday life were shaped by industrialization, depending on the level of industrial development in a particular location.

> II. Europe experienced rapid population growth and urbanization, leading to social dislocations.
>
> III. Over time, the Industrial Revolution altered the family structure and relations for bourgeois and working-class families.
>
> IV. A heightened consumerism developed as a result of the Second Industrial Revolution.

3.3 The problems of industrialization provoked a range of ideological, governmental, and collective responses.

II. Governments responded to the problems created or exacerbated by industrialization by expanding their functions and creating modern bureaucratic states.

VARIETIES OF LATE NINETEENTH-CENTURY WOMEN'S EXPERIENCES

- Women remained second-class citizens in the nineteenth century. Through marriage, many women lost their individual legal identities and suffered tremendous disadvantages that limited their freedom to work, to save, and to move from one location to another.
- During the Second Industrial Revolution, the jobs available to women expanded and more married women withdrew from the workforce. The jobs available to women were usually low-paying jobs that did not require training or skills. New cultural ideas that connected prosperity with women not working outside the home took root in the middle classes.

AP® KEY CONCEPTS
3.2 The experiences of everyday life were shaped by industrialization, depending on the level of industrial development in a particular location.

III. Over time, the Industrial Revolution altered the family structure and relations for bourgeois and working-class families.

3.3 The problems of industrialization provoked a range of ideological, governmental, and collective responses.

III. Political movements and social organizations responded to the problems of industrialization.

JEWISH EMANCIPATION

- Jews saw gains in political equality and social status in the nineteenth century, but changes came slowly. The conditions for Jews improved after the revolutions of 1848, especially in Western Europe. Jews and Christians were granted roughly equal laws by Joseph II in 1782, and in France, the National Assembly recognized Jews as French citizens in 1789. Traditional prejudices against Jews continued in eastern Europe until World War I; in Russia, Jews were treated as foreigners and were restricted in all aspects of their daily lives.
- Anti-Semitism reared its head in the late-nineteenth century, as critics attributed economic stagnation to Jewish bankers and financial institutions.

AP® KEY CONCEPTS
3.3. The problems of industrialization provoked a range of ideological, governmental, and collective responses.

III. Political movements and social organizations responded to the problems of industrialization.

LABOR, SOCIALISM, AND POLITICS TO WORLD WAR I

- After 1848, workers turned to new institutions and ideologies to seek change. Trade unions emerged in the latter part of the nineteenth century, and through them some workers attempted to gain an overall improvement of wages and working conditions. Most European workers were not represented by unions during this period, but unions did help those workers they represented bargain collectively for improvements to their employment.

- Universal male suffrage was extended during this era in many countries, so the voices of lower-class workers carried more political weight than they had previously. Socialist movements of many kinds emerged throughout Europe.
- The organized political party arose at this time. Karl Marx spoke at the First International (International Working Men's Association) of 1864, a group of radicals, socialists, anarchists, and Polish nationalists organized by a group of British and French trade unionists.
- From the activities of the First International, Marxism emerged as a new kind of socialism, and it became popular in Germany. In Britain, Fabianism and early welfare programs took root. French and German socialists emerged at this time, forming the Socialist Party and the German Social Democratic Party, respectively. In Russia, Vladimir Lenin emerged as a prominent socialist, and the Bolsheviks seized power.

AP® KEY CONCEPTS

3.2 The experiences of everyday life were shaped by industrialization, depending on the level of industrial development in a particular location.

    I. Industrialization promoted the development of new classes in the industrial regions of Europe.

3.3 The problems of industrialization provoked a range of ideological, governmental, and collective responses.

    I. Ideologies developed and took root throughout society as a response to industrial and political revolutions.

3.4 European states struggled to maintain international stability in an age of nationalism and revolutions.

    II. The breakdown of the Concert of Europe opened the door for movements of national unification in Italy and Germany, as well as liberal reforms elsewhere.

Multiple-Choice Questions

Questions 1–3 refer to the following map.

Patterns of Global Migration, 1840–1900

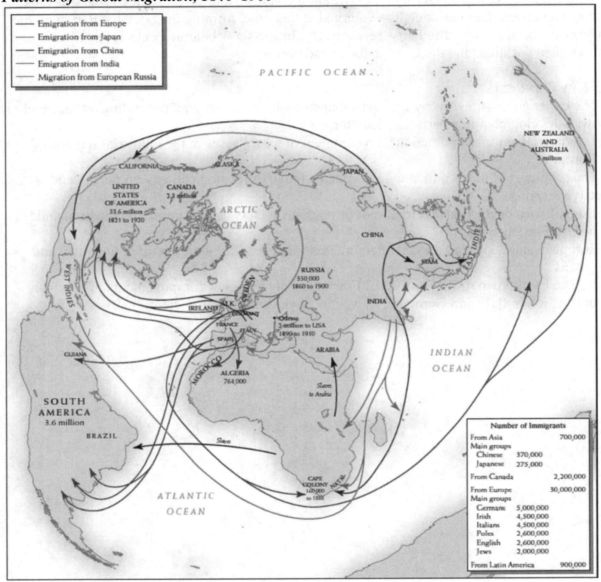

1. 1. In this period, which of these had the highest rate of emigration?
   A. Latin America
   B. Asia
   C. Europe
   D. Canada

2. Which of these appears to have had substantial internal migration?
   A. Europe
   B. Africa
   C. China
   D. Latin America

3. Emigration from Africa in this period was mostly
   A. to Europe.
   B. composed of slaves.
   C. across the Indian Ocean.
   D. to Asia.

Questions 4–5 refer to the following map.

European Industrialization in 1860

185

4. Which of these had the highest per capita industrial output in 1860?
   A. the British Isles
   B. France
   C. Austria-Hungary
   D. Italy

5. Which of these regions was least industrialized in 1860?
   A. western Europe
   B. southern Europe
   C. northern Europe
   D. eastern Europe

Questions 6–7 refer to the following map.

European Industrialization in 1913

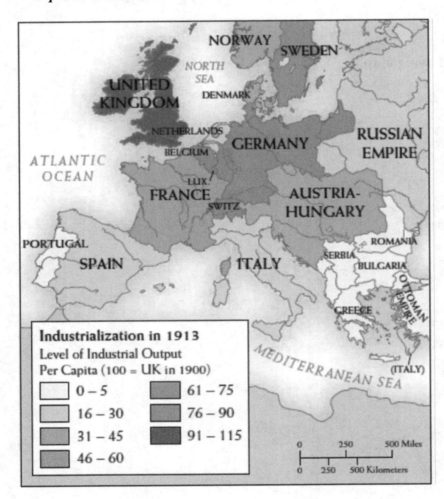

6. Given the map of industrialization in 1860, which of these areas showed the most surprising level of industrialization in 1913?
   A. England
   B. Italy
   C. Germany
   D. Russia

7. Which of these experienced the least growth in per capita industrial output between 1860 and 1913?
   A. the British Isles
   B. the Balkans
   C. France
   D. Italy

Questions 8–9 refer to the following table.

Growth of Major European Cities

GROWTH OF MAJOR EUROPEAN CITIES (FIGURES IN THOUSANDS)

	1850	1880	1910
Berlin	419	1,122	2,071
Birmingham	233	437	840
Frankfurt	65	137	415
London	2,685	4,470	7,256
Madrid	281	398	600
Moscow	365	748	1,533
Paris	1,053	2,269	2,888
Rome	175	300	542
Saint Petersburg	485	877	1,962
Vienna	444	1,104	2,031
Warsaw	160	339	872

8. Which of these experienced the highest rate of growth between 1850 and 1880?
   A. Madrid
   B. Berlin
   C. London
   D. Birmingham

9. Comparing 1850 and 1910, which of these is true of Europe's cities?
   A. A major shift occurred, with southern capitals rapidly outstripping other cities.
   B. Most cities kept their ranking.
   C. Industrialization had little impact on urbanization.
   D. Western capitals grew faster than eastern capitals.

Questions 10–12 refer to the following excerpt.

From the Autobiography of Emmeline Pankhurst

I had called upon women to join me in striking at the Government through the only thing that governments are really very much concerned about—property—and the response was immediate. Within a few days the newspapers rang with the story of the attack made on letter boxes in London, Liverpool, Birmingham, Bristol, and half a dozen other cities. In some cases the boxes, when opened by postmen, mysteriously burst into flame; in others the letters were destroyed by corrosive chemicals; in still others the addresses were rendered illegible by black fluids. Altogether it was estimated that over 5,000 letters were completely destroyed and many thousands more were delayed in transit.

It was with a deep sense of their gravity that these letter-burning protests were undertaken, but we felt that something drastic must be done in order to destroy the apathy of the men of England who view with indifference the suffering of women oppressed by unjust laws. . . .

In only a few cases were the offenders apprehended, and one of the few women arrested was a helpless cripple, a woman who could move about only in a wheeled chair. She received a sentence of eight months in the first division, and, resolutely hunger striking, was forcibly fed with unusual brutality, the prison doctor deliberately breaking one of her teeth in order to insert a gag. In spite of her disabilities and her weakness, the crippled girl persisted in her hunger strike and her resistance to prison rules, and within a short time had to be released. The excessive sentences of the other pillar box destroyers resolved themselves into very short terms because of the resistance of the prisoners, every one of whom adopted the hunger strike. . . .

It was at this time, February, 1913, less than two years ago as I write these words, that militancy, as it is now generally understood by the public, began—militancy in the sense of continued, destructive, guerilla warfare against the Government through injury to private property. . . . We had tried every other measure . . . and our years of work and suffering and sacrifice had taught us that the Government would not yield to right and justice. . . . Now our task was to show the Government that it was expedient to yield to the women's just demands. In order to do that we had to make England and every department of English life insecure and unsafe. We had to make English law a failure and the courts farce comedy theatres; we had to discredit the Government and Parliament in the eyes of the world; we had to spoil English sports, hurt business, destroy valuable property, demoralise the world of society, shame the churches, upset the whole orderly conduct of life.

That is, we had to do as much of this guerilla warfare as the people of England would tolerate.

10. For Pankhurst, the actions described were legitimate because
    A. they reciprocated violent attacks on women.
    B. the government understood only violence.
    C. earlier methods had failed.
    D. the activists were running out of time.

11. Attacks on mailboxes (letter boxes) were undertaken with the goal of
    A. stopping mail delivery.
    B. leading to arrests.
    C. frightening postal workers.
    D. getting the government's attention.

12. Pankhurst and her group could be considered terrorists because of their
    A. attacks on the postal system.
    B. use of hunger strikes.
    C. destruction of property.
    D. use of fear.

Questions 13–15 refer to the following excerpt.

Eduard Bernstein, from **Evolutionary Socialism,** *1899*

Social conditions have not developed to such an acute opposition of things and classes as is depicted in the [Communist] Manifesto. . . . The number of members of the possessing classes is today not smaller but larger. The enormous increase of social wealth is not accompanied by a decreasing number of large capitalists but by an increasing number of capitalists of all degrees. . . .

In all advanced countries we see the privileges of the capitalist bourgeoisie yielding step by step to democratic organizations. . . .

The conquest of political power by the working classes, the expropriation of capitalists, are not ends in certain aims and endeavours. . . .

Democracy is in principle the suppression of class government, though it is not yet the actual suppression of classes. . . . The right to vote in a democracy makes its members virtually partners in the community, and this virtual partnership must in the end lead to real partnership. . . .

Universal franchise is, from two sides, the alternative to a violent revolution. But universal suffrage is only a part of democracy, although a part which in time must draw the other parts after it as the magnet attracts to itself the scattered portions of iron. It certainly proceeds more slowly than many would wish, but in spite of that it is at work. And social democracy cannot further this work better than by taking its stand unreserved only the theory of democracy—on the ground of universal suffrage with all the consequences resulting therefrom to its tactics. . . .

Is there any sense . . . in maintaining the phrase of the "dictatorship of the proletariat" at a time when in all possible places representatives of social democracy have placed themselves practically in the arena of Parliamentary work, have declared for the proportional representation of the people, and for direct legislation—all of which is inconsistent with a dictatorship.

13. Like Marx, for Bernstein the main enemy was(were)
    A. capitalists.
    B. the workers.
    C. the franchise.
    D. democracy.

14. Unlike Marx, Bernstein rejects which of these as an essential element of a socialist victory?
    A. democracy
    B. the workers
    C. violent revolution
    D. triumph over capitalism

15. When Bernstein speaks of a virtual partnership becoming a real partnership, he is referring to
    A. the transition from socialism to communism.
    B. the creation of an egalitarian society.
    C. the movement from democracy to socialism.
    D. implementing the dictatorship of the proletariat.

Short-Answer Question

Socialism became an important thread in European politics in the mid- to late-nineteenth century.

a. Choose ONE of the following and explain why your choice represents the key factor leading to this development.

- Industrialization took hold in Europe in the 1800s.
- Trade unionism flourished in the same period.
- The influence of the middle classes grew in the same period.

b. Contrast your choice against ONE of the other options, demonstrating why that option is not as significant as your choice.

Long-Essay Question

Was the Second Industrial Revolution a continuation of the Industrial Revolution that began in the eighteenth century or a new development?

ANSWERS AND EXPLANATIONS: AP® PRACTICE TEST

Multiple-Choice Questions

1. **C** European emigration was by far the highest.
2. **C** One arrow in China indicates significant migration from rural central China to more urbanized areas.
3. **B** The only significant emigration from Africa in this period was to feed the desire for slaves in the Americas and in Muslim lands.
4. **A** Britain far outstripped other nations, largely due to its early start in industrialization.
5. **D** In 1860, eastern Europe was the least industrialized, with a per capita industrial output less than 10 percent of England's output.
6. **C** In 1860, Germany essentially lacked industry, but was one of Europe's leaders in 1913.
7. **B** The Balkans and the Ottoman Empire remained without industry in 1913, while most of the rest of Europe had begun to industrialize.
8. **A** While most of these cities increased by about half, Berlin more than doubled.
9. **B** With few exceptions, cities grew proportionately. For instance, London was still by far the largest city.
10. **C** Pankhurst argues that earlier, more peaceful, methods had been tried and had failed.
11. **D** The activists reasoned that attacking government property would get the government's attention.
12. **D** The activists deliberately sought to frighten ordinary citizens and upset everyday life.
13. **A** In broad terms, Bernstein and Marx were in agreement.
14. **C** The key point of disagreement between Bernstein and Marx was that Bernstein did not believe a violent revolution was necessary.
15. **B** Bernstein thought that if workers got the vote, society would consequently become more egalitarian.

Long-Essay Question

Was the Second Industrial Revolution a continuation of the Industrial Revolution that began in the eighteenth century or a new development?

(Key topics to focus and elaborate on)
- differences: where, products, sources of power
- impacts: workers, politics, economies

CHAPTER 16

The Birth of Modern European Thought

THE NEW READING PUBLIC

- By 1900, 85 percent of people could read in Britain, France, Belgium, the Netherlands, Germany, and Scandinavia, thanks largely to improvements in primary education. Improvements in literacy led to greater secondary education opportunities in many countries.
- The amount of printed matter available to the public increased dramatically during this time; some of the materials catered to the marginally literate or the lowest levels of public taste.
- Literacy enabled Europeans to gain knowledge and improve their social situations.

AP® KEY CONCEPTS

3.3 The problems of industrialization provoked a range of ideological, governmental, and collective responses.
  II. Governments responded to the problems created or exacerbated by industrialization by expanding their functions and creating modern bureaucratic states.

SCIENCE AT MIDCENTURY

- The philosophy of **positivism** of Auguste Comte (1798–1857) influenced the field of science.
- Charles Darwin's 1859 book, *The Origin of Species,* formulated the principle of **natural selection**, which explained how species evolved over time. In his 1871 work, *The Descent of Man,* Darwin explored the principle of natural selection in the context of human beings, helping establish a new theory of evolutionary ethics that came to be known as **social Darwinism**.

AP® KEY CONCEPTS

3.5 A variety of motives and methods led to the intensification of European global control and increased tensions among the Great Powers.
  I. European nations were driven by economic, political, and cultural motivations in their new imperial ventures in Asia and Africa.
  III. Imperial endeavors significantly affected society, diplomacy, and culture in Europe and created resistance to foreign control abroad.
3.6 European ideas and culture expressed a tension between objectivity and scientific realism on one hand, and subjectivity and individual expression on the other.
  II. Following the revolutions of 1848, Europe turned toward a realist and materialist worldview.

CHRISTIANITY AND THE CHURCH UNDER SIEGE

- Historical scholarship in the nineteenth century attacked Christianity on many grounds. David Friedrich Strauss in *The Life of Jesus* questioned the historical evidence of Jesus' existence. Julius Wellhausen, Ernst Renan, and William Robertson argued that human authors had written and edited the books of the Bible.

- The progress of science undermined the Christian underpinning of the doctrine of Creation by determining the actual age of the earth. Other scientists proposed that religious thought was just like any other phenomena, not spiritually inspired nor did it reveal "the truth."
- Friedrich Nietzsche also attacked Christianity, accusing it of promoting weakness and not glorifying strength.
- There was more conflict between church and state throughout Europe at this time. In England, there was increased hostility between the Anglican Church and other Protestant denominations; in France, where the Catholic Church was frequently at odds with the Third Republic, the Ferry Laws (sponsored by Jules Ferry) replaced religious instruction in the public schools with civil training. In Germany, Bismarck removed Catholic and Protestant clergy from overseeing local education in Prussia. He instituted the May Laws of 1873, which demanded that priests be educated in German schools and universities and gave control of the appointment of priests to the state. This **Kulturkampf**, or "cultural struggle," failed, and Bismarck retreated from his policies.

AP® KEY CONCEPTS

3.3 The problems of industrialization provoked a range of ideological, governmental, and collective responses.

III. Political movements and social organizations responded to the problems of industrialization.

3.5 A variety of motives and methods led to the intensification of European global control and increased tensions among the Great Powers.

I. European nations were driven by economic, political, and cultural motivations in their new imperial ventures in Asia and Africa.

3.6 European ideas and culture expressed a tension between objectivity and scientific realism on one hand, and subjectivity and individual expression on the other.

I. Romanticism broke with neoclassical forms of artistic representation and with rationalism, placing more emphasis on intuition and emotion.

TOWARD A TWENTIETH-CENTURY FRAME OF MIND

- The scientists Ernst Mach, Henri Poincaré, and Hans Vaihinger urged that scientists consider their theories hypothetical constructs of the physical world. Scientists like Wilhelm Roentgen, Henri Becquerel, J.J. Thompson, Marie Curie, and Ernest Rutherford established the important properties and uses of radioactive materials. Albert Einstein researched relativity, and Werner Heisenberg published his uncertainty principle.
- In literature, realism and naturalism became dominant themes. Flaubert used realism to portray life without adornment in his *Madame Bovary* and Zola set forth realism as a movement. Henrik Ibsen and George Bernard Shaw brought realism into the depiction of domestic life and romantic ideals.
- From the 1870s onward, a new movement of **modernism** was captured in works by artists trying to break away from traditional forms. Igor Stravinsky broke from tradition with his Rite of Spring musical composition, Picasso brought the art world to modernism with cubist forms, and members of the Bloomsbury Group challenged this in literature. Virginia Woolf challenged the structure of traditional literature and the assumptions of Victorian culture.

- Marcel Proust, James Joyce, Thomas Mann, and T.S. Eliot were just a few of the important literary modernists of this era.
- Sigmund Freud (1856–1939) introduced psychoanalysis to the modern period. He became interested in the idea that dreams expressed the repressed desires of everyday life, and he developed a theory of infantile sexuality. Freud's former student, Carl Jung, advanced his own ideas of collective memories constituting human souls and relied on Romanticism in his work.
- The influential German sociologist Max Weber advanced his belief in noneconomic factors that might account for major developments in history and his faith in the role of the individual in society. Weber differed from many of his peers, who considered collective behavior more of a factor in society. These scientists included Émile Durkheim, Georges Sorel, Gustave LeBon, Vilfredo Pareto, and Graham Wallas.
- Racial thinking in this century supported the ideas of superior and inferior races (in Europe and beyond) and led to racist ideology. An outgrowth of this ideology was anti-Semitism.

AP® KEY CONCEPTS

3.3 The problems of industrialization provoked a range of ideological, governmental, and collective responses.

    I. Ideologies developed and took root throughout society as a response to industrial and political revolutions.

3.6 European ideas and culture expressed a tension between objectivity and scientific realism on one hand, and subjectivity and individual expression on the other.

    II. Following the revolutions of 1848, Europe turned toward a realist and materialist worldview.

    III. A new relativism in values and the loss of confidence in the objectivity of knowledge led to modernism in intellectual and cultural life.

WOMEN AND MODERN THOUGHT

- The biological role of women as mothers became more entrenched in social views of women during this century. Misogyny was not uncommon in the fiction and art of this period.
- Women were excluded from the scientific community, as their alleged "inferiority" made them ineligible for participation. Freud's views helped perpetuate these ideas, and his theories were later debunked by distinguished psychoanalysts such as Melanie Klein and Karen Horney.
- Feminists of this era supported wider sexual freedom for women and advocated contraception. Some women became active in socialist groups; others sought to carve out careers for themselves in professions that had previously been unavailable to them.

AP® KEY CONCEPTS

3.3 The problems of industrialization provoked a range of ideological, governmental, and collective responses.

    III. Political movements and social organizations responded to the problems of industrialization.

3.6 European ideas and culture expressed a tension between objectivity and scientific realism on one hand, and subjectivity and individual expression on the other.

    II. Following the revolutions of 1848, Europe turned toward a realist and materialist worldview.

CHAPTER 16: AP® PRACTICE TEST

Multiple-Choice Questions

Questions 1–3 refer to the following excerpt.

T.H. Huxley, from **Evolution and Ethics,** *1893*

Men in society are undoubtedly subject to the cosmic process. As among other animals, multiplication goes on without cessation, and involves severe competition for the means of support. The struggle for existence tends to eliminate those less fitted to adapt themselves to the circumstances of their existence. The strongest, the most self-assertive, tend to tread down the weaker. But the influence of the cosmic process on the evolution of society is the greater the more rudimentary its civilization. Social progress means a checking of the cosmic process at every step and the substitution for it of another, which may be called the ethical process; the end of which is not the survival of those who may happen to be the fittest, in respect of the whole of the conditions which obtain, but of those who are ethically the best.

As I have already urged, the practice of that which is ethically best—what we call goodness or virtue— involves a course of conduct which, in all respects, is opposed to that which leads to success in the cosmic struggle for existence. In place of ruthless self-assertion it demands self-restraint; in place of thrusting aside, or treading down, all competitors, it requires that the individual shall not merely respect, but shall help his fellows; its influence is directed, not so much to the survival of the fittest, as to the fitting of as many as possible to survive. It repudiates the gladiatorial theory of existence.

It is from neglect of these plain considerations that the fanatical individualism of our time attempts to apply the analogy of cosmic nature to society. . . .

Let us understand, once for all, that the ethical progress of society depends, not on imitating the cosmic process, still less in running away from it, but in combating it.

1. For Huxley, the cosmic process was equated with
   A. evolution.
   B. human society.
   C. creation.
   D. death.

2. Considering the idea of social Darwinism, Huxley
   A. agreed with it.
   B. invented it.
   C. rejected it.
   D. was unconcerned with it.

3. Which of these does Huxley equate with the "gladiatorial theory of existence"?
   A. Christianity
   B. social progress
   C. social Darwinism
   D. ethical progress

Questions 4–5 refer to the following excerpt.

Karl Pearson, from **National Life from the Standpoint of Science,** *1907*

History shows me one way, and one way only, in which a state of civilisation has been produced, namely, the struggle of race with race, and the survival of the physically and mentally fitter race. This dependence of progress on the survival of the fitter race, terribly black as it may seem to some of you, gives the struggle for existence its redeeming features; it is the fiery crucible out of which comes the finer metal. You may hope for a time when the sword shall be turned into the ploughshare, when American and German and English traders shall no longer compete in the markets of the world for raw materials, for their food supply, when the white man and the dark shall share the soil between them, and each till it as he lists. But, believe me, when that day comes mankind will no longer progress; there will be nothing to check the fertility of inferior stock; the relentless law of heredity will not be controlled and guided by natural selection. Man will stagnate. . . . The path of progress is strewn with the wreck of nations; traces are everywhere to be seen of the hecatombs of inferior races, and of victims who found not the narrow way to the greater perfection. Yet these dead peoples are, in very truth, the stepping stones on which mankind has arisen to the higher intellectual and deeper emotional life of today.

4. For Pearson, compared to his contemporary society, earlier vanished cultures were
   A. stronger.
   B. roughly similar.
   C. infertile.
   D. inferior.

5. Which of these would Pearson have equated with peace among nations?
   A. victory
   B. stagnation
   C. history
   D. progress

Questions 6–7 refer to the following excerpt.

Leo XIII from **Rerum Novarum,** *1891*

The great mistake that is made in the matter now under consideration is to possess oneself of the idea that class is naturally hostile to class; that rich and poor are intended by Nature to live at war with one another. So irrational and so false is this view that the exact contrary is the truth. . . . Each requires the other; capital cannot do without labour, nor labour without capital. Mutual agreement results in pleasantness and good order; perpetual conflict necessarily produces confusion and outrage. Now, in preventing such strife as this, and in making it impossible, the efficacy of Christianity is marvelous and manifold. . . . Religion teaches the labouring man and the workman to carry out honestly and well all equitable agreements freely made; never to injure capital, or to outrage the person of an employer; never to employ violence in representing his own cause, or to engage in riot or disorder; and to have nothing to do with men of evil principles, who work upon the people with artful promises and raise hopes which usually end in disaster and in repentance when too late. Religion teaches the rich man and the employer that their work people are not their slaves; that they must respect in every man his dignity as a man and as a Christian; that labour is nothing to be ashamed of, if we listen to right reason and to Christian philosophy, but is an honourable employment, enabling a man to sustain his life in an upright and creditable way; and that it is shameful and inhuman to treat men like chattels to make money by, or to look upon them merely as so much muscle or physical power. Thus, again, Religion teaches that, as among the workman's concerns are Religion herself and things spiritual and mental, the employer is bound to see that he has time for the duties of piety; that he be not exposed to corrupting influences and dangerous occasions; and that he be not led away to neglect his home and family or to squander his wages. Then, again, the employer must never tax his work people beyond their strength, nor employ them in work unsuited to their sex or age. His great and principal obligation is to give every one that which is just.

6. Leo XIII would have agreed with socialists that
   A. a social revolution would take place.
   B. capitalists should improve working conditions.
   C. the existing social order was divinely sanctioned.
   D. wealth should be redistributed.

7. The ideas of Leo XIII and Karl Marx concerning social reform were
   A. essentially the same.
   B. almost identical.
   C. diametrically opposed.
   D. unrelated.

Questions 8–9 refer to the following excerpt.

Émile Zola, from "J'accuse," 1898

I accuse Lt-Col du Paty de Clam of having been the diabolical agent of a miscarriage of justice (though unwittingly, I am willing to believe) and then of having defended his evil deed for the past three years through the most preposterous and most blameworthy machinations. I accuse General Mercier of having been an accomplice, at least by weak-mindedness, to one of the most iniquitous acts of this century. I accuse General Billot of having had in his hands undeniable proof that Dreyfus was innocent and of having suppressed it, of having committed this crime against justice and against humanity for political purposes, so that the General Staff, which had been compromised, would not lose face. I accuse Generals de Boisdeffre and Gonse of having been accomplices to this same crime, one out of intense clerical conviction, no doubt, and the other perhaps because of the esprit de corps which makes the War Office the Holy of Holies and hence unattackable. . . . I accuse the three handwriting experts . . . of having submitted fraudulent and deceitful reports— unless a medication examination concludes that their eyesight and their judgment were impaired. I accuse the War Office of having conducted an abominable campaign in the press . . . in order to cover up its misdeeds and lead public opinion astray. Finally, I accuse the first court martial of having violated the law by sentencing a defendant on the basis of documents which remained secret, and I accuse the second court martial of having covered up that illegal action, on order, by having, in its own turn, committed the judicial crime of knowingly acquitting a guilty man. In making these accusations, I am fully aware that my action comes under Articles 30 and 31 of the law of 29 July 1881 on the press, which makes libel a punishable offence. I deliberately expose myself to that law. As for the persons I have accused, I do not know them: I have never seen them: I feel no rancour or hatred towards them. To me, they are mere entities, mere embodiments of social malfeasance. And the action I am taking here is merely a revolutionary means to hasten the revelation of truth and justice. . . . Let them dare to summon me before a court of law! Let the inquiry be held in broad daylight! I am waiting.

8. For Zola, the perpetrator(s) of this crime was(were)
    A. numerous.
    B. mostly civilians.
    C. Alfred Dreyfus.
    D. the press.

9. In making these accusations, Zola was open to charges of
    A. treason.
    B. perjury.
    C. bearing false witness.
    D. libel.

Questions 10–12 refer to the following excerpt.

Theodor Herzl, from **The Jewish State,** *1904*

This century has given the world a wonderful renaissance by means of its technical acquisitions; but at the same time its miraculous improvements have not been employed in the service of humanity. . . .

Now, I am of the opinion that electric light was not invented for the purpose of illuminating the drawing-rooms of a few snobs, but rather for the purpose of throwing light on some of the dark problems of humanity. One of these problems, and not the least of them, is the Jewish question. In solving it, we are working not only for ourselves, but for many other over-burdened and oppressed beings also.

The Jewish question . . . is a remnant of the Middle Ages, which civilized nations do not even yet seem able to shake off, try as they will. . . . The Jewish question exists wherever Jews live in perceptible numbers. Where it does not exist, it is carried by Jews in the course of their migrations. We naturally move to those places where we are not persecuted, and there our presence produces persecution. This is the case in every country, and will remain so, even in those most highly civilized—France itself being no exception—till the Jewish question finds a solution on a political basis. . . .

We have honestly endeavored everywhere to merge ourselves in the social life of surrounding communities, and to preserve only the faith of our fathers. It has not been permitted to us. In vain are we loyal patriots, our loyalty in some places running to extremes; in vain do we make the same sacrifices of life and property as our fellow citizens; in vain do we strive to increase the fame of our native land in science and art, or her wealth by trade and commerce. In countries where we have lived for centuries we are still cried down as strangers, and often by those whose ancestors were not yet domiciled in the land where Jews had already made experience of suffering. The majority may decide which are the strangers; for this, as indeed every point which arises in the commerce of nations, is a question of might. . . . In the world of today, and for an indefinite period it will probably remain so, might precedes right. Therefore it is useless for us to be loyal patriots.

10. For Herzl, the "Jewish question" can be solved by
    A. moving to a more tolerant nation, such as France.
    B. creating a Jewish nation.
    C. more equitable laws.
    D. Jews trying harder to assimilate.

11. In this excerpt, Herzl contrasts
    A. Christianity and Judaism.
    B. faith and reason.
    C. modern improvements and the medieval inheritance.
    D. intolerance and tolerance.

12. This essay argues that the greatest weakness of the Jews is that they
    A. have hesitated to take part in their countries' culture.
    B. are defined by their religion.
    C. are a minority.
    D. have recently arrived in their countries.

Questions 13–15 refer to the following excerpt.

Virginia Woolf, from a 1928 Lecture

A thousand pens are ready to suggest what you should do and what effect you will have. My own suggestion is a little fantastic, I admit; I prefer, therefore, to put it in the form of fiction.

I told you in the course of this paper that Shakespeare had a sister; but do not look for her in Sir Sidney Lee's life of the poet. She died young—alas, she never wrote a word. She lies buried where the omnibuses now stop, opposite the Elephant and Castle [a London intersection]. Now my belief is that this poet who never wrote a word and was buried at the cross-roads still lives. She lives in you and in me, and in many other women who are not here to-night, for they are washing up the dishes and putting the children to bed. But she lives; for great poets do not die; they are continuing presences; they need only the opportunity to walk among us in the flesh. This opportunity, as I think, it is now coming within your power to give her. For my belief is that if we live another century or so—I am talking of the common life which is the real life and not of the little separate lives which we live as individuals—and have five hundred [pounds income] a year each of us and rooms of our own; if we have the habit of freedom and the courage to write exactly what we think; if we escape a little from the common sitting-room and see human beings not always in their relation to each other but in relation to reality; and the sky, too, and the trees or whatever it may be in themselves; . . . if we face the fact, for it is a fact, that there is no arm to cling to, but that we go alone and that our relation is to the world of reality and not only to the world of men and women, then the opportunity will come and the dead poet who was Shakespeare's sister will put on the body which she has so often laid down. Drawing her life from the lives of the unknown who were her forerunners, as her brother did before her, she will be born. As for her coming without that preparation, without that effort on our part, without that determination that when she is born again she shall find it possible to live and write her poetry, that we cannot expect, for that would be impossible. But I maintain that she would come if we worked for her, and that so to work, even in poverty and obscurity, is worthwhile.

13. In this essay, Shakespeare's sister symbolizes
    A. successful female writers.
    B. unfulfilled human potential.
    C. attempts to hinder women's progress.
    D. English literature.

14. For Woolf, the "common sitting-room" represents
    A. women's habitual domain.
    B. freedom.
    C. creative potential.
    D. death.

15. In this analysis, the role of men in women's lives is
    A. positive.
    B. destructive.
    C. nonexistent.
    D. irrelevant.

Short-Answer Question

In Germany, conflict with the Catholic Church emerged as the *Kulturkampf*.

    a. Choose ONE of the following and explain why your choice represents the key factor leading to this development.

- the doctrine of the Catholic Church
- German nationalism
- the Reformation

    b. Contrast your choice against ONE of the other options, demonstrating why that option is not as significant as your choice.

Long-Essay Question

What were the most important influences that shaped the main currents of European intellectual life in the late-nineteenth century?

Multiple-Choice Questions

1. A   Huxley opposes the "cosmic process," or evolution, with the "ethical process," under human control.
2. C   Huxley rejected the idea that human society should be shaped by evolutionary forces.
3. C   For Huxley, allowing societies to fight it out and kill each other is akin to watching gladiators combat to the death.
4. D   Pearson implies that older cultures died out because they were weaker, inferior.
5. B   For the author, the end of competition and conflict would mean the end of progress, and stagnation.
6. B   There is considerable overlap between the goals of the pope and the goals of socialists.
7. C   While Marx and Engels concentrated on violent revolution, the pope thought that progress and improvement can take place peacefully.
8. A   Zola names a number of men that he blames for the conviction of Dreyfus, most of them in the military.
9. D   If Zola wrongly accused these men, he could be charged with libel.
10. B   The author argues that many means of assimilation have been attempted, and that only a Jewish nation would bring Jews peace.
11. C   For Herzl, although there are many modern innovations, medieval attitudes towards the Jews persist.
12. C   Herzl argues that it is their numbers that make the Jews permanently vulnerable; by extension that means that they would be safe only in a country that was majority Jewish.
13. B   In this literary take on feminism, Woolf uses Shakespeare's sister to symbolize someone who is unknown because she was female.
14. A   This phrase refers to the area of the house usually associated with middle-class women.
15. D   Woolf presents the image of women living entirely independently, with no reference to men.

Long-Essay Question

What were the most important influences that shaped the main currents of European intellectual life in the late-nineteenth century?

(Key topics to focus and elaborate on)
- science: Darwin, Einstein, Freud
- reaction to Romanticism
- attitudes towards religion

CHAPTER 17

The Age of Western Imperialism

THE CLOSE OF THE AGE OF EARLY MODERN COLONIZATION

- The era of early modern European expansion that lasted from the late fifteenth to the late eighteenth centuries witnessed the encounter, conquest, settlement, and exploitation of the American continents by the Spanish, Portuguese, French, and English; the establishment of modest trading posts by European countries in Africa and Asia; the Dutch dominance in the East Indies (modern Indonesia); and the British domination of India.

- During these three centuries, the European powers had largely conducted their colonial rivalries within the context of the mercantilist economic assumptions discussed in Chapter 16. Each empire was, at least in theory and largely in fact, closed to the commerce of other nations. Furthermore, in the Americas, from New England to the Caribbean and then throughout Latin America, slavery was a major fact of economic life with most slaves imported from Africa.

AP® KEY CONCEPTS

3.5 A variety of motives and methods led to the intensification of European global control and increased tensions among the Great Powers.

    I. European nations were driven by economic, political, and cultural motivations in their new imperial ventures in Asia and Africa.

THE AGE OF BRITISH IMPERIAL DOMINANCE

- During the first half of the nineteenth century, no one doubted that Great Britain was the single power that could exert its influence virtually around the world. During this half century, Britain fostered the settlements that became the nations of Canada, Australia, and New Zealand and expanded its control of India.

- The early nineteenth-century British Empire also included smaller colonies and islands in the Caribbean and the Pacific and Indian Oceans. However, until the 1860s and 1870s, except in India and western Canada, Britain did not seek additional territory. Rather, it extended its influence through what historians call the **Imperialism of Free Trade**.

AP® KEY CONCEPTS

3.5 A variety of motives and methods led to the intensification of European global control and increased tensions among the Great Powers.

    I. European nations were driven by economic, political, and cultural motivations in their new imperial ventures in Asia and Africa.

INDIA—THE JEWEL IN THE CROWN OF THE BRITISH EMPIRE

- Until its independence in 1947, India was the most important part of the British Empire and provided the base for British military and economic power throughout Asia. The protection of the commercial and military routes to India would be the chief concern of British imperial strategy during the nineteenth century.

- Other nations, particularly Russia, believed they could threaten Britain by bringing military pressure to bear on India. As we shall see later in the chapter, Britain largely became involved in Africa in the late nineteenth century to protect India.

AP® KEY CONCEPTS

3.5 A variety of motives and methods led to the intensification of European global control and increased tensions among the Great Powers.

    I. European nations were driven by economic, political, and cultural motivations in their new imperial ventures in Asia and Africa.

    III. Imperial endeavors significantly affected society, diplomacy, and culture in Europe and created resistance to foreign control abroad.

THE "NEW IMPERIALISM," 1870–1914

- In the last third of the nineteenth century, European states expanded their control over one-fifth of the world's land and one-tenth of its population. This expansion was driven by developments in science, agriculture, technology, communication, transportation, and military weapons. This movement, known as **New Imperialism,** had numerous motives.

AP® KEY CONCEPTS

3.5 A variety of motives and methods led to the intensification of European global control and increased tensions among the Great Powers.

    I. European nations were driven by economic, political, and cultural motivations in their new imperial ventures in Asia and Africa.

    III. Imperial endeavors significantly affected society, diplomacy, and culture in Europe and created resistance to foreign control abroad.

MOTIVES FOR THE NEW IMPERIALISM

- The many interpretations of motives for New Imperialism include an economic theory advanced by both J. A. Hobson and Valdimir Lenin. They each viewed imperialism as a monopolistic form of capitalism. Others argue that these undeveloped nations had raw materials and provided markets, and still others claim that imperialism was an effort to cure the depression of 1873–1896. None of these theories has been proven. Some view the imperialism as an effort to extend European culture and Christianity to less-industrialized regions. Some advocates of imperialism viewed these regions as inferior and "backward," and they resolved to bring them culture in the form of religion and domestic reform. Some believed that the colonies would attract Europe's surplus population, but in fact European emigrants preferred areas not controlled by their home countries, including North and South America.

AP® KEY CONCEPTS

3.5 A variety of motives and methods led to the intensification of European global control and increased tensions among the Great Powers.

    I. European nations were driven by economic, political, and cultural motivations in their new imperial ventures in Asia and Africa.

III. Imperial endeavors significantly affected society, diplomacy, and culture in Europe and created resistance to foreign control abroad.

THE PARTITION OF AFRICA

- For almost fifty years inter-European rivalries played out in regions far away from Europe itself and nowhere more intensely than in Africa. During the so-called "Scramble for Africa," which occurred between the late 1870s and about 1912, the European powers sought to maximize their strategic control of African territory, markets, and raw materials. Motivated by intense competition, the imperial powers eventually divided almost all the continent among themselves (see Map 17-2). The short- and long-term consequences were complex and in most cases devastating for the Africans. One of the long-term effects was that European control forcibly integrated largely agrarian African societies into the modern world industrial economy. In the process, new forms of agrarian production, market economies, social organizations, political structures, and religious allegiances emerged that would form the basis for the post-colonial African nations (see Map 17-3).

- The European partition of Africa was not based on a universal policy, and each power acquired and administered its new possessions in different ways. Their goals, however, were the same: to gain control, or at least dominance, through diplomacy or force and then either to place Europeans directly in charge of administering the territories or to compel local rulers to accept European "advisers" who would exercise real authority.

AP® KEY CONCEPTS

3.5 A variety of motives and methods led to the intensification of European global control and increased tensions among the Great Powers.

I. European nations were driven by economic, political, and cultural motivations in their new imperial ventures in Asia and Africa.
II. Industrial and technological developments (i.e., the Second Industrial Revolution) facilitated European control of global empires.
III. Imperial endeavors significantly affected society, diplomacy, and culture in Europe and created resistance to foreign control abroad.

RUSSIAN EXPANSION IN MAINLAND ASIA

- The British presence in India was intimately related to Russian expansion across mainland Asia in the nineteenth century, which eventually brought huge territories and millions of people of a variety of ethnicities and religions under tsarist rule. This expansion of Russian imperialism is one of the chief sources of the ethnic tensions that exist today in the Russian Federation and in particular between that federation and Chechnya and other parts of the Caucasus.

AP® KEY CONCEPTS

3.5 A variety of motives and methods led to the intensification of European global control and increased tensions among the Great Powers.

I. European nations were driven by economic, political, and cultural motivations in their new imperial ventures in Asia and Africa.
III. Imperial endeavors significantly affected society, diplomacy, and culture in Europe and created resistance to foreign control abroad.

WESTERN POWERS IN ASIA

- While merchants had established the British interest in India and South Asia, French interest in Indochina arose because of the activity of Roman Catholic missionaries. The French domain in Indochina eventually consisted of Vietnam, Cambodia, and Laos.
- In 1853, a U.S. naval squadron under Commodore Matthew C. Perry (1794–1858) arrived in Japanese waters to open Japanese markets to American goods. In 1867, American interest in the Pacific again manifested itself when the United States bought Alaska from Russia. For the next twenty-five years, the United States assumed a fairly passive role in foreign affairs, but it had established its presence in the Pacific.
- From late 1899 through the autumn of 1901, a Chinese group called The Righteous and Harmonious Society of Fists, better known in the West as the Boxers, attempted to resist the Western incursions. The Boxers, who were supported by a faction at the Qing court, hated missionaries whom they saw as agents of the imperial powers and killed thousands of their Chinese converts.

AP® KEY CONCEPTS

3.5 A variety of motives and methods led to the intensification of European global control and increased tensions among the Great Powers.

> I. European nations were driven by economic, political, and cultural motivations in their new imperial ventures in Asia and Africa.
> III. Imperial endeavors significantly affected society, diplomacy, and culture in Europe and created resistance to foreign control abroad.

TOOLS OF IMPERIALISM

- The domination that Europe and peoples of European descent came to exert over the entire globe by 1900 is extraordinary. It had not existed a century earlier and would not exist a century later. At the time, many Europeans, as well as Americans who worked their way across the North American continent in what many regarded as manifest destiny, saw this domination as evidence of cultural or racial superiority.
- Western domination was based on distinct and temporary technological advantages, what one historian called the "tools of empire." These tools gave Westerners the capacity to conquer and dominate vast areas of the world. Steamboats, the conquest of tropical diseases, and the technological advantage of Western firearms, can all be considered "tools of imperialism."

AP® KEY CONCEPTS

3.5 A variety of motives and methods led to the intensification of European global control and increased tensions among the Great Powers.

> II. Industrial and technological developments (i.e., the Second Industrial Revolution) facilitated European control of global empires.

THE MISSIONARY FACTOR

- The modern Western missionary movement, which continues to the present day, originated in Great Britain in the late eighteenth century as a direct outgrowth of the rise of evangelical Christianity. Evangelicalism, which influenced Protestant communities from Central Europe to the United States, emphasized the authority of the Bible, the importance of a personal conversion experience, and the duty to spread the Gospel. Many Evangelicals were also concerned about preparing the world for the Second Coming of Jesus by carrying the message of Christian redemption to peoples who had not heard it. British Evangelicals first looked to unchurched groups in their own nation as the primary field for bearing Christian witness, but by the close of the eighteenth century, in a largely new departure for Protestants, small groups of Evangelicals began to be active in the non-Western world. Roman Catholics later copied these early Protestant missionary efforts. The result of this widespread nineteenth-century missionary campaign was the establishment of large Christian communities in Africa and Asia, which today thrive and continue to expand.

AP® KEY CONCEPTS

3.5 A variety of motives and methods led to the intensification of European global control and increased tensions among the Great Powers.

I. European nations were driven by economic, political, and cultural motivations in their new imperial ventures in Asia and Africa.

III. Imperial endeavors significantly affected society, diplomacy, and culture in Europe and created resistance to foreign control abroad.

SCIENCE AND IMPERIALISM

- The early modern European encounter with the non-Western world from the fifteenth-century voyages of discovery onward had been associated with the expansion of natural knowledge. The same would be true of Western imperialism in the nineteenth and early twentieth centuries. Commencing in 1768, Captain James Cook (1728–1779) had undertaken his famous voyages to the South Pacific under the patronage of the Royal Society of London to observe the transit of the planet Venus. Sir Joseph Banks (1744–1820), later president of the Royal Society, went with him to collect specimens of plants and animals unknown in Europe. Other British, French, and Spanish naval expeditions also carried scientists with their crews.
- Scientific societies often cooperated with military forces to carry out their research. For example, dozens of French scholars accompanied Napoleon's invasion of Egypt in 1798.

AP® KEY CONCEPTS

3.5 A variety of motives and methods led to the intensification of European global control and increased tensions among the Great Powers.

I. European nations were driven by economic, political, and cultural motivations in their new imperial ventures in Asia and Africa.

II. Industrial and technological developments (i.e., the Second Industrial Revolution) facilitated European control of global empires.

Multiple-Choice Questions

Questions 1–2 refer to the following excerpt.

Lin Tse-hsü to Queen Victoria, 1839

. . . after a long period of commercial intercourse, there appear among the crowd of barbarians [that is, foreigners trading in China] both good persons and bad, unevenly. Consequently there are those who smuggle opium to seduce the Chinese people and so cause the spread of the poison to all provinces . . . His Majesty the Emperor, upon hearing of this, is in a towering rage. .

. . The wealth of China is used to profit the barbarians. . . . By what right do they then in return use the poisonous drug to injure the Chinese people? . . . Let us ask, where is your conscience? I have heard that smoking of opium is very strictly forbidden by your country; that is because the harm caused by opium is clearly understood. Since it is not permitted to do harm to your own country, then even less should you let it be passed on to the harm of other countries—how much less to China! Of all that China exports to foreign countries, there is not a single thing which is not beneficial to people. . . .

Even if you do not sell opium, you still have this threefold profit. How can you bear to go further, selling products injurious to others in order to fulfill your insatiable desire? . . .

Now we have set up regulations governing the Chinese people. He who sells opium shall receive the death penalty and he who smokes it also the death penalty. . . . [I]n the new regulations, in regard to those barbarians who bring opium to China, the penalty is fixed at decapitation or strangulation. This is what is called getting rid of a harmful thing on behalf of mankind. . . .

The barbarian merchants of your country, if they wish to do business for a prolonged period, are required to obey our statutes respectfully and to cut off permanently the source of opium. They must by no means try to test the effectiveness of the law with their lives. May you, O King, check your wicked and sift your vicious people before they come to China, in order to guarantee the peace of your nation . . . to let the two countries enjoy together the blessings of peace.

1. 1. In this letter, Lin Tse-hsü asks Queen Victoria to
   A. cut off trade with China.
   B. uphold Chinese law.
   C. stop the opium trade.
   D. end the Opium War.

2. Which of these most likely explains the continued trade with China following this letter, in spite of the harsh penalties imposed?
   A. the desirability of Chinese goods
   B. the weakness of the Chinese government
   C. the greed of Chinese merchants
   D. the lack of Chinese export goods

Questions 3–4 refer to the following maps.

British India, 1820 to 1856

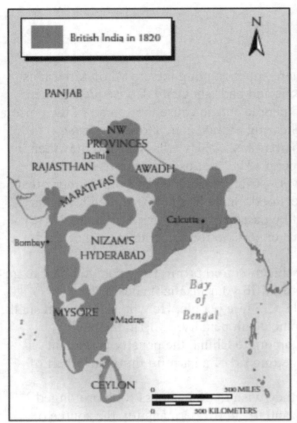 

3. Looking at these maps, the British plan for India is best described as
   A. a plan of conquest from north to south.
   B. the wholesale military conquest of the subcontinent.
   C. a decision to remain out of India.
   D. opportunistic.

4. What was the probable political situation in India, as reflected by this map?
   A. a strongly centralized government
   B. chaos
   C. fragmentation
   D. division under several foreign powers

Questions 5–7 refer to the following excerpt.

Gandhi on Civilization

Let us first consider what state of things is described by the word "civilisation." Its true test lies in the fact that people living in it make bodily welfare the object of life. The people of Europe today live in better built houses than they did a hundred years ago. This is considered an emblem of civilisation, and this is also a matter to promote bodily happiness. Formerly, they wore skins, and used as their weapons spears. Now they wear long trousers, and for embellishing their bodies, they wear a variety of clothing, and, instead of spears, they carry with them revolvers. . . . If people of a certain country, who have hitherto not been in the habit of wearing much clothing, boots, etc., adopt European clothing, they are supposed to have become civilised out of savagery. . . . Formerly, when people wanted to fight with one another, they measured between them their bodily strength; now it is possible to take away thousands of lives by one man working behind a gun from a hill. This is civilization. Formerly, men worked in the open air only as much as they liked. Now thousands of workmen meet together and for the sake of maintenance work in factories or mines. Their condition is worse than that of beasts. They are obliged to work, at the risk of their lives, at most dangerous occupations, for the sake of millionaires. Formerly, men were made slaves under physical compulsion. Now they are enslaved by temptation of money and of luxuries that money can buy. Formerly, people had two or three meals consisting of home-made bread and vegetables; now, they require something to eat every two hours so that they have hardly leisure for anything else. . . . These are all true tests of civilisation. . . . Even a child can understand that in all I have described above there can be no inducement to morality. Civilisation seeks to increase bodily comforts, and it fails miserably even in doing so.

This civilisation is irreligion, and it has taken such a hold on the people in Europe that those who are in it appear to be half mad. They lack real physical strength or courage. They keep up their energy by intoxication. They can hardly be happy in solitude.

Women, who should be the queens of households, wander in the streets or they slave away in factories. For the sake of a pittance, half a million women in England alone are labouring under trying circumstances in factories or similar institutions. This awful fact is one of the causes of the daily growing suffragette movement.

This civilisation is such that one has only to be patient and it will be self-destroyed. . . . Civilisation is not an incurable disease, but it should never be forgotten that the English are at present afflicted by it.

5. The word "civilisation" is used repeatedly in this excerpt with a sense of
   A. tragedy.
   B. praise.
   C. irony.
   D. comedy.

6. Gandhi attributes the calls for women's suffrage to
   A. liberal values.
   B. poor working conditions.
   C. economic opportunity.
   D. universal manhood suffrage.

7. Which of these best summarizes Gandhi's assessment of the importance of clothing?
   A. As Indians have adopted European-style clothing, they have become more civilized.
   B. Civilization and more elaborate clothing go hand in hand.
   C. Material conditions are the best measure of a culture's sophistication.
   D. Civilization does not depend on having more.

Questions 8–9 refer to the following map.

Imperial Expansion in Africa to 1880

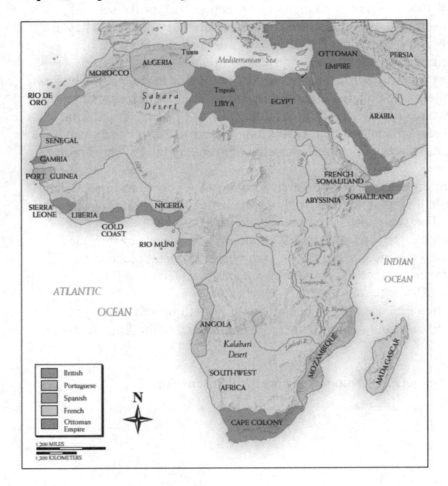

8. In 1880, European colonization in Africa is best described as
   A. extensive.   C. limited.
   B. complete.   D. greatest in the south.

9. Which of these had established the most colonies in Africa by 1880?
   A. Britain
   B. France
   C. Portugal
   D. Spain

Questions 10–11 refer to the following excerpt.

Gustav Schmoller Makes the Case for German Imperial Expansion

In various States, arrogant, reckless, cold-blooded daring bullies, men who possess the morals of a captain of pirates . . . push themselves more and more forward into the Government. . . . We must not forget that it is in the freest States, England and North America, where the tendencies of conquest, Imperial schemes, and hatred against new economic competitors are growing up amongst the masses. The leaders of these agitations are great speculators, who have the morals of a pirate, and who are at the same time party leaders and Ministers of State. . . . The conquest of Cuba and the Philippines by the United States alters their political and economical basis. Their tendency to exclude Europe from the North and South American markets must needs lead to new great conflicts. . . . These bullies, these pirates and speculators à la Cecil Rhodes, act like poison within their State. They buy the press, corrupt ministers and the aristocracy, and bring on wars for the benefit of a bankrupt company or for the gain of filthy lucre. . . . We mean to extend our trade and industries far enough to enable us to live and sustain a growing population. We mean to defend our colonies, and, if possible, to acquire somewhere agricultural colonies. We mean to prevent extravagant mercantilism everywhere, and to prevent the division of the earth among the three world powers, which would exclude all other countries and destroy their trade. In order to attain this modest gain we require today so badly a large fleet. The German Empire must become the centre of a coalition of States, chiefly in order to be able to hold the balance in the death-struggle between Russia and England, but that is only possible if we possess a stronger fleet than that of today. . . . We must wish that at any price a German country, peopled by twenty to thirty million Germans, should grow up in Southern Brazil. Without the possibility of energetic proceedings on the part of Germany our future over there is threatened. . . . We do not mean to press for an economic alliance with Holland, but if the Dutch are wise, if they do not want to lose their colonies someday, as Spain did, they will hasten to seek our alliance.

10. The "bullies" referred to by Schmoller are
    A. European imperialists.
    B. European governments.
    C. African governments.
    D. Arab merchants

11. The alliance envisioned by Schmoller appears to be planned in order to
    A. bring about greater cooperation among European merchants.
    B. impose rules in international commerce.
    C. turn England and Russia into allies.
    D. balance the trading power of dominant European states.

Questions 12–13 refer to the following excerpt.

Anatole France on Imperialism

Imperialism is the most recent form of barbarism, the end of the line for civilization. I do not distinguish between the two terms—imperialism and barbarism—for they mean the same thing.

We Frenchmen, a thrifty people, who see to it that we have no more children than we are able to support easily, careful of adventuring into foreign lands, we Frenchmen who hardly ever leave our own gardens, for what in the world do we need colonies? What can we do with them? What are the benefits for us? It has cost France much in lives and money so that the Congo, Cochinchina, Annam, Tonkin, Guinea, and Madagascar may be able to buy cotton from Manchester, liquors from Danzig, and wine from Hamburg. For the last seventy years France has attacked and persecuted the Arabs so that Algeria might be inhabited by Italians and Spaniards!

The French people get nothing from the colonial lands of Africa and Asia. But their government finds it profitable. Through colonial conquest the military people get promotions, pensions, and awards, in addition to the glory gained by quelling the natives. Shipowners, army contractors, and shady politicians prosper. The ignorant mob is flattered because it believes that an overseas empire will make the British and Germans green with envy.

Will this colonial madness never end? I know well that nations are not reasonable. Considering their composition, it would be strange, indeed, if they were. But sometimes they know instinctively what is bad for them. Through long and bitter experience they will come to see the mistakes they have made. And, one day, they will realize that colonies bring only danger and ruin.

12. In this essay, imperialism is criticized mainly because it is
    A. unethical.
    B. unprofitable.
    C. racist.
    D. un-Christian.

13. For Anatole France, colonization is most beneficial to
    A. individuals in the military and in the government.
    B. France as a whole.
    C. colonized peoples.
    D. the Arabs.

Questions 14–15 refer to the following map.

Partition of Africa, 1880–1914

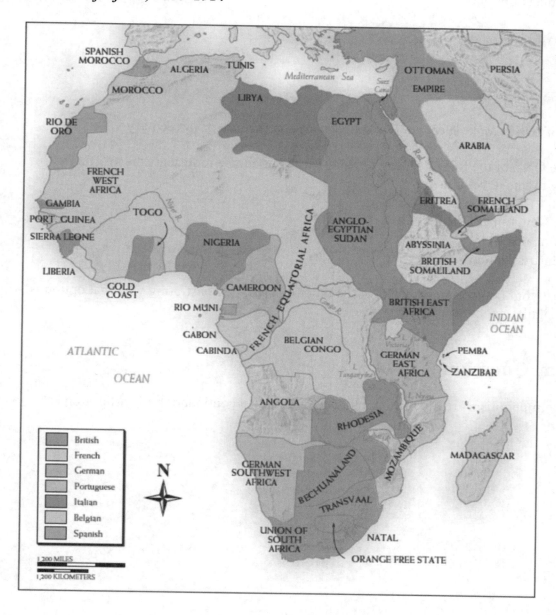

14. The two greatest competitors for control of Africa in 1914 were
    A. Germany and Spain.
    B. Portugal and Spain.
    C. France and Britain.
    D. France and Germany.

15. Which of these remained free of European control in 1914?
    A. Libya
    B. Abyssinia (Ethiopia)
    C. Egypt
    D. South Africa

Short-Answer Question

The partition of Africa took place in a few decades around the turn of the century.

a. Choose ONE of the following and explain why your choice represents the key factor leading to this development.

- the New Imperialism
- nationalism
- industrialization

b. Contrast your choice against ONE of the other options, demonstrating why that option is not as significant as your choice.

Long-Essay Question

Was the "New Imperialism" really something new, or simply a continuation of earlier trends?

Multiple-Choice Questions

1. B   The official asks that Victoria ensure that English merchants uphold Chinese law.
2. A   The consistent, strong demand for Chinese goods in Europe meant that European merchants continued the trade even when threatened with death.
3. D   The British encroachment in India was not governed by a long-range plan, but took place whenever an opportunity presented itself.
4. C   India was politically fragmented, which explains the piecemeal pattern of British conquest.
5. C   Gandhi seeks to weaken the common criticism of the Indians as "uncivilised," by showing that the British themselves are uncivilized.
6. B   Gandhi ties women's work to the demands for women's suffrage.
7. D   One of Gandhi's most important critiques of European culture is the assumption that having more—or wearing more—means a higher level of civilization.
8. C   Up until the late 1800s, Europeans were not able to penetrate far beyond the coasts of Africa.
9. A   Already by this period, the British led the way in African colonization; the French were their principal rivals.
10. A   Schmoller refers to European imperialists as "pirates" and as "bullies," and argues that they have a great deal of influence over their governments.
11. D   The author hopes to create a coalition—with Germany at its head—that would overcome the great power of Britain and other states.
12. B   Although other critiques are mentioned, the focus here is on the fact that colonization does not profit most French people.
13. A   Only some individuals benefit from imperialism, according to France.
14. C   Between them, France and Britain controlled well over half of the continent.
15. B   Abyssinia managed to remain free of European imperialism until invaded by Germany in 1936.

Long-Essay Question

Was the "New Imperialism" really something new, or simply a continuation of earlier trends?

(Key topics to focus and elaborate on)
- motives
- actors
- means

CHAPTER 18

Alliances, War, and a Troubled Peace

EMERGENCE OF THE GERMAN EMPIRE AND THE ALLIANCE SYSTEMS (1873–1890)

- In 1873, Bismarck formed the Three Emperors' League, which brought together Germany, Austria, and Russia. The league soon collapsed because of the Austro-Russian rivalry in the Balkans.
- The Congress of Berlin resulted in Russia's significant loss of territory, and a new tension arose between Germany and Russia. Germany and Austria signed the Dual Alliance, whereby they would protect each other if either country was attacked by Russia.
- Russia soon joined and renewed the Three Emperors' League in 1881. Another series of alliances between Austria, Germany, and Italy were arranged, but the rise of William II to the German throne in 1888 upset these delicate balances and led to the dismissal of Bismarck.
- New alliances and tensions led to a Franco-Russian alliance in 1894, and a new tension arose between Britain and Germany. Britain concluded agreements with the French in 1902 known as the *Entente Cordiale*.
- The Triple Entente, consisting of Britain, France, and Russia, was now posed against the Triple Alliance of Germany, Austria, and Italy. These relationships and shifting conflicts in the region pushed Europe closer to war.

AP® KEY CONCEPTS

3.4 European states struggled to maintain international stability in an age of nationalism and revolutions.
    III. The unification of Italy and Germany transformed the European balance of power and led to efforts to construct a new diplomatic order.

WORLD WAR I

- A series of Balkan crises precipitated war. Both Serbia and Austria-Hungary wanted to expand into the Balkans. Austria annexed Bosnia-Herzegovina in 1908, and proceeded to alienate Russia, which sided with Serbia in the crisis. Germany joined Austria's cause to keep the Russian threat in check.
- A second crisis in Morocco occurred in 1911, when Germany protested French occupation of the region and sent the Panther gunboat to protect German interests. This action irritated Britain, which pledged its support to France. Negotiations allowed France to establish a protectorate in Morocco and gave Germany some land in the French Congo. However, the more important outcome was an increase of British fear and hostility toward Germany, and a closer alliance with France.
- The June 28, 1914, assassination of Archduke Ferdinand, Austrian heir to the throne, by a

Bosnian nationalist was the spur to the outbreak of war. Serbia's involvement with the plot provoked outrage in Europe. Germany agreed to support Austria in an attack on Serbia, and war was declared in July—but not begun until August. Russia was not eager for war, but Pan-Slav nationalists demanded action, and the government ordered partial mobilization. France and Britain were not eager for war, but their alliance with Russia required their assistance.

AP® KEY CONCEPTS

3.4 European states struggled to maintain international stability in an age of nationalism and revolutions.

    III. The unification of Italy and Germany transformed the European balance of power and led to efforts to construct a new diplomatic order.

4.1 Total war and political instability in the first half of the twentieth century gave way to a polarized state order during the Cold War, and eventually to efforts at transnational union.

    I. World War I, caused by a complex interaction of long- and short-term factors, resulted in immense losses and disruptions for both victors and vanquished.

THE RUSSIAN REVOLUTION

- In March 1917, a Russian revolution overthrew the tsarist government of Nicholas II. The war put too many demands on Russia's resources, and peasant discontent had plagued the country for many years. Strikes and worker demonstrations erupted, the tsar abdicated, the government fell to the members of the reconvened *Duma,* and a provisional government was formed composed of Constitutional Democrats with Western sympathies. This government remained loyal to the tsarist alliances and decided to continue war against Germany.

- The Bolshevik wing of the Social Democratic Party had been working against the provisional government. Vladimir Lenin demanded that political power go to the *soviets,* which were councils of workers and soldiers controlled by the Menshevik wing, a group of orthodox Marxists. With Lenin's help, Leon Trotsky organized a coup that concluded with the Bolshevik rule of Russia.

AP® KEY CONCEPTS

4.2 The stresses of economic collapse and total war engendered internal conflicts within European states and created conflicting conceptions of the relationship between the individual and the state, as demonstrated in the ideological battle among liberal democracy, communism, and fascism.

    I. The Russian Revolution created a regime based on Marxist-Leninist theory.

THE END OF WORLD WAR I

- In March 1918, Germany agreed to accept defeat and sought peace on the basis of Woodrow Wilson's **Fourteen Points**, which included the creation of the **League of Nations**. The Great War came to an end with some 4 million dead and 8.3 million wounded among the Central Powers and 5.4 million dead and 7 million wounded among the Allies.

4.1 Total war and political instability in the first half of the twentieth century gave way to a polarized state order during the Cold War, and eventually to efforts at transnational union.

    I. World War I, caused by a complex interaction of long- and short-term factors, resulted in immense losses and disruptions for both victors and vanquished.

    II. The conflicting goals of the peace negotiators in Paris pitted diplomatic idealism against the desire to punish Germany, producing a settlement that satisfied few.

    VII. The process of decolonization occurred over the course of the century with varying degrees of cooperation, interference, or resistance from European imperialist states.

4.2 The stresses of economic collapse and total war engendered internal conflicts within European states and created conflicting conceptions of the relationship between the individual and the state, as demonstrated in the ideological battle among liberal democracy, communism, and fascism.

    I. The Russian Revolution created a regime based on Marxist-Leninist theory.

THE SETTLEMENT AT PARIS

- The Paris settlement consisted of five separate treaties between victors and the defeated powers. The Soviet Union (as Russia was called after the Bolshevik victory) and Germany were not included in the peace conference.
- The League of Nations was established, and its covenant was an important part of the peace treaty. France won Alsace-Lorraine, Germany was disarmed, and the United States and Britain agreed to protect France from any future German aggression.
- The Austro-Hungarian Empire disappeared, giving way to five small states. Germany was required to pay $5 billion annually in reparations until 1921.

AP® KEY CONCEPTS
4.1 Total war and political instability in the first half of the twentieth century gave way to a polarized state order during the Cold War, and eventually to efforts at transnational union.

    I. World War I, caused by a complex interaction of long- and short-term factors, resulted in immense losses and disruptions for both victors and vanquished.

    II. The conflicting goals of the peace negotiators in Paris pitted diplomatic idealism against the desire to punish Germany, producing a settlement that satisfied few.

    VII. The process of decolonization occurred over the course of the century with varying degrees of cooperation, interference, or resistance from European imperialist states.

Multiple-Choice Questions

Questions 1–3 refer to the following map.

The Balkans 1912–1913

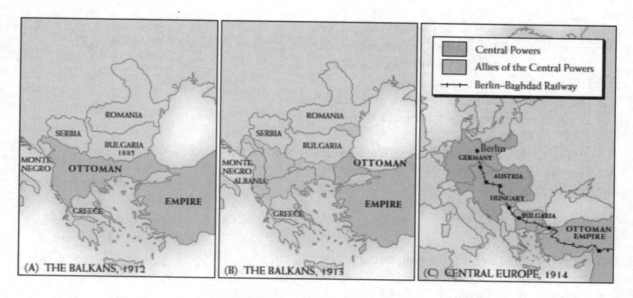

1. The crises in the Balkans in the 1910s were largely the product of changes in
   A. the German Empire.
   B. the Ottoman Empire.
   C. Austria-Hungary.
   D. France.

2. The independence movements reflected in these maps were spurred primarily by
   A. religious sentiment.
   B. German aggression.
   C. nationalism.
   D. Austrian expansion.

Questions 3–4 refer to the following excerpt.

The Austrian Ambassador Gets a "Blank Check" from the Kaiser

After lunch, when I again called attention to the seriousness of the situation, the Kaiser authorised me to inform our gracious Majesty that we might in this case, as in all others, rely upon Germany's full support. He must, as he said before, first hear what the Imperial Chancellor has to say, but he did not doubt in the least that Herr von Bethmann-Hollweg would agree with him. Especially as far as our action against Serbia was concerned. But it was his [Kaiser

Wilhelm's] opinion that this action must not be delayed. Russia's attitude will no doubt be hostile but to this he had been for years prepared, and should a war between Austria-Hungary and Russia be unavoidable, we might be convinced that Germany, our old faithful ally, would stand at our side. Russia at the present time was in no way prepared for war, and would think twice before it appealed to arms. But it will certainly set other powers on to the Triple Alliance and add fuel to the fire in the Balkans. He understands perfectly well that His Apostolic Majesty [the Austrian Emperor Franz Josef] in his well-known love of peace would be reluctant to march into Serbia; but if we had really recognised the necessity of warlike action against Serbia, he [Kaiser Wilhelm] would regret if we did not make use of the present moment which is all in our favour.

3. Which of these best describe the German leader's stance, as reflected in this excerpt?
    A. The kaiser wants to go to war soon.
    B. The kaiser is committed to peace.
    C. The kaiser is waiting for Russia to declare war.
    D. The kaiser prefers negotiations to war.

4. According to this author, if Austria were to attack Serbia, Russia would
    A. become involved.
    B. declare war.
    C. side with Austria.
    D. also attack Serbia.

Questions 5–7 refer to the following excerpt.

Austrian Demands to Serbia, July 1914
     The results brought out by the inquiry no longer permit the Imperial and Royal Government to maintain the attitude of patient tolerance which it has observed for years toward those agitations which center at Belgrade and are spread thence into the territories of the Monarchy. Instead, these results impose upon the Imperial and Royal Government the obligation to put an end to those intrigues, which constitute a standing menace to the peace of the Monarchy.
     In order to attain this end, the Imperial and Royal Government finds itself compelled to demand that the Serbian Government give official assurance that it will condemn the propaganda directed against Austria-Hungary, that is to say, the whole body of the efforts whose ultimate object it is to separate from the Monarchy territories that belong to it; and that it will obligate itself to suppress with all the means at its command this criminal and terroristic propaganda. . . .
     1. to suppress every publication which shall incite to hatred and contempt the Monarchy, and the general tendency of which shall be directed against the territorial integrity of the latter;
     2. to proceed at once to the dissolution of the Narodna Odbrana [a Serbian nationalist propaganda and paramilitary organization], confiscate all of its means of propaganda, and in the same manner to proceed against the other unions and associations in Serbia which occupy themselves with propaganda against Austria-Hungary; the Royal Government will take such measures as are necessary to make sure that the dissolved associations may not continue their activities under other names in other forms;

3. to eliminate without delay from public instruction in Serbia, everything, whether connected with the teaching corps or with the methods of teaching, that serves or may serve to nourish the propaganda against Austria-Hungary;

4. to remove from the military and administrative service in general all officers and officials who have been guilty of carrying on the propaganda against Austria-Hungary, whose names the Imperial and Royal Government reserve the right to make known to the Royal Government . . . ;

5. to agree to the cooperation in Serbia of the organs of the Imperial Royal Government in the suppression of the subversive movement directed against the integrity of the Monarchy;

6. to institute a judicial inquiry against every participant in the conspiracy of the twenty-eighth of June who may be found in Serbian territory; the organs of the Imperial and Royal Government delegated for this purpose will take part in the proceedings held for this purpose;

7. to undertake with all haste the arrest of Major Voislav Tankositch and of one Milan Ciganovitch, a Serbian official, who have been compromised by the results of the inquiry . . . ;

10. to inform the Imperial and Royal Government without delay of the execution of the measures comprised in the foregoing points. The Imperial and Royal Government awaits the reply of the Royal Government by Saturday, the twenty-fifth instant, at 6 p.m., at the latest.

5. Which of these is the focus of these demands?
   A. Serbia will become part of the Austrian Empire.
   B. Serbia will gain its independence.
   C. Serbia will respect the integrity of the Austrian Empire.
   D. Serbia will demilitarize.

6. What triggered these demands?
   A. the Austrian "blank check" given to Germany
   B. the outbreak of World War I
   C. the assassination of Franz Ferdinand
   D. the creation of Serbia

7. What is Austria's rationale for making these demands?
   A. Serbia and Austria are allies.
   B. Austria's security is threatened.
   C. The "blank check" is being invoked.
   D. Serbia is part of the Austrian Empire.

Questions 8–9 refer to the following map.

The Schlieffen Plan of 1905

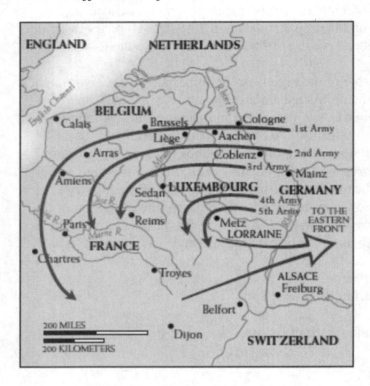

8. What is the first stage of the strategy shown here?
   A. to defeat Belgium and France
   B. to attack Russia
   C. to defeat England
   D. to expand into eastern Europe

9. According to this plan, what posed the greatest threat to Germany?
   A. France
   B. Russia
   C. England
   D. Belgium

Questions 10–11 refer to the following map.

The Western Front 1914–1918

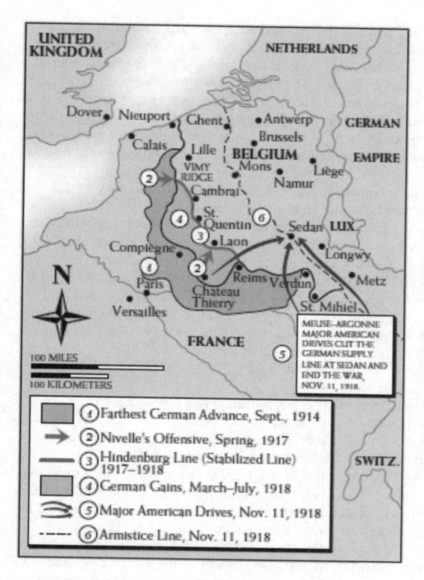

10. Where did most of the fighting of the western front take place?
    A. Belgium
    B. Germany
    C. Switzerland
    D. France

11. Between 1914 and 1918, roughly how far did the western front move?
    A. 10 miles
    B. 500 miles
    C. 50 miles
    D. 100 miles

Questions 12–13 refer to the following excerpt.

The Outbreak of the Russian Revolution, 1917

At half-past eight this morning, just as I finished dressing, I heard a strange and prolonged din which seemed to come from the Alexander Bridge. I looked out: there was no one on the bridge, which usually presents such a busy scene. But, almost immediately, a disorderly mob carrying red flags appeared at the end which is on the right bank of the Neva, and a regiment came towards it from the opposite side. It looked as if there would be a violent collision, but on the contrary the two bodies coalesced. The army was fraternizing with revolt.

Shortly afterwards, someone came to tell me that the Volhynian regiment of the Guard had mutinied during the night, killed its officers and was parading the city, calling on the people to take part in the revolution and trying to win over the troops who still remain loyal.

At ten o'clock there was a sharp burst of firing, and flames could be seen rising somewhere on the Liteïny Prospekt which is quite close to the embassy. Then silence. Accompanied by my military attaché, Lieutenant-Colonel Lavergne, I went out to see what was happening. Frightened inhabitants were scattering through the streets. There was indescribable confusion at the corner of the Liteïny. Soldiers were helping civilians to erect a barricade. Flames mounted from the Law Courts. The gates of the arsenal burst open with a crash. Suddenly the crack of machine-gun fire split the air: it was the regulars who had just taken up position near the Nevsky Prospekt. The revolutionaries replied. I had seen enough to have no doubt as to what was coming. Under a hail of bullets I returned to the embassy with Lavergne who had walked calmly and slowly to the hottest corner out of sheer bravado.

About half-past eleven I went to the Ministry for Foreign Affairs, picking up Buchanan [the British ambassador to Russia] on the way.

I told Pokrovski [the Russian foreign minister] everything I had just witnessed.

"So it's even more serious than I thought," he said.

But he preserved unruffled composure, flavoured with a touch of skepticism, when he told me of the steps on which the ministers had decided during the night:

"The sitting of the Duma has been prorogued to April and we have sent a telegram to the Emperor, begging him to return at once. With the exception of M. Protopopov [the Minister of the Interior, in charge of the police], my colleagues and I all thought that a dictatorship should be established without delay; it would be conferred upon some general whose prestige with the army is pretty high, General Russky for example."

I argued that, judging by what I saw this morning, the loyalty of the army was already too heavily shaken for our hopes of salvation to be based on the use of the "strong hand," and that the immediate appointment of a ministry inspiring confidence in the Duma seemed to me more essential than ever, as there is not a moment to lose. I reminded Pokrovski that in 1789, 1830, and 1848, three French dynasties were overthrown because they were too late in realizing the significance and strength of the movement against them. I added that in such a grave crisis the representative of allied France had a right to give the Imperial Government advice on a matter of internal politics.

Buchanan endorsed my opinion.

Pokrovski replied that he personally shared our views, but that the presence of Protopopov in the Council of Ministers paralyzed action of any kind.

I asked him: "Is there no one who can open the Emperor's eyes to the real situation?"

He heaved a despairing sigh. "The Emperor is blind!" Deep grief was writ large on the face of the honest man and good citizen whose uprightness, patriotism and disinterestedness I can never sufficiently extol.

12. According to this assessment, which of these groups was pivotal in advancing the Russian Revolution?
    A. the proletariat
    B. the government itself
    C. the military
    D. diplomats

13. For the author, which of these would be able to halt the Revolution?
    A. a strong government
    B. the police
    C. the army
    D. outside intervention

Questions 14–15 refer to the following excerpt.

Relative Strengths of the Combatants in World War I

	POPULATION (TOTAL)	SOLDIERS POTENTIALLY AVAILABLE	MILITARY EXPENDITURES (1913–1914)	BATTLESHIPS IN SERVICE OR BEING BUILT	CRUISERS	SUBMARINES	MERCHANT SHIPS (TONS)
GREAT BRITAIN	Overseas Emp. 390 Million 45,000,000	711,000	250,000,000	64	121	64	20,000,000
FRANCE	Overseas Emp. 58 Million 40,000,000	1,250,000	185,000,000	28	34	73	2,000,000
ITALY	Overseas Emp. 2 Million 35,000,000	750,000	50,000,000	14	22	12	1,750,000
RUSSIA	164,000,000	1,200,000	335,000,000	16	14	29	750,000
BELGIUM	7,500,000	180,000	13,750,000				
ROMANIA	7,500,000	420,000	15,000,000				
GREECE	5,000,000	120,000	3,750,000				
SERBIA	5,000,000	195,000	5,250,000				
MONTE-NEGRO	500,000						
UNITED STATES	92,000,000	150,000	150,000,000	37	35	25	4,500,000
GERMANY	65,000,000	2,200,000	300,000,000	40	57	23	5,000,000
AUSTRIA-HUNGARY	50,000,000	810,000	110,000,000	16	12	6	1,000,000
OTTOMAN EMPIRE	20,000,000	360,000	40,000,000				
BULGARIA	4,500,000	340,000	5,500,000				

14. Which of these would have had the advantage in the case of a land war?
    A. France
    B. Germany
    C. Russia
    D. Great Britain

15. Compared to the Allies, the naval power of the Axis was
    A. roughly equal.
    B. much larger.
    C. insignificant.
    D. far outmatched.

Short-Answer Question

In the 1910s, a series of crises in the Balkans helped to precipitate World War I.

    a. Choose ONE of the following and explain why your choice represents the key factor leading to this development.

- weakness of the Ottoman Empire
- growth of nationalism
- German aggression

    b. Contrast your choice against ONE of the other options, demonstrating why that option is not as significant as your choice.

Long-Essay Question

Analyze the significance of the 1904 Entente Cordiale between France and Britain.

ANSWERS AND EXPLANATIONS: AP® PRACTICE TEST

Multiple-Choice Questions

1. **B** As the Ottoman Empire lost control of the Balkans, hostilities broke out between ethnicities in the region.
2. **C** The patchwork of ethnicities was not new, but with the rise of nationalism, each national group sought independence.
3. **A** According to this excerpt, the kaiser wanted to go to war soon, arguing that the moment is favorable.
4. **A** The author knows that Russia would not tolerate attacks on Serbia, but argues that Russia was unlikely to go to war in the short term.
5. **D** The demands are intended to stop Serbian nationalists from encouraging Serbian separatists within the Austrian Empire.
6. **C** The demands resulted from an investigation into the death of Franz Ferdinand and a demand Serbia take action against Serbians that may have been involved.
7. **B** Austria claims that Serbian radicals continue to threaten "the peace of the Monarchy (Austria.)"
8. **A** The first step of the Schlieffen Plan was to defeat Belgium and France quickly, before turning east.
9. **A** Germany had to first defeat France before it could go on and turn to the eastern front.
10. **D** Soon after the outbreak of World War I, the western front got bogged down in northeastern France.
11. **D** The front moved only about 100 miles in four years.
12. **C** Many members of the military joined the revolution, which made it difficult to halt its spread.
13. **A** The author believes that the government needs to gain the trust of the Duma to save the situation.
14. **B** Germany had many more soldiers than any other power, and sizeable military expenditures.
15. **D** While Germany had developed a powerful navy, it was still far behind the joint forces of Britain and France.

Long-Essay Question

Analyze the significance of the 1904 Entente Cordiale between France and Britain.

(Key topics to focus and elaborate on)
- end of British isolation
- shift in alliances
- threat to Germany

CHAPTER 19

The Interwar Years: The Challenges of Dictators and Depression

AFTER VERSAILLES: DEMANDS FOR REVISION AND ENFORCEMENT

- There were numerous postwar economic problems partly brought on by the many casualties of war and Europe's loss of its financial dominance. The reparations and debt structure of the peace made the economies of many European nations—even victorious ones—uncertain.
- Market and trade conditions changed radically, as much of Europe's infrastructure had been damaged or destroyed in the war. The United States also became less dependent on European production and was a major competitor. Slow postwar economic growth and an overall decline of economic activity lowered international demand for European goods. The prominence of labor during the war gave unions a greater role in national government.

AP® KEY CONCEPTS

4.1 Total war and political instability in the first half of the twentieth century gave way to a polarized state order during the Cold War, and eventually to efforts at transnational union.

II. The conflicting goals of the peace negotiators in Paris pitted diplomatic idealism against the desire to punish Germany, producing a settlement that satisfied few.

TOWARD THE GREAT DEPRESSION IN EUROPE

- Reparations and war debts made international trade, capital investment, and day-to-day business difficult for European nations. After the Dawes Plan was put into effect, more American money flowed into Europe, but that changed in 1928 after the stock market crash. This triggered the **Great Depression**.
- In 1931, President Hoover put a year-long moratorium on payments of international debts, which was a blow to the French economy. In 1932, the Lausanne Conference effectively ended all payment of reparations. Problems in agricultural commodities during this time also brought about a downturn in production and trade.

AP® KEY CONCEPTS

4.2 The stresses of economic collapse and total war engendered internal conflicts within European states and created conflicting conceptions of the relationship between the individual and the state, as demonstrated in the ideological battle among liberal democracy, communism, and fascism.

III. The Great Depression, caused by weaknesses in international trade and monetary theories and practices, undermined Western European democracies and fomented radical political responses throughout Europe.

THE SOVIET EXPERIMENT

- The Bolshevik gains in Russia resulted in a communist party in the Soviet Union. Communist leaders sought to spread their ideology around the world; fear of communism and resolve to stop its spread became a major force in Europe and the United States.
- The Bolsheviks rapidly developed authoritarian policies in response to internal and foreign military opposition. They formed the *Cheka,* a new secret police, and political and economic administrations became highly centralized. Under an economic policy of war, the Bolsheviks took control of all the major industries, financial institutions, and transportation.
- After Lenin's death in 1924, two factions emerged in struggles for leadership of the party. Leon Trotsky and Joseph Stalin were on opposite sides—with Trotsky speaking for the "left wing" and urging agricultural **collectivization**, rapid industrialization, and new revolutions in other nations. A right-wing faction emerged with Nikolai Bukharin as its chief voice and Stalin manipulating the group that called for continuation of Lenin's NEP and slow industrialization. Stalin began to amass power and in the mid-1920s, he supported Bukharin and denounced Trotsky for his vision of international revolution, endorsing the doctrine of "socialism in one country." Stalin defeated Trotsky and controlled the Soviet State.
- In 1919, the Soviet Communists founded the Third International of the European Socialist movement, known as the *Comintern.* In 1920, the Comintern imposed Twenty-one Conditions on any socialist party that wanted to join it. This effort to destroy democratic socialism split every major European socialist party, divided the political left, and created a vacuum of power for right-wing politicians, which led to the rise of Fascists and **Nazis**.

AP® KEY CONCEPTS

4.2 The stresses of economic collapse and total war engendered internal conflicts within European states and created conflicting conceptions of the relationship between the individual and the state, as demonstrated in the ideological battle among liberal democracy, communism, and fascism.

    I. The Russian Revolution created a regime based on Marxist-Leninist theory.

THE FASCIST EXPERIMENT IN ITALY

- In a response to the threat of Bolshevism, Benito Mussolini became prominent as a proponent of *fascism,* a term used to describe right-wing dictators that rose in Europe between the wars. These governments claimed to hold back Bolshevism and were antidemocratic, anti-Marxist, antiparliamentary, and often anti-Semitic. Fascist movements were nationalistic.
- In October 1922, Fascists marched on Rome, an event that became known as the Black Shirt March and that led to Mussolini's becoming prime minister. The Fascist Party came to dominate Italy's political structure at every level.

AP® KEY CONCEPTS

4.2 The stresses of economic collapse and total war engendered internal conflicts within European states and created conflicting conceptions of the relationship between the individual and the state, as demonstrated in the ideological battle among liberal democracy, communism, and fascism.

II. The ideology of fascism, with roots in the pre-World War I era, gained popularity in an environment of postwar bitterness, the rise of communism, uncertain transitions to democracy, and economic instability.

GERMAN DEMOCRACY AND DICTATORSHIP

- The Weimar Republic took shape in the aftermath of World War I; its constitution was written in August of 1919. While the Weimar constitution guaranteed civil liberties and provided for direct election, it had flaws that allowed its liberal institutions to be overthrown.

- Adolf Hitler (1889–1945) arrived on the political scene around the time when the French occupation of the Ruhr sent inflation soaring, and unemployment had spread throughout Germany. Hitler affiliated with the Christian Social Party in Vienna and absorbed much of its rabid German nationalism and anti-Semitism. He moved to Munich and became involved with a small, nationalistic, anti-Semitic party known as the National Socialist German Workers' party, or the *Nazis*.

- During the chancellorship of Gustav Stresemann, Germany recovered from some of its losses. Under Stresemann, a new reparations payment plan, called the Dawes Plan, was instituted, giving Germany a flexible form of payment that varied according to the German economy. In 1925, the Locarno Agreements accepted Paris as the western frontier, and Britain and Italy agreed to intervene against whichever side violated the frontier or if Germany sent troops into the Rhineland. No such agreement existed for Germany's eastern frontier. France supported Germany's membership in the League of Nations. The Locarno Treaty, which pleased all of the European powers, would not solve the tensions that continued to fester.

- Hitler consolidated his control almost as soon as he took office by crushing alternative political groups, purging his rivals in the Nazi Party, and capturing full legal authority of Germany. Hitler quickly outlawed all other political parties and arrested the leaders of offices, banks, and the newspapers of free trade unions. He effectively eliminated all institutions of opposition and began moving against the governments of individual federal states in Germany. Hitler had key SA leaders murdered to gain support from the German army officer corps. After the death of Hindenburg, Hitler combined the position of chancellor and president and became head of state and head of the government.

- Hitler oversaw the control of Germany as a police state. Police surveillance units, known as the SS *(Schutzstaffel),* terrorized much of Germany and focused its hatred against German Jews. The Nazis based their anti-Semitic views on biological racial theories rather than on religious discrimination. Jews were robbed of their citizenship, their opportunities to earn a living, and their civil liberties, and they were repeatedly persecuted and harassed. Ultimately, they were killed in Hitler's efforts to eliminate Jews in Europe. More than 6 million Jews were murdered in the Holocaust.

- Hitler effectively handled the German economic problem by subordinating all economic enterprise to the goals of the state. He instituted a massive program of spending and public works, many of which related to rearmament. In 1935, Hitler renounced the provisions of the Treaty of Versailles and began open rearmament to prepare for his next aggression.

4.1 Total war and political instability in the first half of the twentieth century gave way to a polarized state order during the Cold War, and eventually to efforts at transnational union.

II. The conflicting goals of the peace negotiators in Paris pitted diplomatic idealism against the desire to punish Germany, producing a settlement that satisfied few.

4.2 The stresses of economic collapse and total war engendered internal conflicts within European states and created conflicting conceptions of the relationship between the individual and the state, as demonstrated in the ideological battle among liberal democracy, communism, and fascism.

II. The ideology of fascism, with roots in the pre-World War I era, gained popularity in an environment of postwar bitterness, the rise of communism, uncertain transitions to democracy, and economic instability.

III. The Great Depression, caused by weaknesses in international trade and monetary theories and practices, undermined Western European democracies and fomented radical political responses throughout Europe.

4.4 Demographic changes, economic growth, total war, disruptions of traditional social patterns, and competing definitions of freedom and justice altered the experiences of everyday life.

I. The twentieth century was characterized by large-scale suffering brought on by warfare and genocide, as well as tremendous improvements in the standard of living.

II. The lives of women were defined by family and work responsibilities, economic changes, and feminism.

TRIALS OF THE SUCCESSOR STATES IN EASTERN EUROPE

- The "successor states" was the name given to the lands that emerged after the breakup of the German, Austro-Hungarian, and Russian empires. Many of the postwar states (Czechoslovakia, Poland, Germany, Austria) faced major economic difficulties; except for Czechoslovakia, all of them depended on foreign loans to finance their economic rebuilding. The collapse of the old empires allowed ethnic groups to pursue nationalistic goals.

AP® KEY CONCEPTS

4.2 The stresses of economic collapse and total war engendered internal conflicts within European states and created conflicting conceptions of the relationship between the individual and the state, as demonstrated in the ideological battle among liberal democracy, communism, and fascism.

II. The ideology of fascism, with roots in the pre-World War I era, gained popularity in an environment of postwar bitterness, the rise of communism, uncertain transitions to democracy, and economic instability.

III. The Great Depression, caused by weaknesses in international trade and monetary theories and practices, undermined Western European democracies and fomented radical political responses throughout Europe.

Multiple-Choice Questions

Questions 1–3 refer to the following table.

Total Casualties in the First World War

Country	Dead	Wounded	Total Killed as a Percentage of Population
France	1,398,000	2,000,000	3.4
Belgium	38,000	44,700	0.5
Italy	578,000	947,000	1.6
British Empire	921,000	2,090,000	1.7
Romania	250,000	120,000	3.3
Serbia	278,000	133,000	5.7
Greece	26,000	21,000	0.5
Russia	1,811,000	1,450,000	1.1
Bulgaria	88,000	152,000	1.9
Germany	2,037,000	4,207,000	3.0
Austria-Hungary	1,100,000	3,620,000	1.9
Turkey	804,000	400,000	3.7
United States	114,000	206,000	0.1

Source: Niall Ferguson, *The Pity of War* (New York: Basic Books, 1998).

1. Which of these explain the relatively low percentage for Russia in this table?
    A. Russia's role in World War I
    B. the outbreak of the Russian Revolution
    C. the lack of activity on the eastern front
    D. the small size of the Russian population

2. Which of these lost the most as a percentage of its population?
    A. France
    B. Britain
    C. Turkey
    D. Serbia

3. Which of these explain the low percentage for the United States?
    A. the small population of the United States
    B. the refusal of the United States to enter the war
    C. the non-combatant role of most U.S. troops
    D. the late entry of the United States into the war

Questions 4–6 refer to the following excerpt.

John Maynard Keynes from **The General Theory of Employment, Interest and Money,** *1936*

In some respects the foregoing theory is moderately conservative in its implications. For whilst it indicates the vital importance of establishing certain central controls in matters which are now left in the main to individual initiative, there are wide fields of activity which are unaffected. The State will have to exercise a guiding influence on the propensity to consume partly through its scheme of taxation, partly by fixing the rate of interest, and partly, perhaps, in other ways. Furthermore, it seems unlikely that the influence of banking policy on the rate of interest will be sufficient by itself to determine an optimum rate of investment. I conceive, therefore, that a somewhat comprehensive socialisation of investment will prove the only means of securing an approximation to full employment; though this need not exclude all manner of compromises and of devices by which public authority will co-operate with private initiative. But beyond this, no obvious case is made out for a system of State Socialism which would embrace most of the economic life of the community. It is not the ownership of the instruments of production which it is important for the State to assume. If the State is able to determine the aggregate amount of resources devoted to augmenting the instruments and the basic rate of reward to those who own them, it will have accomplished all that is necessary. . . .

To put the matter concretely, I see no reason to suppose that the existing system seriously misemploys the factors of production which are in use. There are, of course, errors of foresight; but these would not be avoided by centralizing decisions. When 9,000,000 men are employed out of 10,000,000 willing and able to work, there is no evidence that the labour of these 9,000,000 men is misdirected. The complaint against the present system is not that these 9,000,000 men ought to be employed on different tasks, but that tasks should be available for the remaining 1,000,000 men. It is in determining the volume, not the direction, of actual employment that the existing system has broken down.

4. Which of these best summarizes Keynes' principles concerning state and private action in the economy?
    A. The state should stay out of the economic sphere.
    B. A healthy economy requires constant government intervention.
    C. Intervention is generally bad, but is occasionally necessary.
    D. Private investors should direct state economic policy.

5. For Keynes, which of these would be most resistant to the actions of the private sector?
   A. unemployment
   B. lack of innovation
   C. productivity
   D. outsourcing

6. Keynes distinguishes between socialism and socialization, supporting socialization which
   A. concerns only the young.
   B. affects only a small segment of life.
   C. runs counter to socialism.
   D. is a cradle-to-grave program.

Questions 7–9 refer to the following excerpt.

Mussolini on Political Liberalism, 1923

Liberalism is not the last word, nor does it represent the definitive formula on the subject of the art of government. . . . Liberalism is the product and the technique of the nineteenth century. . . . It does not follow that the Liberal scheme of government, good for the nineteenth century, for a century, that is, dominated by two such phenomena as the growth of capitalism and the strengthening of the sentiment of nationalism, should be adapted to the twentieth century, which announces itself already with characteristics sufficiently different from those that marked the preceding century. . . .

I challenge Liberal gentlemen to tell if ever in history there has been a government that was based solely on popular consent and that renounced all use of force whatsoever. A government so constructed there has never been and never will be. Consent is an ever-changing thing like the shifting sand on the sea coast, it can never be permanent: It can never be complete. . . . If it be accepted as an axiom that any system of government whatever creates malcontents, how are you going to prevent this discontent from overflowing and constituting a menace to the stability of the State? You will prevent it by force. By the assembling of the greatest force possible. By the inexorable use of this force whenever it is necessary. Take away from any government whatsoever force—and by force is meant physical, armed force—and leave it only its immortal principles, and that government will be at the mercy of the first organized group that decides to overthrow it. Fascism now throws these lifeless theories out to rot. . . . The truth evident now to all who are not warped by [liberal] dogmatism is that men have tired of liberty. They have made an orgy of it. Liberty is today no longer the chaste and austere virgin for whom the generations of the first half of the last century fought and died. For the gallant, restless and bitter youth who face the dawn of a new history there are other words that exercise a far greater fascination, and those words are: order, hierarchy, discipline. . . .

Know then, once and for all, that Fascism knows no idols and worships no fetishes. It has already stepped over, and if it be necessary it will turn tranquilly and step again over, the more or less putrescent corpse of the Goddess of Liberty.

7. Mussolini proposes to replace liberty with
   A. rights.
   B. force.
   C. nationalism.
   D. democracy.

8. For Mussolini, Liberalism is
   A. outdated.
   B. dead.
   C. his guiding principle.
   D. the enemy of liberty.

9. Which of these are likely to be the cornerstone of the kind of government Mussolini envisages here?
   A. the legislature
   B. the church
   C. the military
   D. the judiciary

Questions 10–12 refer to the following excerpt.

Hitler on the Versailles Treaty, 1923

 With the armistice begins the humiliation of Germany. If the Republic on the day of its foundation had appealed to the country: "Germans, stand together! Up and resist the foe! The Fatherland, the Republic expects of you that you fight to your last breath," then millions who are now the enemies of the Republic would be fanatical Republicans. Today they are the foes of the Republic not because it is a Republic but because this Republic was founded at the moment when Germany was humiliated, because it so discredited the new flag that men's eyes must turn regretfully towards the old flag.

 It was no Treaty of Peace which was signed, but a betrayal of Peace.

 The Treaty was signed which demanded from Germany that she should perform what was forever impossible of performance. But that was not the worst; after all that was only a question of material values. This was not the end: Commissions of Control were formed! For the first time in the history of the modern world there were planted on a State agents of foreign Powers to act as Hangmen and German soldiers were set to serve the foreigner. And if one of these Commissions was "insulted," a company of the German army had to defile before the French flag. We no longer feel the humiliation of such an act; but the outside world says, "What a people of curs!"

 So long as this Treaty stands there can be no resurrection of the German people: no social reform of any kind is possible! The Treaty was made in order to bring 20 million Germans to their deaths and to ruin the German nation. But those who made the Treaty cannot set it aside. At its foundation our Movement formulated three demands;

  1. Setting aside of the Peace Treaty.
  2. Unification of all Germans.
  3. Land and soil to feed our nation.

Our Movement could formulate these demands, since it was not our Movement which caused the War, it has not made the Republic, it did not sign the Peace Treaty.

There is thus one thing which is the first task of this Movement: it desires to make the German once more National, that his Fatherland shall stand for him above everything else. It desires to teach our people to understand afresh the truth of the old saying: He who would not be a hammer must be an anvil. An anvil are we today, and that anvil will be beaten until out of the anvil we fashion once more a hammer, a German sword!

10. For Hitler, the German Republic is discredited because it
    A. has not been able to protect individual rights.
    B. is led by his political rivals.
    C. was created in the peace process.
    D. was far right.

11. When Hitler refers to "what was forever impossible of performance," he is most likely referring to
    A. the creation of the Weimar Republic.
    B. the German defeat in World War I.
    C. foundation of the Nazi Party.
    D. reparation payments.

12. When Hitler writes that "those who made the Treaty cannot set it aside," he is implying that
    A. his movement alone can move Germany forward.
    B. the current Republic should repudiate the Versailles Treaty.
    C. he should head the Republic.
    D. a new treaty should be concluded.

Questions 13–15 refer to the following excerpt.

Hitler on Emancipation

The slogan "Emancipation of women" was invented by Jewish intellectuals and its content was formed by the same spirit. In the really good times of German life the German woman had no need to emancipate herself. She possessed exactly what nature had necessarily given her to administer and preserve; just as the man in his good times had no need to fear that he would be ousted from his position in relation to the woman. . . .

If the man's world is said to be the State, his struggle, his readiness to devote his powers to the service of the community, then it may perhaps be said that the woman's is a smaller world. For her world is her husband, her family, her children, and her home. But what would become of the greater world if there were no one to tend and care for the smaller one? How could the greater world survive if there were no one to make the cares of the smaller world the content of their lives? No, the greater world is built on the foundation of this smaller world. This great world cannot survive if the smaller world is not stable. Providence has entrusted to the woman the cares of that world which is her very own, and only on the basis of this smaller world can the man's world be formed and built up. The two worlds are not antagonistic. They complement each other, they belong together just as man and woman belong together.

We do not consider it correct for the woman to interfere in the world of the man, in his main sphere. We consider it natural if these two worlds remain distinct. To the one belongs the strength of feeling, the strength of the soul. To the other belongs the strength of vision, of toughness, of decision, and of the willingness to act. In the one case this strength demands the willingness of the woman to risk her life to preserve this important cell and to multiply it, and in the other case it demands from the man the readiness to safeguard life. . . .

So our women's movement is for us not something which inscribes on its banner as its programme the fight against men, but something which has as its programme the common fight together with men. For the new National Socialist national community acquires a firm basis precisely because we have gained the trust of millions of women as fanatical fellow combatants, women who have fought for the common life in the service of the common task of preserving life. . . .

Whereas previously the programmes of the liberal, intellectualist women's movements contained many points, the programme of our National Socialist Women's movement has in reality but one single point, and that point is the child, that tiny creature which must be born and grow strong and which alone gives meaning to the whole life-struggle.

13. Hitler's vision of women's role is based on
    A. liberalism.
    B. the past.
    C. nationalism.
    D. fascism.

14. Which of these models of gender roles is employed in this excerpt?
    A. separate spheres
    B. Mary Magdalen
    C. the philosophe
    D. suffragette

15. What public role does Hitler envision for women?
    A. teaching
    B. public office
    C. none
    D. factory work

Short-Answer Question

The interwar period saw the emergence of dictatorships in several European countries.

a. Choose ONE of the following and explain why your choice represents the key factor leading to this development.

- World War I
- the Great Depression
- the Bolshevik Revolution

b. Contrast your choice against ONE of the other options, demonstrating why that option is not as significant as your choice.

Long-Essay Question

Did Nazism and Bolshevism present more contrasts or commonalities?

ANSWERS AND EXPLANATIONS: AP® PRACTICE TEST

Multiple-Choice Questions

1. B When the Russian Revolution broke out, Russia withdrew from the war.
2. D Although Serbia's numbers were low, as a percentage of its population, its losses were higher than any other nation.
3. D The United States entered the war very late, and the U.S. entry was followed fairly soon by the end of the war.
4. C While Keynes is primarily against state intervention, he believed that in some cases private action would not be enough to keep the economy going.
5. A Keynes believed indirect policies such as setting interest rates may not be effective in ending an unemployment crisis.
6. B Keynes opposes the intervention of the state in a broad swath of private life, but supports "socialisation" which involves only limited government intervention in the economy.
7. B Rejecting Enlightenment values, Mussolini utterly rejects liberty, arguing that force is preferable.
8. A Mussolini argues that Liberalism was the product of the nineteenth century, but is outmoded in the twentieth century.
9. C Praising the virtues of "order, hierarchy, discipline," Mussolini would prefer military discipline to the individual freedoms of Liberalism.
10. C For Hitler, the peace treaty was a disaster, and he utterly rejected the government that had been created by the peace process.
11. D It appears that Hitler is referring to the impossibly high reparation payments imposed on Germany as part of the peace treaty.
12. A Hitler is arguing that the Weimar Republic cannot do anything about the treaty, and that only his own movement, standing outside the government, can bring any progress.
13. B Hitler argues that in some fictitious past men and women were happy in their distinct spheres.
14. A Hitler revives the idea of women and men occupying separate, but equally important spheres.
15. C Although he would later reverse this stance when women were needed as wartime laborers, in this essay Hitler confines women to the household alone.

Long-Essay Question

Did Nazism and Bolshevism present more contrasts or commonalities?

(Key topics to focus and elaborate on)
- relationship of both to classic socialism and liberalism
- role of state
- economy
- role of individuals
- use of force

CHAPTER 20

World War II

AGAIN THE ROAD TO WAR (1933–1939)

- Hitler envisioned enlarging Germany beyond its 1914 borders and wanted to bring the entire German people, the *Volk,* into one nation.
- In 1935, Mussolini attacked Ethiopia, which engendered anger in the international community. Britain and France did not want to alienate Mussolini, but in the end he turned to Germany and in 1936 the Rome-Berlin Axis was born. Hitler marched into the demilitarized Rhineland in 1936 and seized control, registering only weak protests in the form of a policy of appeasement from Britain and France.
- Hitler and Mussolini supported Francisco Franco in his bid to take control of Spain. Hundreds of thousands of Spaniards died in the Spanish Civil War. Japan joined the Axis powers.
- Germany and Austria entered into an *Anschluss,* or union, that had profound implications for Czechoslovakia, which was surrounded by Germany. The Czechs appealed to France, England, and Russia for aid, but the British prime minister, Neville Chamberlain, was committed to the policy of appeasement and did not want Britain in another war.
- In 1939, Hitler invaded Prague, putting an end to the Czech state. Hitler began aggressive acts in Poland, and England and France considered allying with the Russians to prevent him. But in 1939, a Nazi-Soviet nonaggression pact was revealed. This pact divided Poland between the two nations and allowed Russia to occupy the Baltic states. This pact effectively led to the French and English commitment to go to war.

AP® KEY CONCEPTS

4.1 Total war and political instability in the first half of the twentieth century gave way to a polarized state order during the Cold War, and eventually to efforts at transnational union.

> III. In the interwar period, fascism, extreme nationalism, racist ideologies, and the failure of appeasement resulted in the catastrophe of World War II, presenting a grave challenge to European civilization.

WORLD WAR II (1939–1945)

- Germany's attack on Poland was swift—a *Blitzkrieg*—or "lightning warfare."
- Hitler invaded Denmark and Norway in 1940, and a month later, he attacked Belgium, the Netherlands, and Luxembourg. British and French armies in Belgium fled to the English Channel and escaped from the beaches of Dunkirk, saving thousands of lives. The Maginot Line, an imaginary line that ran from Switzerland to the Belgian frontier, was exposed on its left flank after Hitler remilitarized the Rhineland, and Hitler's advance through Belgium avoided French defense. Mussolini staged an invasion of southern France, and less than a week later, France, led by Marshal Pétain, asked for an armistice.
- Britain was isolated after the fall of France, but the rise to power of Prime Minister Winston Churchill ended the government's days of appeasement. Churchill established a connection with President Franklin D. Roosevelt, and the United States aided the British before it

entered the war.

- Hitler invaded Britain in 1940, bombing London and destroying much of the city. British morale grew during this time and united the nation against Hitler.
- War was thrust on the Americans in 1941 when Japan, an Axis member, launched an attack on the U.S. naval base at Pearl Harbor, in Hawaii. The next day, the United States and Britain declared war on Japan; three days later, Germany and Italy declared war on the United States. In 1942, the Allies gained control of the Mediterranean Sea, and in 1943 they conquered German-controlled Italy, gaining the new leader of the government as an ally against Germany. In the Battle of Stalingrad in 1942, the Russians lost more soldiers than the United States lost in combat in the entire war, but they prevailed against Germany, and Hitler's army was destroyed.
- In 1943, the American and British began a series of day and night bombings of German cities. On June 6, 1944, "D-Day," American, British, and Canadian troops landed on the coast of Normandy, France, and penetrated the German defense. France was liberated by September. The Battle of the Bulge in December of 1944 resulted in heavy Allied losses, but the Allies pushed on and crushed German resistance. By May 1, 1945, the German resistance was completely defeated and Berlin was occupied. Japan refused to surrender, and in 1945, American warplanes dropped an atomic bomb on the city of Hiroshima, killing a third of its residents. Two days later, another atomic bomb was dropped on Nagasaki. The Japanese government under Emperor Hirohito surrendered on August 14, 1945.

AP® KEY CONCEPTS

4.1 Total war and political instability in the first half of the twentieth century gave way to a polarized state order during the Cold War, and eventually to efforts at transnational union.

> III. In the interwar period, fascism, extreme nationalism, racist ideologies, and the failure of appeasement resulted in the catastrophe of World War II, presenting a grave challenge to European civilization.

4.3 During the twentieth century, diverse intellectual and cultural movements questioned the existence of objective knowledge, the ability of reason to arrive at truth, and the role of religion in determining moral standards.

> II. Science and technology yielded impressive material benefits but also caused immense destruction and posed challenges to objective knowledge.

4.4 Demographic changes, economic growth, total war, disruptions of traditional social patterns, and competing definitions of freedom and justice altered the experiences of everyday life.

> I. The twentieth century was characterized by large-scale suffering brought on by warfare and genocide as well as tremendous improvements in the standard of living.
>
> II. The lives of women were defined by family and work responsibilities, economic changes, and feminism.

RACISM AND THE HOLOCAUST

- Hitler hoped to extinguish Jews from his new Germany, to reunite the German people of the old Habsburg Empire, and to seize land from neighboring countries—beginning with Poland and Ukraine. He also targeted other groups, including Slavs, the disabled, homosexuals, and the Roma.
- Poland had a large Jewish population that had thrived under the leadership of Jozef Pilsudski. The tendency of Nazis to equate Judaism and Bolshevism led to a large-scale attempt to kill all European Jews.

4.1 Total war and political instability in the first half of the twentieth century gave way to a polarized state order during the Cold War, and eventually to efforts at transnational union.

III. In the interwar period, fascism, extreme nationalism, racist ideologies, and the failure of appeasement resulted in the catastrophe of World War II, presenting a grave challenge to European civilization.

4.4 Demographic changes, economic growth, total war, disruptions of traditional social patterns, and competing definitions of freedom and justice altered the experiences of everyday life.

I. The twentieth century was characterized by large-scale suffering brought on by warfare and genocide as well as tremendous improvements in the standard of living.

THE DOMESTIC FRONTS

- In Germany, the economy remained buoyant until the army's failure to overwhelm the Russians, after which time a wartime economy took over. Germany suffered severe food shortages and demanded major sacrifices from its people. The manufacture of armaments replaced the production of consumer goods, and food rationing began in 1942. Women, teenagers, and retired men were required to work in factories, and thousands of people from conquered lands were forced to labor in Germany. Political propaganda intensified in Germany, and the role of women became important to the German ideology.

- In France, the Vichy government that followed Germany's aggression was a source of national controversy. It encouraged an intense nationalism that fostered anti-Semitism. Internal resistance to the Vichy government developed in 1942, but a large-scale movement did not arise until 1944, when General Charles de Gaulle, who had fled to Britain, urged the French people to resist their conquerors and to support the French National Committee of Liberation. In 1945, France voted to end the Third Republic, and the Fourth Republic was formed with a new constitution.

4.1 Total war and political instability in the first half of the twentieth century gave way to a polarized state order during the Cold War, and eventually to efforts at transnational union.

III. In the interwar period, fascism, extreme nationalism, racist ideologies, and the failure of appeasement resulted in the catastrophe of World War II, presenting a grave challenge to European civilization.

PREPARATIONS FOR PEACE

- In spite of wartime cooperation, a deep rift separated the Western powers and the Soviet Union.

- In 1941, the Atlantic Charter was concluded between Roosevelt and Churchill. Based on the Fourteen Points, this agreement laid the foundation for a lasting Anglo-American understanding.

- In a series of meetings, at Tehran, Yalta, and Potsdam, the leaders of the Soviet Union, Britain, and the United States made plans for winning the war and for a postwar settlement. Key issues included plans for Eastern Europe, for a conquered Germany, and for an enduring global forum: the United Nations.

AP® Key Concepts

4.1 Total war and political instability in the first half of the twentieth century gave way to a polarized state order during the Cold War, and eventually to efforts at transnational union.

IV. As World War II ended, a Cold War between the liberal democratic West and the communist East began, lasting nearly half a century.

Multiple-Choice Questions

Questions 1–3 refer to the following map.

North African Campaigns, 1942–1945

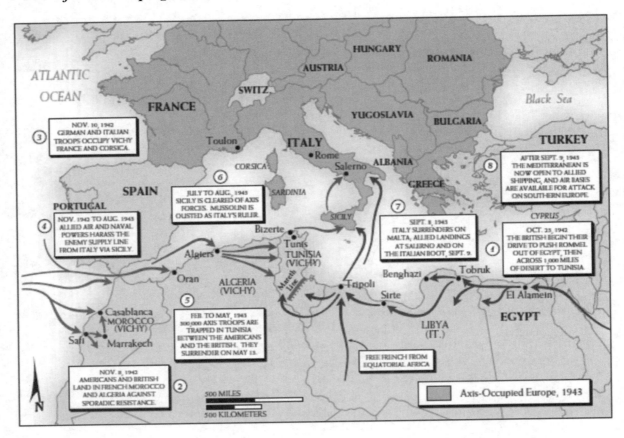

1. In 1943, Axis control of Europe was
   A. extensive.
   B. complete.
   C. over.
   D. ending.

2. The Allied invasion of Europe began through
   A. France.
   B. Britain.
   C. Italy.
   D. Spain.

3. Which of these best summarizes the role of North Africa in World War II campaigns?
   A. pivotal
   B. marginal
   C. irrelevant
   D. decisive

Questions 4–6 refer to the following map.

Partitions of Czechoslovakia and Poland, 1938–1939

4. The partition of Poland benefited
   A. Germany only.
   B. the Soviet Union only.
   C. Germany and Austria.
   D. the Soviet Union and Germany.

5. Which of these gained from the destruction of Czechoslovakia?
   A. Germany and Hungary
   B. the Soviet Union and Germany
   C. Germany and Austria
   D. Germany only

6. Which of these was a key principle for the division of Czechoslovakia?
   A. geography
   B. nationality
   C. the expansion of the Soviet Union
   D. the partition of Poland

Questions 7–8 refer to the following excerpt.

Winston Churchill on the Munich Agreement

I will begin by saying what everybody would like to ignore or forget but which must nevertheless be stated, namely, that we have sustained a total and unmitigated defeat, and that France has suffered even more than we have. . . .

We really must not waste time after all this long Debate upon the difference between the positions reached at Berchtesgaden, at Godesberg and at Munich. They can be very simply epitomized, if the House will permit me to vary the metaphor. One pound was demanded at the pistol's point. When it was given, £2 were demanded at the pistol's point. Finally, the dictator consented to take £1 17s. 6d. and the rest in promises of good will for the future. . . .

All is over. Silent, mournful, abandoned, broken, Czechoslovakia recedes into the darkness. She has suffered in every respect by her association with the Western democracies and with the League of Nations, of which she has always been an obedient servant. . . .

We have been reduced in these five years from a position of security so overwhelming and so unchallengeable that we never cared to think about it. We have been reduced from a position where the very word "war" was considered one which could be used only by persons qualifying for a lunatic asylum. We have been reduced from a position of safety and power— power to do good, power to be generous to a beaten foe, power to make terms with Germany, power to give her proper redress for her grievances, power to stop her arming if we chose, power to take any step in strength or mercy or justice which we thought right—reduced in five years from a position safe and unchallenged to where we stand now. . . .

[T]he responsibility must rest with those who have had the undisputed control of our political affairs. They neither prevented Germany from rearming, nor did they rearm ourselves in time. They quarreled with Italy without saving Ethiopia. They exploited and discredited the vast institution of the League of Nations and they neglected to make alliances and combinations which might have repaired previous errors, and thus they left us in the hour of trial without adequate national defense or effective international security. . . .

We are in the presence of a disaster of the first magnitude which has befallen Great Britain and France. Do not let us blind ourselves to that. It must now be accepted that all the countries of Central and Eastern Europe will make the best terms they can with the triumphant Nazi power. The system of alliances in Central Europe upon which France has relied for her safety has been swept away, and I can see no means by which it can be reconstituted. The road down the Danube Valley to the Black Sea, the road which leads as far as Turkey, has been opened.

7. In Churchill's assessment, Hitler is likened to a
   A. skillful diplomat.
   B. robber.
   C. faithful ally.
   D. traitor.

8. For Churchill, which of these would have halted Hitler?
   A. German rearmament
   B. support for the Weimar Republic
   C. international cooperation
   D. stronger British sanctions against Germany

Questions 9–11 refer to the following map.

Axis Europe, 1941

9. By 1941, the position of Britain and the Soviet Union can be said to have been
   A. strong.
   B. fatal.
   C. growing stronger.
   D. precarious.

10. As so often in history, in 1941 the political situation in the Balkans is best characterized as
    A. a solid Slavic bloc.
    B. a patchwork.
    C. under Turkish rule.
    D. dominated by democracies.

11. Which of these tied together greater Germany?
    A. Catholic traditions
    B. a strong tradition of fascist rule
    C. nationalism
    D. religion

Questions 12–13 refer to the following map.

World War II in the Pacific

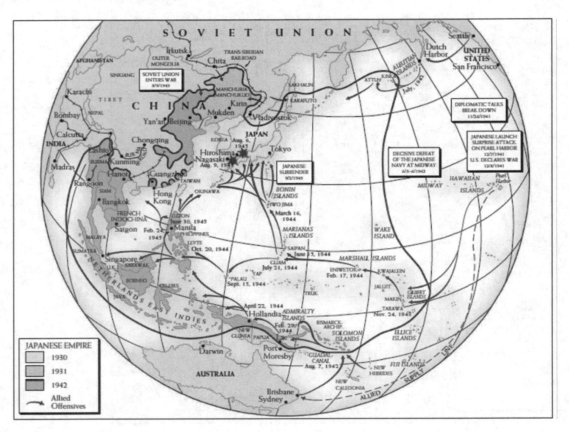

12. At its greatest extent, the Japanese Empire comprised
    A. all of Asia.
    B. most of mainland Asia.
    C. most of Pacific Asia.
    D. all of Pacific Asia.

13. The primary Allied offensive against Japan took place via
    A. the Pacific.
    B. Siberia.
    C. China.
    D. India.

Questions 14–15 refer to the following map.

Yalta to the Surrender

14. By 1945, which of these dominated most of Eastern Europe?
    A. the Soviet Union
    B. Germany
    C. the Axis
    D. Austria

15. Between the Yalta conference and Germany's surrender, the eastern front
    A. did not move.
    B. moved to the east.
    C. moved west.
    D. disappeared.

Short-Answer Question

Plans for postwar Europe were shaped by meetings of the "Big Three": Stalin, Churchill, and Franklin Roosevelt.

a. Choose ONE of the following and explain why your choice represents the key factor leading to this development.

- rise of Nazi Germany
- the Bolshevik Revolution
- situation at the end of World War II

b. Contrast your choice against ONE of the other options, demonstrating why that option is not as significant as your choice.

Long-Essay Question

When did the Cold War alignment of Britain and the United States versus the Soviet Union begin?

ANSWERS AND EXPLANATIONS: AP® PRACTICE TEST

Multiple-Choice Questions

1. A   By 1943, the Axis controlled much of continental Europe.
2. C   The first phase of the Allied invasion of Europe took place through Italy, launched from North Africa and the Mediterranean.
3. A   When the Allies won in North Africa, they were able to pursue the Axis into Europe, winning the war.
4. D   Poland was partitioned in an agreement in which the Soviet Union and Nazi Germany temporarily made common cause.
5. A   The relatively new country of Czechoslovakia was broken up into several parts, most consumed by Germany, but a large chunk went to Hungary.
6. B   The division of Czechoslovakia was largely along ethnic lines; for instance Slovakia nominally gained its independence.
7. B   Churchill uses the metaphor of Britain being robbed at gunpoint, and then cooperating with the robber.
8. C   Churchill blames European powers for squabbling among themselves, while ignoring the threat of Hitler.
9. D   Although these two powers still had great resources and advantages, by 1941 they remained as the main Allied powers in Europe.
10. B   As always, the situation in the Balkans was complex, with some nations siding with Hitler, and some that had opposed him under German occupation.
11. C   Although many other nationalities existed in this region, greater Germany brought together many lands with a strong tradition of German culture.
12. D   The Japanese Empire only included a small portion of mainland Asia, but did include almost all of Southeast Asia.
13. A   While a Soviet offensive moved into northern China, most of the Allied defeat of Japan took place in the Pacific.
14. A   Most of Eastern Europe was held by the Soviet Union, with the rest falling under Allied control. This meant that the Soviet Union was in a very strong position in 1945.
15. C   The eastern front moved about 150 miles in this last phase of the war.

Long-Essay Question

When did the Cold War alignment of Britain and the United States versus the Soviet Union begin?

(Key topics to focus and elaborate on)
- Bolshevik Revolution
- Atlantic Charter
- Soviet control of Eastern Europe
- Nazi-Soviet Pact

CHAPTER 21

The Cold War Era, Decolonization, and the Emergence of the New Europe

THE EMERGENCE OF THE COLD WAR

- The Soviet Union and the United States entered into a tense relationship at the end of World War II. The United States pursued a policy of **containment** to prevent Soviet expansion into Eastern Europe.
- In 1947, President Truman set forth what has been called the Truman Doctrine, and Americans also devised the **Marshall Plan**—a program that restored prosperity to Western Europe by providing broad economic aid to European states working together for their mutual benefit.
- In 1949, the Western nations formed the North Atlantic Treaty Organization in 1949, which was a commitment to mutual assistance in the event of an attack.
- The state of Israel was created in 1948, and the Arab-Israeli conflict over this disputed territory involved Europe and the United States. The Soviet Union became an ally of Arab states, and the United States continued to support Israel, further intensifying existing tensions.
- The Korean conflict in 1950 brought the United States and the Soviet Union on opposite sides of yet another international dilemma.

AP® KEY CONCEPTS

4.1 Total war and political instability in the first half of the twentieth century gave way to a polarized state order during the Cold War, and eventually to efforts at transnational union.

> IV. As World War II ended, a Cold War between the liberal democratic West and the communist East began, lasting nearly half a century.

4.2 The stresses of economic collapse and total war engendered internal conflicts within European states and created conflicting conceptions of the relationship between the individual and the state, as demonstrated in the ideological battle among liberal democracy, communism, and fascism.

> V. Eastern European nations were defined by their relationship with the Soviet Union, which oscillated between repression and limited reform, until Mikhail Gorbachev's policies led to the collapse of communist governments in Eastern Europe and the fall of the Soviet Union.

THE KHRUSHCHEV ERA IN THE SOVIET UNION

- The leadership of Nikita Khrushchev led to a move away from Stalin's policies. While the Communist Party still controlled political life, somewhat more freedom of expression was allowed. In 1956, Khrushchev denounced Stalin's regime in a secret speech to the Communist Party.
- The Suez Intervention, which involved French and British intervention in the war between Egypt and Israel, proved that without U.S. support, nations of Western Europe could not use military force to impose their will on the rest of the world.
- Poland's efforts toward independence temporarily caused a crisis of Soviet troop movements in the region, but the country managed to be led by a Communist figure, Wladyslaw Gomulka, who was approved by the Soviet Communist Party.
- After the rise to power of Imre Nagy in Hungary, Soviet troops invaded the country and deposed Nagy. The United States did not liberate Hungary as they had promised in the Truman Doctrine.

AP® KEY CONCEPTS

4.1 Total war and political instability in the first half of the twentieth century gave way to a polarized state order during the Cold War, and eventually to efforts at transnational union.

    IV. As World War II ended, a Cold War between the liberal democratic West and the communist East began, lasting nearly half a century.

4.2 The stresses of economic collapse and total war engendered internal conflicts within European states and created conflicting conceptions of the relationship between the individual and the state, as demonstrated in the ideological battle among liberal democracy, communism, and fascism.

    V. Eastern European nations were defined by their relationship with the Soviet Union, which oscillated between repression and limited reform, until Mikhail Gorbachev's policies led to the collapse of communist governments in Eastern Europe and the fall of the Soviet Union.

LATER COLD WAR CONFRONTATIONS

- The 1960 Paris Summit talks (intended to promote the peaceful coexistence of the Soviet Union and the United States) collapsed. The aborted conference produced the most difficult period of the Cold War, as the East Germans closed the wall along the border between East and West Berlin, shutting the two parts of the city off from each other.
- The Cuban Missile Crisis, which followed in 1962, tested John F. Kennedy's presidency. The threat of a Soviet ally just 100 miles from the United States was ratcheted up when it was discovered that the Soviet Union was storing nuclear weapons in Cuba. After a standoff between the United States and the Soviet Union, the Soviets backed down after a week of tense negotiations. In 1963, the Soviet Union and the United States concluded a nuclear test ban treaty that marked the beginning of reduced tensions.

4.1 Total war and political instability in the first half of the twentieth century gave way to a polarized state order during the Cold War, and eventually to efforts at transnational union.

> IV. As World War II ended, a Cold War between the liberal democratic West and the communist East began, lasting nearly half a century.

THE BREZHNEV ERA

- In 1968, Leonid Brezhnev declared the right of the Soviet Union to interfere in the domestic policies of other communist countries, after the Soviet Union sent troops into Czechoslovakia to repress a more liberal form of communism. This **Brezhnev Doctrine** sought to sustain the communist governments of Eastern Europe and to prevent liberalization.
- The United States, under Richard Nixon, initiated a period of **détente**, leading to talks with the Soviet Union on arms and trade.
- In 1979, the Soviet Union invaded Afghanistan, enmeshing the Soviets in a protracted and unsuccessful war.
- In 1980 the Solidarity movement emerged in Poland, challenging communist control.
- Under Ronald Reagan, U.S. policy towards the Soviet Union included both increased diplomacy, and the characterization of the Soviet Union as the "evil empire."

AP® KEY CONCEPTS
4.1 Total war and political instability in the first half of the twentieth century gave way to a polarized state order during the Cold War, and eventually to efforts at transnational union.

> IV. As World War II ended, a Cold War between the liberal democratic West and the communist East began, lasting nearly half a century.

4.2 The stresses of economic collapse and total war engendered internal conflicts within European states and created conflicting conceptions of the relationship between the individual and the state, as demonstrated in the ideological battle among liberal democracy, communism, and fascism.

> V. Eastern European nations were defined by their relationship with the Soviet Union, which oscillated between repression and limited reform, until Mikhail Gorbachev's policies led to the collapse of communist governments in Eastern Europe and the fall of the Soviet Union.

4.3 During the twentieth century, diverse intellectual and cultural movements questioned the existence of objective knowledge, the ability of reason to arrive at truth, and the role of religion in determining moral standards.

> III. Organized religion continued to play a role in European social and cultural life, despite the challenges of military and ideological conflict, modern secularism, and rapid social changes.

DECOLONIZATION: THE EUROPEAN RETREAT FROM EMPIRE

- Many European empires broke away from their colonies after World War II, in a mass act of **decolonization** that was as much a result of war as it was a response to the nationalist movements in Africa, Asia, and the Middle East. The one exception to this rule was the Soviet Union. Many of the states that became newly independent were called the Third World, because they were aligned neither with the United States nor with the Soviet Union.

AP® KEY CONCEPTS

4.1 Total war and political instability in the first half of the twentieth century gave way to a polarized state order during the Cold War, and eventually to efforts at transnational union.

> VII. The process of decolonization occurred over the course of the century with varying degrees of cooperation, interference, or resistance from European imperialist states.

THE TURMOIL OF FRENCH DECOLONIZATION

- France's withdrawal from Algeria was both protracted and bloody.
- France's decolonization became an important part of the Cold War, as the United States became involved in the war in Vietnam. The United States became involved from 1956 and began sending in troops in 1961. The war became a major Cold War conflict. In 1975, after American troops were withdrawn, North and South Vietnam were united.

AP® KEY CONCEPTS

4.1 Total war and political instability in the first half of the twentieth century gave way to a polarized state order during the Cold War, and eventually to efforts at transnational union.

> IV. As World War II ended, a Cold War between the liberal democratic West and the communist East began, lasting nearly half a century.
>
> VII. The process of decolonization occurred over the course of the century with varying degrees of cooperation, interference, or resistance from European imperialist states.

THE COLLAPSE OF EUROPEAN COMMUNISM

- Communism collapsed in Europe in part because of changing Soviet Union policy advanced by Mikhail Gorbachev. Gorbachev wanted to revive the Russian economy. Under the policy of **perestroika**, he proposed major reforms to the centralized economic ministries. He also abandoned traditional Marxist ideology by advocating private ownership of property and moving toward free market ideology. When these policies did not achieve all the economic gains Gorbachev desired, he pursued bold political reform, such as his policy of **glasnost**, or "openness."
- Throughout 1989, one after another Eastern European country moved toward independence. The Berlin Wall fell in 1989 as well, and in the coming months and years, communism and the Soviet Union crumbled. Gorbachev was unseated by a coup in 1991.

- As president of Russia, Boris Yeltsin dominated the post-Soviet Commonwealth of Independent States. He continued the move from communism to a market economy.

AP® KEY CONCEPTS
4.1 Total war and political instability in the first half of the twentieth century gave way to a polarized state order during the Cold War, and eventually to efforts at transnational union.
> IV. As World War II ended, a Cold War between the liberal democratic West and the communist East began, lasting nearly half a century.

4.2 The stresses of economic collapse and total war engendered internal conflicts within European states and created conflicting conceptions of the relationship between the individual and the state, as demonstrated in the ideological battle among liberal democracy, communism, and fascism.
> V. Eastern European nations were defined by their relationship with the Soviet Union, which oscillated between repression and limited reform, until Mikhail Gorbachev's policies led to the collapse of communist governments in Eastern Europe and the fall of the Soviet Union.

THE COLLAPSE OF YUGOSLAVIA AND CIVIL WAR

Yugoslavia, created in the wake of World War I, was an artificial entity composed of several different nationalities. In the 1980s, this union fell apart, leading to a series of bloody ethnic conflicts.

AP® KEY CONCEPTS
4.1 Total war and political instability in the first half of the twentieth century gave way to a polarized state order during the Cold War, and eventually to efforts at transnational union.
> IV. As World War II ended, a Cold War between the liberal democratic West and the communist East began, lasting nearly half a century.

4.2 The stresses of economic collapse and total war engendered internal conflicts within European states and created conflicting conceptions of the relationship between the individual and the state, as demonstrated in the ideological battle among liberal democracy, communism, and fascism.
> V. Eastern European nations were defined by their relationship with the Soviet Union, which oscillated between repression and limited reform, until Mikhail Gorbachev's policies led to the collapse of communist governments in Eastern Europe and the fall of the Soviet Union.

PUTIN AND THE RESURGENCE OF RUSSIA

- Vladimir Putin became president of the Russian Federation in 2000. He dealt harshly with Chechen separatists, reimposing Russian control of the region.
- Under Putin, the Russian economy grew stronger. Putin also sought to both more strongly centralize the Russian government and to recapture Georgia, formerly a part of the Soviet Union.

AP® KEY CONCEPTS

4.1 Total war and political instability in the first half of the twentieth century gave way to a polarized state order during the Cold War, and eventually to efforts at transnational union.

VI. Nationalist and separatist movements, along with ethnic conflict and ethnic cleansing, periodically disrupted the post-World War II peace.

THE RISE OF POLITICAL ISLAMISM

- Radical Islamism spread, with long-range effects in the United States and Europe.
- Emerging as a response to secular Arab nationalism, radical Islamism looked instead to the region's Muslim traditions. The Iranian Revolution of 1979 was an example of this development. Founded on Muslim reformism, the revolution sought to establish a purified form of Islam, in a modern context.

The Soviet invasion of Afghanistan similarly sparked a **jihad** against the invaders in that country. Success in repelling the Soviet Union, and the U.S. involvement in the Persian Gulf War of 1991 turned radical Muslims' attention to the United States.

AP® KEY CONCEPTS

4.1 Total war and political instability in the first half of the twentieth century gave way to a polarized state order during the Cold War, and eventually to efforts at transnational union.

VI. Nationalist and separatist movements, along with ethnic conflict and ethnic cleansing, periodically disrupted the post-World War II peace.

4.3 During the twentieth century, diverse intellectual and cultural movements questioned the existence of objective knowledge, the ability of reason to arrive at truth, and the role of religion in determining moral standards.

I. The widely held belief in progress characteristic of much of nineteenth-century thought began to break down before World War I; the experience of war intensified a sense of anxiety that permeated many facets of thought and culture, giving way by the century's end to a plurality of intellectual frameworks.

A TRANSFORMED WEST

- The collapse of communism and the emergence of the European Union fundamentally altered the political, social, and economic landscape of contemporary Europe, and Europe today faces renewed challenges to its role in the world.
- George W. Bush launched a "war on terrorism," and led the invasion of Afghanistan and Iraq. The Iraq war was controversial both in the United States and challenged the long-standing alliances between the United States and European nations.

4.3 During the twentieth century, diverse intellectual and cultural movements questioned the existence of objective knowledge, the ability of reason to arrive at truth, and the role of religion in determining moral standards.

> I. The widely held belief in progress characteristic of much of nineteenth-century thought began to break down before World War I; the experience of war intensified a sense of anxiety that permeated many facets of thought and culture, giving way by the century's end to a plurality of intellectual frameworks.

Multiple-Choice Questions

Questions 1–2 refer to the following map.

Vladimir Putin on Russia's Future, 2008

The desire of millions of our citizens for individual freedom and social justice is what defines the future of Russia's political system. The democratic state should become an effective instrument for civil society's self-organization. . . .

Russia's future political system will be centered on several large political parties that will have to work hard to maintain or affirm their leading positions, be open to change and broaden their dialogue with the voters.

Political parties must not forget their immense responsibility for Russia's future, for the nation's unity and for our country's stable development.

No matter how fierce the political battles and no matter how irreconcilable the differences between parties might be, they are never worth so much as to bring the country to the brink of chaos.

Irresponsible demagogy and attempts to divide society and use foreign help or intervention in domestic political struggles are not only immoral but are illegal. They belittle our people's dignity and undermine our democratic state. . . .

No matter what their differences, all of the different public forces in the country should act in accordance with one simple but essential principle: do nothing that would damage the interests of Russia and its citizens and act only for Russia's good, act in its national interests and in the interest of the prosperity and security of all its people. . . .

It is now clear that the world has entered a new spiral in the arms race. This does not depend on us and it is not we who began it. . . .

NATO itself is expanding and is bringing its military infrastructure ever closer to our borders. We have closed our bases in Cuba and Vietnam, but what have we got in return? New American bases in Romania and Bulgaria, and a new missile defense system with plans to install components of this system in Poland and the Czech Republic soon it seems. . . .

We are effectively being forced into a situation where we have to take measures in response, where we have no choice but to make the necessary decisions. . . .

Russia has a response to these new challenges and it always will. Russia will begin production of new types of weapons over these coming years, the quality of which is just as good and in some cases even surpasses those of other countries.

1. In this analysis, what has taken the place of the United States in a renewed arms race?
   A. the Soviet Union
   B. the European Union
   C. Russia
   D. NATO

2. Which of these best summarizes Putin's stance on political parties?
   A. He believes one-party rule should be reinstated.
   B. He gives precedence to the Communist Party, but will allow other parties to exist.
   C. He supports a multiparty system, as long as the parties place Russia's international position first.
   D. He places no restraints on political parties in a multiparty system.

Questions 3–5 refer to the following excerpt.

Statement of the Cominform, 1947

Fundamental changes have taken place in the international situation as a result of the Second World War and in the post-war period. These changes are characterized by a new disposition of the basic political forces operating in the world arena, by a change in the relations among the victor states in the Second World War, and their realignment. . . .

The Soviet Union and the other democratic countries regarded as their basic war aims the restoration and consolidation of democratic order in Europe, the eradication of fascism and the prevention of the possibility of new aggression on the part of Germany, and the establishment of a lasting all-round cooperation among the nations of Europe. The United States of America, and Britain in agreement with them, set themselves another aim in the war: to rid themselves of competitors on the markets (Germany and Japan) and to establish their dominant position. . .

Thus two camps were formed—the imperialist and anti-democratic camp having as its basic aim the establishment of world domination of American imperialism and the smashing of democracy, and the anti-imperialist and democratic camp having as its basic aim the undermining of imperialism, the consolidation of democracy, and the eradication of the remnants of fascism. . .

. . . the imperialist camp and its leading force, the United States, are displaying particularly aggressive activity. . . . The Truman-Marshall Plan is only a constituent part . . . of the general plan for the policy of global expansion pursued by the United States in all parts of the World. . . .

To frustrate the plan of imperialist aggression the efforts of all the democratic anti-imperialist forces of Europe are necessary. The right-wing Socialists are traitors to this cause. . . . and primarily the French Socialists and the British Labourites . . . by their servility and sycophancy are helping American capital to achieve its aims, provoking it to resort to extortion and impelling their own countries on to a path of vassal-like dependence on the United States of America.

This imposes a special task on the Communist Parties. They must take into their hands the banner of defense of the national independence and sovereignty of their countries. . . .

The principle danger for the working class today lies in underestimating their own strength and overestimating the strength of the imperialist camp.

3. For the authors of this statement, the goals of the United States and Western European powers are essentially
   A. political.
   B. commercial.
   C. military.
   D. theoretical.

4. Which of these are defined in this document as "anti-democratic"?
   A. the Western powers
   B. Britain only
   C. the United States only
   D. the Soviet Union

5. According to this assessment, the Marshall Plan is a(n)
   A. aid package.
   B. act of aggression.
   C. failure.
   D. violation of the Geneva Code.

Questions 6–8 refer to the following excerpt.

National Security Council Paper 68, 1950

The fundamental design of those who control the Soviet Union and the international communist movement is to retain and solidify their absolute power, first in the Soviet Union and second in the areas now under their control. . . . The design, therefore, calls for the complete subversion or forcible destruction of the machinery of government and structure of society in the countries of the non-Soviet world and their replacement by an apparatus and structure subservient to and controlled from the Kremlin. . . .

Our overall policy at the present time may be described as one designed to foster a world environment in which the American system can survive and flourish. It therefore rejects the concept of isolation and affirms the necessity of our positive participation in the world community.

This broad intention embraces two subsidiary policies. One is a policy which we would probably pursue even if there were no Soviet threat. It is a policy of attempting to develop a healthy international community. The other is the policy of "containing" the Soviet system. . . .

As for the policy of "containment," it is one which seeks by all means short of war to (1) block further expansion of Soviet power, (2) expose the falsities of Soviet pretensions, (3) induce a retraction of the Kremlin's control and influence, and (4) in general, so foster the seeds of destruction within the Soviet system that the Kremlin is brought at least to the point of modifying its behavior to conform to generally accepted international standards. . . .

One of the most important ingredients of power is military strength. . . . Without superior aggregate military strength . . . a policy of "containment"—which is in effect a policy of calculated and gradual coercion—is no more than a policy of bluff.

At the same time, it is essential to the successful conduct of a policy of "containment" that we always leave open the possibility of negotiation with the USSR . . .

In "containment" it is desirable to exert pressure in a fashion which will avoid so far as possible directly challenging Soviet prestige, to keep open the possibility for the USSR to retreat before pressure with a minimum loss of face and to secure political advantage from the failure of the Kremlin to yield or take advantage of the openings we leave it.

6. The basic goal of the policies outlined here is to
   A. undermine communism.
   B. create a good environment for global commerce.
   C. promote the spread of the American political system.
   D. foster international cooperation.

7. A secondary goal outlined in this document is to
   A. create a stronger Europe.
   B. reduce the Soviet Union's sphere of influence.
   C. end the Cold War.
   D. work through the United Nations.

8. Which of these methods is rejected here?
   A. war
   B. diplomacy
   C. coercion
   D. a military buildup

Questions 9–10 refer to the following map.

Occupied Germany and Austria

9. When the war ended, Germany was divided into how many occupied sectors?
    A. four
    B. five
    C. two
    D. seven

10. In 1945, the position of the Soviet Union in Eastern Europe is best characterized as
    A. weak.
    B. strong.
    C. in complete control.
    D. challenged by Austria.

Questions 11–12 refer to the following map.

Major Cold War Alliance Systems

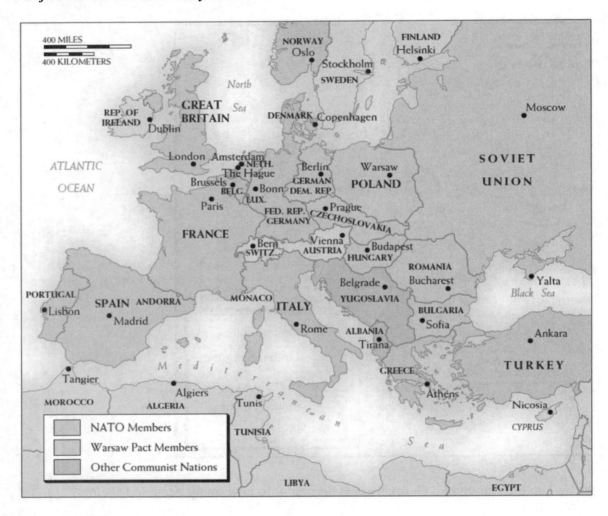

11. Which of these nations was unaligned during the Cold War?
    A. Poland
    B. Spain
    C. Italy
    D. Ireland

12. Which of these nations was communist, but not part of the Soviet bloc?
    A. the Soviet Union
    B. Finland
    C. Turkey
    D. Yugoslavia.

Questions 13–15 refer to the following excerpt.

Khrushchev's Secret Speech, 1956

Stalin acted not through persuasion, explanation, and patient cooperation with people, but by imposing his concepts and demanding absolute submission to his opinion. Whoever opposed this concept or tried to prove his viewpoint and the correctness of his position was doomed to removal from the leading collective [group] and to subsequent moral and physical annihilation. . . .

Stalin originated the concept of "enemy of the people." This term automatically rendered it unnecessary that the ideological errors of a man or men engaged in a controversy be proved; this term made possible the usage of the most cruel repression violating all norms of revolutionary legality, against anyone who in any way disagreed with Stalin, against those who were only suspected of hostile intent, against those who had bad reputations.

This concept "enemy of the people" actually eliminated the possibility of any kind of ideological fight or the making of one's views known on this or that issue, even those of a practical character. In the main, and in actuality, the only proof of guilt used, against all norms of current legal science, was the "confession" of the accused himself; and, as a subsequent probing proved, "confessions" were acquired through physical pressures against the accused. . . .

Lenin used severe methods only in the most necessary cases, when the exploiting classes were still in existence and were vigorously opposing the revolution, when the struggle for survival was decidedly assuming the sharpest forms, even including civil war.

Stalin, on the other hand, used extreme methods and mass repressions at a time when the revolution was already victorious, when the Soviet State was strengthened, when the exploiting classes were already liquidated and Socialist relations were rooted solidly in all phases of national economy, when our party was politically consolidated and had strengthened itself both numerically and ideologically. It is clear that here Stalin showed in a whole series of cases his intolerance, his brutality and his abuse of power. Instead of proving his political correctness and mobilizing the masses, he often chose the path of repression and physical annihilation, not only against actual enemies, but also against individuals who had not committed any crimes against the party and the Soviet Government.

13. According to this analysis, an "enemy of the people" was in fact often a(n)
    A. enemy of Stalin.
    B. religious figure.
    C. scientist.
    D. foreigner.

14. According to Khrushchev, unlike Stalin, Lenin
   A. never used force as Stalin had.
   B. was justified in his use of force.
   C. was an enemy of the people.
   D. was a true communist.

15. What is apparently meant by "physical annihilation" here?
   A. exile
   B. torture
   C. imprisonment
   D. death

Short-Answer Question

The Cold War became a global conflict soon after the end of World War II.

   a. Choose ONE of the following and explain why your choice represents the key factor leading to this development.

   - decolonization
   - dominance of super powers
   - conflicting ideologies

   b. Contrast your choice against ONE of the other options, demonstrating why that option is not as significant as your choice.

Long-Essay Question

To what extent did the United States replace the European powers as the process of decolonization unfolded?

ANSWERS AND EXPLANATIONS: AP® PRACTICE TEST

Multiple-Choice Questions

1. D   Putin argues that NATO is forcing Russia into an arms race.
2. C   He supports a multiparty system, but says that Russia's interests should always come first, implying substantial limits on individual freedoms.
3. B   The authors claim that the real motive of the Western power is to dominate global markets.
4. A   The authors place the imperialist, anti-democratic nations on one side, with the democratic Soviet Union and its allies on the other.
5. B   The author places the Marshall Plan in the context of aggressive imperialist activities.
6. C   The document states "Our overall policy at the present time may be described as one designed to foster a world environment in which the American system can survive and flourish."
7. B   One of the planks of this policy is to "induce a retraction of the Kremlin's control and influence."
8. A   Although it is advised that military strength is essential, the document advises measures include "all means short of war."
9. A   France, the Soviet Union, Britain, and the United States each occupied a region of Germany.
10. B   Already in 1945, the Soviet Union was in a very strong position, but it was not yet in complete control.
11. D   The Republic of Ireland was one of a handful of unaligned European nations during the Cold War.
12. C   Yugoslavia was unique in adopting communism, yet remaining free of Soviet control.
13. A   Khrushchev rightly states that many that were branded as "enemies of the people" were often really Stalin's political allies.
14. B   Khrushchev justifies Lenin's use of force, in saving the revolution from its opponents.
15. D   Khrushchev apparently uses this term as a euphemism for the mass assassinations that took place under Stalin.

Long-Essay Question

To what extent did the United States replace the European powers on the global scene as the process of decolonization unfolded?

(Key topics to focus and elaborate on)
- dominance versus colonization
- examples of Vietnam, Korea, Middle East
- American motives

CHAPTER 22

Social, Cultural, and Economic Challenges in the West through the Present

THE TWENTIETH-CENTURY MOVEMENT OF PEOPLES

■ World War II created a terrible refugee problem as millions of people were displaced from their homes. Between 1945 and 1960, half a million Europeans left Europe each year.

AP® KEY CONCEPTS

4.4 Demographic changes, economic growth, total war, disruptions of traditional social patterns, and competing definitions of freedom and justice altered the experiences of everyday life.

> I. The twentieth century was characterized by large-scale suffering brought on by warfare and genocide as well as tremendous improvements in the standard of living.
> II. The lives of women were defined by family and work responsibilities, economic changes, and feminism.
> III. New voices gained prominence in political, intellectual, and social discourse.

TOWARD A WELFARE STATE

■ The emergence of a modern European welfare state evolved after the economic dislocation, unemployment, rise of authoritarian states, and the devastating effects of World War II. After World War II, the concept that social insurance against risks should be available to all citizens came into being. Britain created the first welfare state, with universal health coverage for all citizens.

■ Western European attitudes toward providing social security and coverage to their citizens grew in response to communist promises (largely unfounded) of the same.

AP® KEY CONCEPTS

4.2 The stresses of economic collapse and total war engendered internal conflicts within European states and created conflicting conceptions of the relationship between the individual and the state, as demonstrated in the ideological battle among liberal democracy, communism, and fascism.

> IV. Postwar economic growth supported an increase in welfare benefits; however, subsequent economic stagnation led to criticism and limitation of the welfare state.

NEW PATTERNS IN THE WORK AND EXPECTATIONS OF WOMEN

■ Women in the years since World War II have made important gains in the workplace. More women are in managerial positions and have better opportunities, but gender inequality remains a problem.

AP® KEY CONCEPTS

4.4 Demographic changes, economic growth, total war, disruptions of traditional social patterns, and competing definitions of freedom and justice altered the experiences of everyday life.

    II. The lives of women were defined by family and work responsibilities, economic changes, and feminism.

TRANSFORMATIONS IN KNOWLEDGE AND CULTURE

- Many intellectuals in the 1930s viewed communism as a vehicle for protecting humane values. Some did not know of Stalin's terror; others simply ignored it or defended it. Four events that were crucial to the transformation of intellectual thought with regard to communism: the Spanish Civil War, the great public purge trials of the 1930s, the Nazi-Soviet pact, and the Soviet invasion of Hungary in 1956.
- Many intellectuals remained fans of Marxism, which they distinguished from the agenda of the Communist Party. Another powerful intellectual trend during this time was **existentialism**, which had its roots in the thinking of Søren Kierkegaard and Frederick Nietzsche.
- The university populations in Europe expanded in the postwar years, with higher education available to women throughout Europe.
- In the postwar years, the American military presence in Europe, tourism, and student exchanges have all led to the Americanization of Europe.

AP® KEY CONCEPTS

4.4 Demographic changes, economic growth, total war, disruptions of traditional social patterns, and competing definitions of freedom and justice altered the experiences of everyday life.

    III. New voices gained prominence in political, intellectual, and social discourse.

ART SINCE WORLD WAR II

- Broadly speaking, the influence of the Cold War was mirrored in artistic developments.
- **Socialist realism** dominated in the Soviet Union, focusing on the heroic.
- In Western Europe and the United States, abstract styles continued to dominate.

AP KEY CONCEPTS

4.3 During the twentieth century, diverse intellectual and cultural movements questioned the existence of objective knowledge, the ability of reason to arrive at truth, and the role of religion in determining moral standards.

    I. The widely held belief in progress characteristic of much of nineteenth-century thought began to break down before World War I; the experience of war intensified a sense of anxiety that permeated many facets of thought and culture, giving way by the century's end to a plurality of intellectual frameworks.

    IV. During the twentieth century, the arts were defined by experimentation, self-expression, subjectivity, and the increasing influence of the United States in both elite and popular culture.

THE CHRISTIAN HERITAGE

- Christianity continues to struggle against the **forces of secularization** in contemporary society. Strands of neo-orthodoxy and liberalism are evident in contemporary Christianity.

- The Roman Catholic Church has remained generally traditionalist, but some popes, such as John XXIII attempted sweeping reforms.

AP® KEY CONCEPTS

4.3 During the twentieth century, diverse intellectual and cultural movements questioned the existence of objective knowledge, the ability of reason to arrive at truth, and the role of religion in determining moral standards.

> III. Organized religion continued to play a role in European social and cultural life, despite the challenges of military and ideological conflict, modern secularism, and rapid social changes.

LATE TWENTIETH-CENTURY TECHNOLOGY: THE ARRIVAL OF THE COMPUTER

- The importance of the computer in the twentieth century cannot be underestimated. It altered forever the way business was done, and it effectively brought the world closer together, with new means of technological communication like email and the Internet.

AP® KEY CONCEPTS

4.3 During the twentieth century, diverse intellectual and cultural movements questioned the existence of objective knowledge, the ability of reason to arrive at truth, and the role of religion in determining moral standards.

> II. Science and technology yielded impressive material benefits but also caused immense destruction and posed challenges to objective knowledge.

THE CHALLENGES OF EUROPEAN UNIFICATION

- Much of Western Europe's political power has come from its postwar cooperation.
- In 1957, the members of this group agreed to form a new organization, called the European Economic Community (EEC), or Common Market. This group hoped to achieve the elimination of tariffs, a free flow of capital and labor, and similar benefits in their countries.
- In 1988, the leaders of the EEC had decided that by 1992 the EEC was to be a free-trade zone with no trade barriers or restrictive trade policies. In 1991, the Treaty of Maastricht proposed a series of steps leading to a unified European currency (the Euro) and a strong central bank. In 1993, the EEC was renamed the **European Union**. The **euro** was launched in 1999.
- In 2004, the proposed European Constitution triggered controversy. Opposition to the constitution represented the first major challenge to the steady trend of unification.

AP® KEY CONCEPTS

4.4 Demographic changes, economic growth, total war, disruptions of traditional social patterns, and competing definitions of freedom and justice altered the experiences of everyday life.

> I. The twentieth century was characterized by large-scale suffering brought on by warfare and genocide as well as tremendous improvements in the standard of living.

Multiple-Choice Questions

Questions 1–3 refer to the following excerpt.

Mona Eltahawy Argues Women's Rights Trump Cultural Relativism

Some have likened this issue to Switzerland's move last year to ban the construction of minarets. . . .

Underlying both bans is a dangerous silence: liberal refusal to robustly discuss what it means to be European, what it means to be Muslim, and racism and immigration. Liberals decrying the infringement of women's rights should acknowledge that the absence of debate on these critical issues allowed the political right and the Muslim right to seize the situation.

Europe's ascendant political right is unapologetically xenophobic. It caricatures the religion that I practice and uses those distortions to fan Islamophobia. But ultra-conservative strains of Islam, such as Salafism and Wahhabism, also caricature our religion and use that Islamophobia to silence opposition. . . .

The strains of Islam that promote face veils do not believe in the concept of a woman's right to choose and describe women as needing to be hidden to prove their "worth." . . . There is no choice in such conditioning. That is not a message Muslims learn in our holy book, the Koran, nor is the face veil prescribed by the majority of Muslim scholars.

The French ban has been condemned as anti-liberal and anti-feminist. Where were those howls when niqabs began appearing in European countries, where for years women fought for rights? A bizarre political correctness tied the tongues of those who would normally rally to defend women's rights.

There are several ideological conflicts here: Within Islam, liberal and feminist Muslims refuse to believe that full-length veils are mandatory. . . . Feminist groups run by Muslim women in various Western countries fight misogynistic practices justified in the name of culture and religion. Cultural relativists, they say, don't want to "offend" anyone by protesting the disappearance of women behind the veil—or worse.

1. For this author, the veil symbolizes
    A. freedom of religion.
    B. economic values.
    C. suppression of women's rights.
    D. essentially a political issue.

2. According to this author, which of these is in the wrong in their stance on the use of the veil in Europe?
    A. the political right only
    B. the political left only
    C. both the left and the right
    D. Muslims on the political left

3. For this author, what has kept liberals from opposing the use of the veil?
   A. xenophobia
   B. adherence to cultural relativism
   C. apathy
   D. misunderstandings

Questions 4–6 refer to the following excerpt.

Simone De Beauvoir from **The Second Sex,** *1949*

According to French law, obedience is no longer included among the duties of a wife, and each woman citizen has the right to vote; but these civil liberties remain theoretical as long as they are unaccompanied by economic freedom. . . . It is through gainful employment that woman has traversed most of the distance that separated her from the male; and nothing else can guarantee her liberty in practice. Once she ceases to be a parasite, the system based on her dependence crumbles; between her and the universe there is no longer any need for a masculine mediator. . . .

When she is productive, active, she regains her transcendence; in her projects she concretely affirms her status as subject; in connection with the aims she pursues, with the money and the rights she takes possession of, she makes trial of and senses her responsibility. . . .

There are . . . a fairly large number of privileged women who find in their professions a means of economic and social autonomy. These come to mind when one considers woman's possibilities and her future. . . . [E]ven though they constitute as yet only a minority; they continue to be the subject of debate between feminists and antifeminists. The latter assert that the emancipated women of today succeed in doing nothing of importance in the world and that furthermore they have difficulty in achieving their own inner equilibrium. The former exaggerate the results obtained by professional women and are blind to their inner confusion. There is no good reason . . . to say they are on the wrong road; and still it is certain that they are not tranquilly installed in their new realm: as yet they are only halfway there. The woman who is economically emancipated from man is not for all that in a moral, social, and psychological situation identical with that of man. The way she carried on her profession and her devotion to it depends on the context supplied by the total pattern of her life. For when she begins her adult life she does not have behind her the same past as does a boy; she is not viewed by society in the same way; the universe presents itself to her in a different perspective. The fact of being a woman today poses peculiar problems for an independent human individual.

4. For de Beauvoir, in France key civil liberties for women
   A. cannot be fully put into practice.
   B. should be legislated.
   C. are not obtainable.
   D. have been fully realized.

5. According to the author, complete liberty depends on
   A. a bill of rights.
   B. more stringent legal protections.
   C. economic independence.
   D. a supportive spouse.

6. For de Beauvoir, which of these groups of women have obtained real freedom?
   A. wives
   B. students
   C. the upper classes
   D. professionals

Questions 7–8 refer to the following excerpt.

Sartre Discusses His Existentialism

The existentialist frankly states that man is in anguish. His meaning is as follows—When a man commits himself to anything, fully realizing that he is not only choosing what he will be, but is thereby at the same time a legislator deciding for the whole of mankind—in such a moment a man cannot escape from the sense of complete and profound responsibility. There are many, indeed, who show no such anxiety. But we affirm that they are merely disguising their anguish or are in flight from it. Certainly, many people think that in what they are doing they commit no one but themselves to anything: and if you ask them, "What would happen if everyone did so?," they shrug their shoulders and reply, "Everyone does not do so." But in truth, one ought always to ask oneself what would happen if everyone did as one is doing; nor can one escape from that disturbing thought except by a kind of self-deception. The man who lies in self-excuse, by saying, "Everyone will not do it" must be ill at ease in his conscience, for the act of lying implies the universal value which it denies. By its very disguise his anguish reveals itself. Existentialism is nothing else but an attempt to draw the full conclusions from a consistently atheistic position. Its intention is not in the least that of plunging men into despair. And if by despair one means— as the Christians do—any attitude of unbelief, the despair of the existentialist is something different. Existentialism is not atheist in the sense that it would exhaust itself in demonstration of the nonexistence of God. It declares, rather, that even if God existed that would make no difference from its point of view. Not that we believe God does exist, but we think that the real problem is not that of His existence; what man needs is to find himself again and to understand that nothing can save him from himself, not even a valid proof of the existence of God. In this sense existentialism is optimistic. It is a doctrine of action, and it is only by self-deception, by confusing their own despair with ours, that Christians can describe us as without hope.

7. Which of these best summarizes Sartre's existentialism?
   A. Existentialism is essentially pessimistic.
   B. It is impossible to prove that God does or does not exist.
   C. Humans are incapable of triumphing over their own destinies.
   D. Humans have the capacity to shape their own lives.

8. On the subject of religion, Sartre believes that the existence of God is
    A. irrelevant.
    B. obvious.
    C. easily refuted.
    D. not provable.

Questions 9–10 refer to the following excerpt.

Tatjiana Yablonskaya, **Bread,** *1949*

9. Which of these aspects of this painting ties it to socialist realism?
    A. where this takes place
    B. the kind of work depicted
    C. a focus on women
    D. the difficulties depicted

10. Which of these is exalted in this painting?
    A. wealthy peasants
    B. independence
    C. progress
    D. collective work

Questions 11–13 refer to the following excerpt.

Growth of the European Union

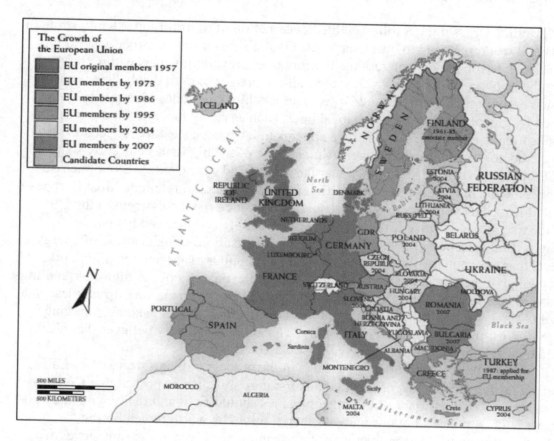

11. Initially, the European Union was essentially
    A. Europe.
    B. western Europe.
    C. western continental Europe.
    D. the World War II allies.

12. By what date did the European Union include much of the former Soviet bloc?
    A. 1957
    B. 1973
    C. 1986
    D. 2004

13. Most of the candidates for European Union membership are in
    A. eastern Europe.
    B. the Balkans.
    C. southern Europe.
    D. the former Soviet Union.

Questions 14–15 refer to the following excerpt.

Richard Lofthouse on the Global Economic Role of Europe

In 1968, rioting across the US followed the assassination of Martin Luther King, while in France students and workers hoped to oust Charles de Gaulle's government. Broadly speaking these tumultuous events concerned generational conflict over prevailing values within the societies where the riots broke out. Forty years later, all the images of civil disobedience such as French fisherman dumping their catches and British hauliers blocking roads illustrate self-interest triggered by global forces rather than local ones, such as rising fuel and food prices.

If globalisation is a bus trip, then, Europe appears to have been steadily reduced in status from driver to conductor to helpless passenger. Almost none of the big issues currently shaping its future are European. In the past six months fear has intensified over China's economic rise and India has become the most seductive destination for entrepreneurial retailers. Most European banks have lost at least half of their value due to wildly misguided risk assessment in the US while most of the rise in the oil price reflects non-Western supply and demand habits.

One might paint Europe as the hapless victim of globalisation. Consideration of energy security suggests that the crunch will worsen as natural gas supplies evaporate (as if high oil prices weren't enough to keep you awake at night). Meanwhile, analysis of the future of retailing suggests that online retailing is set to soar, not least because even Americans are driving less in a bid to keep fuel costs down. Malls might have only just opened their doors in some emerging markets but in the West they face an uncertain future. The aviation industry believes that if oil remains at $135 a barrel, the world's airlines will lose $6.1bn this year.

It seems as if every business model in town is in the process of being wrecked by OPEC, or China's soaring resource demands, or greedy bankers; in reply, citizens protest that Congress or the European Union Commissioner or big oil companies should fix it and really, you know, it is someone else's fault. But that's not our view. In fact, it might be worth remembering Einstein's credo that "the significant problems we have cannot be solved at the same level of thinking with which we created them." This fragment is the basis of most of the entrepreneurship espoused in this publication, and it opens the door to creative solutions to problems that are invariably both global and local.

Europe has a leadership role to play in globalization, providing not just technological solutions to pressing problems such as climate change but perhaps more importantly offering a deep heritage of cultural intelligence and humanity arising from its eighteenth century Enlightenment.

There are hopeful signs to which one may point. A telemetry company is helping hauliers to cut their fuel consumption; an electric car project, backed by both Israel's government and Renault-Nissan, may herald the end of the internal combustion engine as we know it, and a book called WASTEnomics bristles with private sector solutions to excessive waste, the product of our extraordinary affluence.

14. Which of these would provide the best thesis for this excerpt?
    A. Europe is steadily losing out to global competitors.
    B. Europe can play an active role in shaping global commerce.
    C. While in the past it was a leader, Europe will never regain its leadership role.
    D. As a victim of globalization, European business can nevertheless benefit from global economic developments.

15. For the author, the impact of the actions of American financiers and OPEC policies
    A. are significant, but only part of the story.
    B. disastrous for European businesses.
    C. in reality of little consequence.
    D. immoral.

Short-Answer Question

In Europe, conflict has centered on the subject of Muslim practices, especially women's wearing of headscarves.

   a. Choose ONE of the following and explain why your choice represents the key factor leading to this development.

   - decolonization
   - radical Islamism
   - conflict between Islam and Christianity

   b. Contrast your choice against ONE of the other options, demonstrating why that option is not as significant as your choice.

Long-Essay Question

Has European unification been successful?

ANSWERS AND EXPLANATIONS: AP® PRACTICE TEST

Multiple-Choice Questions

1. C   The author argues that those who support the veil are tacitly or openly allowing women's rights to be ignored.
2. B   The author takes to task both those on the right and on the left.
3. B   For this author, cultural relativism has led many liberals to support the veil in an effort to respect Muslim traditions.
4. A   For de Beauvoir, women cannot realize their promise without economic freedom.
5. C   The author says that women cannot become fully free as long as they are economically "parasites."
6. D   De Beauvoir points to professional women that are socially and economically truly independent.
7. D   For Sartre, existentialism is optimistic; humans can direct their own lives.
8. A   Sartre writes that the existence or nonexistence of God is irrelevant, because humans should decide upon their course without reference to religion.
9. B   Socialist realism focused on the everyday, and especially manual labor.
10. D   This scene represents the fondness of socialist realism for collective labor, and happy peasants engaged in hard work.
11. C   The first members were all in Western Europe, with the notable exceptions of Spain, Portugal, and the United Kingdom.
12. D   By 2004, the European Union included most of the former Soviet Union, with the exception of members of the Russian Federation.
13. B   Several states in the Balkans are currently candidates for admission to the European Union, along with Turkey.
14. B   The author argues that Europe should move from victimhood to a more active role where globalization is concerned.
15. A   The author does not deny the impact of actions taken in other countries on European business, but he does deny that these impacts are overwhelming.

Long-Essay Question

Has European unification been successful?

(Key topics to focus and elaborate on)
- define goals of unification
- economic success
- response to constitution

PART III

PRACTICE DOCUMENT-BASED QUESTIONS WITH SAMPLE ESSAYS

On the following pages are six practice Document-based Questions. They mirror the actual section in the AP exam in format and question types. Set aside a time to write essay responses to these questions, timing yourself as you will be timed when you take the actual exam. This will help you prepare for your test-taking experience.

DOCUMENT-BASED QUESTION 1

> ***Defend or refute the following statement: The Protestant Reformation was a unified movement of dissent against the Catholic Church.***

Historical Background: The Protestant Reformation officially began with Martin Luther's posting his "Ninety-five Theses" on the door of Castle Church in Wittenberg in 1517, but discontent with the dogma and policies of the Catholic Church had begun long before that. Luther's act dramatized the internal division in the western church. As this powerful religious movement spread throughout northern Europe, Protestant reformers challenged many aspects of the Catholic Church and traditional religion that they found troublesome and not scripturally sound. These leaders, including Martin Luther, John Calvin, Ulrich Zwingli, and others, sought to worship as Christians in a church free from papal influence and clerical corruption.

DOCUMENT A The Apostles' Creed, official statement of faith for Catholic Church, ca. 1200.

I believe in God, the Father Almighty, the Creator of heaven and earth, and in Jesus Christ, His only Son, our Lord:
Who was conceived of the Holy Spirit, born of the Virgin Mary, suffered under Pontius Pilate, was crucified, died, and was buried.
He descended into hell.
The third day He arose again from the dead.
He ascended into heaven and sits at the right hand of God the Father Almighty, whence He shall come to judge the living and the dead.
I believe in the Holy Spirit, the holy Catholic Church, the communion of saints, the forgiveness of sins, the resurrection of the body, and life everlasting. Amen.

DOCUMENT B Anonymous, caricature of indulgence preacher John Tetzel, 1517.

DOCUMENT C   Martin Luther, German theologian, letter to Albert of Mainz, October 31, 1517.

Finally, works of piety and love are infinitely better than indulgences, and yet these are not preached with such ceremony or such zeal; nay, for the sake of preaching the indulgences they are kept quiet, though it is the first and the sole duty of all bishops that the people should learn the Gospel and the love of Christ, for Christ never taught that indulgences should be preached. How great then is the horror, how great the peril of a bishop, if he permits the Gospel to be kept quiet, and nothing but the noise of indulgences to be spread among his people! Will not Christ say to them, "straining at a gnat and swallowing a camel"? In addition to this, Most Reverend Father in the Lord, it is said in the Instruction to the Commissaries which is issued under your name, Most Reverend Father (doubtless without your knowledge and consent), that one of the chief graces of indulgence is that inestimable gift of God by which man is reconciled to God, and all the penalties of purgatory are destroyed. Again, it is said that contrition is not necessary in those who purchase souls [out of purgatory] or buy confessionalia.

DOCUMENT D   Martin Luther, "Ninety-five Theses," document posted on door of Castle Church, Wittenberg, 1517.

32. Those who believe that they can be certain of their salvation because they have indulgence letters will be eternally damned, together with their teachers.
33. Men must especially be on guard against those who say that the pope's pardons are that inestimable gift of God by which man is reconciled to him.
34. For the graces of indulgences are concerned only with the penalties of sacramental satisfaction established by man.
35. They who teach that contrition is not necessary on the part of those who intend to buy souls out of purgatory or to buy confessional privileges preach unchristian doctrine.
36. Any truly repentant Christian has a right to full remission of penalty and guilt, even without indulgence letters.
37. Any true Christian, whether living or dead, participates in all the blessings of Christ and the church; and this is granted him by God, even without indulgence letters.

DOCUMENT E   "Parody of the Apostles Creed," ca. 1520.

I believe in the Pope, binder and looser in heaven, earth, and hell,
and in Simony, his only son our lord,
Who was conceived by the canon law
and born of the Romish church.
Under his power truth suffered,
was crucified, dead and buried,
and through the ban descended to hell,
rose again through the gospel and Paul
and was brought to Charles,
sitting at his right hand,
who in future is to rule over spiritual and worldly things.
I believe in canon law,

in the Romish church,
in the destruction of faith and of the communion of saints,
in indulgences both for the remission of guilt and penalty in purgatory,
in the resurrection of the flesh in an Epicurean life,
because given to us by the Holy Father, the Pope. Amen.

DOCUMENT F Martin Luther, letter to his wife, October 4, 1529.

Grace and peace in Christ! Dear Käthie—Our friendly conference at Marburg is almost ended, and we have agreed upon nearly all points, except that our opponents maintain that only bread and wine are present in the sacrament, although admitting Christ's spiritual presence in the elements. Today, Landgrave is making every effort to unite us, or at least to make us consider each other brethren and members of Christ's body.

DOCUMENT G Martin Luther, *Against Catholicism,* 1535.

If the pope were the head of the Christian Church, then the Church were a monster with two heads, seeing that St. Paul says that Christ is her head. The pope may well be, and is, the head of the false Church. Where the linnet is, there is also the cuckoo, for he thinks his song a thousand times better than the linnet's. Even thus, the pope places himself in the Church, and so that his song may be heard, overcrowds the Church. The cuckoo is good for something, in that its appearance gives tidings that summer is at hand; so the pope serves to show us that the last day of judgment approaches. There are many that think I am too fierce against popedom; on the contrary, I complain that I am, alas! too mild; I wish I could breathe out lightning against pope and popedom, and that every word were a thunderbolt.

DOCUMENT H John Calvin, Protestant reformer, *Institutes of the Christian Religion,* 1536.

The covenant of life not being equally preached to all, and among those to whom it is preached not always finding the same reception, this diversity discovers the wonderful depth of the Divine judgment. Nor is it to be doubted that this variety also follows, subject to the decision of God's eternal election. If it be evidently the result of the Divine will, that salvation is freely offered to some, and others are prevented from attaining it—this immediately gives rise to important and difficult questions, which are incapable of any other explication, than by the establishment of pious minds in what ought to be received concerning election and predestination—a question, in the opinion of many, full of perplexity; for they consider nothing more unreasonable, than that, of the common mass of mankind, some should be predestinated to salvation, and others to destruction.

DOCUMENT I Philip Melanchthon, German humanist and religious scholar, *Of the Power and Primacy of the Pope,* 1537.

On this account our consciences are sufficiently excused; for the errors of the kingdom of the Pope are manifest. And Scripture with its entire voice exclaims that these errors are a teaching of demons and of Antichrist. The idolatry in the profanation of the masses is manifest, which, besides other faults are shamelessly applied to most shameful gain. The doctrine of repentance has been utterly corrupted by the Pope and his adherents. For they teach that sins are remitted because of the worth of our works. Then they bid us doubt whether the remission takes place. They nowhere teach that sins are remitted freely for Christ's sake, and that by this faith we obtain remission of sins.

Thus they obscure the glory of Christ, and deprive consciences of firm consolation, and abolish true divine services, namely, the exercises of faith struggling with despair concerning the promise of the Gospel. They have obscured the doctrine concerning sin, and have invented a tradition concerning the enumeration of offenses, producing many errors and despair.

They have devised, in addition, satisfactions, whereby they have also obscured the benefit of Christ. From these, indulgences have been born, which are pure lies, fabricated for the sake of gain. Then, how many abuses and what horrible idolatry the invocation of saints has produced! What shameful acts have arisen from the tradition concerning celibacy!

DOCUMENT J   The Forty-two Articles of 1553, issued in England during the reign of Edward VI.

XII. Works before Justification

Works done before the Grace of Christ, and the inspiration of his Spirit, are not pleasant to God, for as much as they spring not of Faith in Jesus Christ; neither do they make Men meet to receive Grace, or (as the School Authors say) deserve Grace of Congruity; yea rather for that they are not done as God hath willed and commanded them to be done, we doubt not but they have the nature of Sin.

DOCUMENT-BASED QUESTION 2

> ### *To what extent was the War of the American Revolution a European conflict?*

Historical Background: European involvement in the colonies of North America had been a source of conflict for some time. French and English settlers had long coveted the various river valleys of the region, but William Pitt's strategic use of military forces enabled Britain to gain control of the North American colonies. When Britain attempted to exert greater control over the colonies in the form of a series of tariffs and taxes, the colonists rebelled against their imperial benefactors. The American Revolution and the colonies' independence followed. The American colonies sought French assistance in their battles against the British, further arousing European resentments and hostilities.

DOCUMENT A   John Locke, English philosopher, *Two Treatises on Civil Government,* 1690.

The reason men enter into society is to protect their property. And the reason they choose a government is to make laws to guard that property…. Certainly society does not want to give the government the power to destroy the very property which it was chosen to protect. Therefore, whenever government tries to take away and destroy the property of the people, or reduce the people to slavery, it puts itself in a state of war with the people. The people are freed from any further obedience to that government … and have the right to establish a new government.

DOCUMENT B British Parliamentary document, *Stamp Act, an Act Applying Certain Stamp Duties in the American Colonies,* March 22, 1765.

Whereas by an act made in the last session of parliament, several duties were granted, continued, and appropriated, toward defraying the expenses of defending, protecting, and securing the British colonies and plantations in America … we, your Majesty's most dutiful and loyal subjects, the commons of Great Britain … have therefore resolved to give and grant unto your Majesty the several rates and duties herein…. For every skin or piece of vellum or parchment, or sheet or piece of paper, on which shall be engrossed, written or printed, any declaration, plea, replication, rejoinder, demurrer, or other pleading, or any copy thereof, in any court of law within the British colonies and plantations in America, a stamp duty of three pence….

DOCUMENT C Transcript of "The Stamp Act Congress," from *Journal of the First Congress of the American Colonies,* 1765.

… IV. That the people of these colonies are not, and cannot, be represented in the House of Commons in Great Britain.
V. That the only representatives of the people of these colonies are persons chosen therein by themselves, and that no taxes ever have been, or can be constitutionally imposed on them, but by their respective legislatures….

DOCUMENT D William Pitt (the Elder), British statesman, *Speech by William Pitt in the House of Commons Opposing Parliament's Right to Tax the American Colonies,* January 16, 1766.

There is an idea in some, that the colonies are virtually represented in the house. I would fain know by whom an American is represented here? Is he represented by any knight of the shire, in any county in this kingdom? Would to God that respectable representation was augmented to a greater number! Or will you tell him that he is represented by any representative of a borough—a borough, which, perhaps, its own representatives never saw. This is what is called the rotten part of the constitution. It cannot continue a century. If it does not drop, it must be amputated. The ideal of a virtual representation of America in this house is the most contemptible idea that ever entered into the head of a man. It does not deserve a serious refutation.

DOCUMENT E Thomas Jefferson, American president, an account of points made at the June 8, 1776, meeting in Congress, prior to the publication of the *Declaration of Independence,* from Jefferson's *Autobiography* (1821).

That the present campaign may be unsuccessful, & therefore we had better propose an alliance while our affairs wear a hopeful aspect:
That to await the event of this campaign will certainly work delay, because during this

summer France may assist us effectually by cutting off those supplies of provisions from England & Ireland on which the enemy's armies here are to depend; or by setting in motion the great power they have collected in the West Indies, & calling our enemy to the defense of the possessions they have there:

That it would be idle to lose time in settling the terms of alliance, till we had first determined we would enter into alliance:

And that the only misfortune is that we did not enter into alliance with France six months sooner, as besides opening their ports for the vent of our last year's produce, they might have marched an army into Germany and prevented the petty princes there from selling their unhappy subjects to subdue us.

DOCUMENT F Thomas Paine, Political theorist, *The American Crisis,* December 23, 1776.

Britain, with an army to enforce her tyranny, has declared that she has a right (not only to TAX) but "to BIND us in ALL CASES WHATSOEVER," and if being bound in that manner, is not slavery, then is there not such a thing as slavery upon earth. Even the expression is impious; for so unlimited a power can belong only to God.

DOCUMENT G *Treaty of Alliance with France* between the American colonial government and Louis XVI of France, February 6, 1778.

ART. 1. If war should break out between France and Great Britain during the continuance of the present war between the United States and England, His Majesty and the said United States shall make it a common cause and aid each other mutually with their good offices, their counsels, and their forces, according to the exigence of conjunctures, as becomes good and faithful allies.

DOCUMENT H *Articles 2 and 3 of the Treaty of Amity and Commerce between the United States and France,* February 6, 1778.

ART. 2.nd The most Christian King, and the United States engage mutually not to grant any particular Favor to other Nations in respect of Commerce and Navigation, which shall not immediately become common to the other Party, who shall enjoy the same Favor freely…

ART. 3.d The Subjects of the most Christian King shall pay in the Port Havens, Roads, Countries Islands, Cities or Towns, of the United States or any of them, no other or greater Duties or Imposts of what Nature soever they may be, or by what Name soever called, than those which the Nations most favoured are or shall be obliged to pay; and they shall enjoy all the Rights, Liberties, Privileges, Immunities and Exemptions in Trade, Navigation and Commerce, whether in passing from one Port in the said States to another, or in going to and from the same, from and to any Part of the World, which the said Nations do or shall enjoy.

DOCUMENT I Treaty between Great Britain and the United States of America, signed at Paris and ending the War of the American Revolution, September 3, 1783.

ART. 1 His Britannic Majesty acknowledges the said United States. viz. New Hampshire, Massachusetts Bay, Rhode Island, and Providence Plantations, Connecticut, New York, New Jersey, Pennsylvania Delaware, Maryland, Virginia, North Carolina, South Carolina, and Georgia, to be free, sovereign, and independent States; that he treats with them as such, and for himself, his heirs, and successors, relinquishes all claims to the Government, propriety and territorial rights of the same, and every part thereof.

DOCUMENT J Exchange of notes between Benjamin Franklin, American statesman and diplomat, and Gravier de Vergennes, French statesman, referring to *Articles 2 and 3 of the Treaty of Amity and Commerce between the United States and France,* September 1784.

Sir: I have the Honour to transmit to your Excellency by Order of Congress a Resolution of theirs, dated the 11th of May last, which is in the Words following, Viz, Resolved, "That Doctor Franklin be instructed to express to the Court of France the constant Desire of Congress to meet their Wishes; That these States are about to form a general System of Commerce by Treaties with other Nations: That at this Time they cannot foresee what Claim might be given to those Nations by the explanatory Propositions from the Count de Vergennes on the **2d & 3d** Articles of our Treaty of Amity & Commerce with His most Christian Majesty; but that he may be assured it will be our constant Care to place no People on more advantageous Ground than the Subjects of his Majesty."
With great Respect I am. Sir, Your Excellency's, most obedient and most humble Servant. VERSAILLES, 9th September, 1784. Benjamin Franklin

Sir: I have received the letter which you did me the honor to write me the third instant. You there declare in the name of Congress that the United States will be careful not to treat any other nation, in matters of commerce, more advantageously than the French nation. This declaration, founded on the treaty of the 6th February, 1778, has been very agreeable to the King; and you, Sir, can assure Congress that the United States shall constantly experience a perfect reciprocity in France. I have the honor to be, etc., GRAVIER DE VERGENNES

DOCUMENT-BASED QUESTION 3

Analyze the political and social forces that helped bring about the Paris Commune of 1871, as well as those that led to its downfall.

Historical Background: The Prussian occupation of Paris that followed the end of the Franco-Prussian War angered many Parisians, who felt that their suffering during the Prussian siege was ignored by the National Government in its negotiation of this occupation in the Frankfurt Treaty. Increasingly, Parisians and residents of the French provinces experienced political divisions. A group of Parisians elected a new municipal government, called the Paris Commune, which was formally proclaimed on March 28, 1871. The Commune was suppressed by the army of the National Assembly on May 28,

1871, after a violent battle that resulted in many deaths and that devastated the Parisian infrastructure.

DOCUMENT A   The First Proclamation of the Government, September 5, 1870.

Frenchmen!

The people have disavowed a Chamber which hesitated to save the country when in danger. It had demanded a Republic. The friends of its representatives are not in power but in peril. The Republic has vanquished the invasion of 1792. The Republic is proclaimed! The Revolution is accomplished in the name of right and public safety. Citizens! Watch over the army confided to you. Tomorrow you will be, with the army, avengers of the country.

DOCUMENT B   *Journal Officiel de la République Française,* editorial, March 21, 1871.

The proletariat, faced with a constant threat to its rights, a total denial of all its legitimate aspirations, along with the imminent destruction of the country and of all its hopes, has realized that it is its imperative duty and absolute right to take its destiny in its own hands by seizing political power.

DOCUMENT C   Edmond de Goncourt, French writer, Journal, March 28, 1871.

In the events taking place the newspapers see only a question of decentralization. Decentralization, indeed! What is happening is very simply the conquest of France by the workers and the enslavement under their despotism of the nobles, the middle lass, and the peasants. The government is leaving the hands of those who have, to go into the hands of those who have not, going from those who have a material interest in conservation of society to those who are completely unconcerned about order, stability, or conservation. Is it possible that in the great law underlying changes here on earth the workers are for modern societies what the Barbarians were for ancient societies, convulsive agents of dissolution and destruction?

DOCUMENT D   Proclamation of the Paris Commune, March 28, 1871.

The Commune is the foundation of all political states, exactly as the family is the embryo of human society. It must have autonomy; that is to say, self-administration and self-government, agreeing with its particular genius, traditions, and wants; preserving, in its political, moral, national, and special groups its entire liberty, its own character, and its complete sovereignty, like a citizen of a free town.

DOCUMENT E   Charles Delescluze, Paris Commune's delegate of war, proclamation at news of entry of Versailles troops, May 22, 1871.

Enough of militarism! No more staff officers bespangled and glided along every seam! Make way for the people, for fighters, for bare arms! The hour for revolutionary warfare has struck. The people know nothing of intricate maneuvers; but when they have a gun in their hand, paving stones underfoot, they have no fear of all the strategies of the monarchical school. To arms! Citizens, to arms! It is now a matter, as you know, of either winning or falling into the hands of the reactionaries and clericals of Versailles, of those wretches who have deliberately handed France over to the Prussians, and who are making us pay the ransom for their treachery.

DOCUMENT F   Appeal by Central Committee of the National Guard to soldiers of Versailles, May 23, 1871.

Soldiers of the Versailles Army,
We are family men. We are fighting so that our children will never have to bend, as you must, under military despotism. One day you will have children too. If you fire on the people today your sons will condemn you, as we condemn the soldiers who massacred the people in June 1848 and December 1851. Two months ago, on 18 March, your brothers of the Paris Army, bitterly resentful of the cowards who had betrayed France, fraternized with the people. We urge you to follow their example. Soldiers, our sons and our brothers, listen to these words and let your conscience decide: *When the orders are immoral, disobedience is a duty.*

DOCUMENT G   Madame Cornélie Morisot to her daughter, Berthe Morisot (French impressionist painter), May 25, 1871.

Paris on fire! This is beyond any description . . . Throughout the day the wind kept blowing in charred papers; some of them were still legible. A vast column of smoke covered Paris, and at night a luminous red cloud, horrible to behold, made it all look like a volcanic eruption. There were continual explosions and detonations; we were spared nothing. They say the insurrection is crushed; but the shooting has not yet stopped. . . . Latest official dispatch: the insurrection is now driven back to a very small part of Paris, the Tuileries is reduced to ashes, the Louvre survives, the part of the Finance ministry building fronting on the Rue de Rivoli is on fire, the Cour des Comptes is burned down, twelve thousand prisoners, Paris strewn with dead.

DOCUMENT H   Marshal MacMahon, French military leader, proclamation of return to order and end of Paris Commune, May 28, 1871.

French Republic—Inhabitants of Paris:
The French Army has come to your rescue.
Paris has been delivered.
At four o'clock our soldiers took over the last rebel positions.
At last the fighting is over; order, work, and security will reign once more.

DOCUMENT I   Sketch, Paris during Prussian siege of 1871.

DOCUMENT J   Vladimir Lenin, Russian Communist leader, speech, "Lessons of the Commune," March 18, 1908.

But despite all its mistakes the Commune was a superb example of the great proletarian movement of the nineteenth century. Marx set a high value on the historic significance of the Commune—if, during the treacherous attempt by the Versailles gang to seize the arms of the Paris proletariat, the workers had allowed themselves to be disarmed without a fight, the disastrous effect of the demoralization that this weakness would have caused in the proletarian movement, would have been far, far greater than the losses suffered by the working class in the battle to defend its arms. The sacrifices of the Commune, heavy as they were, are made up for by its significance for the general struggle of the proletariat: it stilled the Socialist movement throughout Europe, it demonstrated the strength of civil war, it dispelled patriotic illusions, and it destroyed the naïve belief in any efforts of the bourgeoisie for common national aims. The Commune taught the European proletariat to pose concretely the tasks of the Socialist revolution.

DOCUMENT-BASED QUESTION 4

Evaluate the political, social, and cultural reforms Enlightenment thinkers sought in eighteenth century European society.

Historical Background: During the eighteenth century, new convictions began to spread about the possibility for wide economic change and social reform. These attitudes grew over time, and the movement that stimulated such ideas became known as the Enlightenment. The leading figures of the Enlightenment were inspired by the fruits of the Scientific Revolution, and they believed in the power of rational criticism to challenge the intellectual authority of traditional institutions and the Church.

DOCUMENT A John Locke, English philosopher, excerpt from An Essay Concerning Human Understanding, 1690.

Let us then suppose the mind to be, as we say, white paper void of all characters, without any ideas. Whence comes it to be furnished? Whence comes it by that vast store which the busy and boundless fancy of man has painted on it with an almost endless variety? Whence has it all the materials of reason and knowledge? To this I answer, from experience; in that all our knowledge is founded, and from that it ultimately derives itself. Our observation, employed either about external sensible objects, or about the internal operations of our minds perceived and reflected on by ourselves, is that which supplies our understanding with all the materials of thinking. These two are the foundations of knowledge, from whence all the ideas we have, or can naturally have, do spring.

DOCUMENT B Alexander Pope, English poet and satirist, excerpt from An Essay on Man, 1733.

Know then thyself, presume not God to scan;
The proper study of mankind is Man.
Placed on this isthmus of a middle state,
A being darkly wise, and rudely great:
With too much knowledge for the skeptic side,
With too much weakness for the Stoic pride,
He hangs between; in doubt to act, or rest,
In doubt to deem himself a god, or beast;
In doubt his mind or body to prefer;
Born but to die, and reasoning but to err;
Alike in ignorance, his reason such,
Whether he thinks too little, or too much;
Chaos of thought and passion, all confused;
Still by himself abused, or disabused;
Created half to rise, and half to fall;
Great lord of all things, yet a prey to all;
Sole judge of truth, in endless error hurled
The glory, jest, and riddle of the world!

DOCUMENT C Baron de Montesquieu, French political philosopher, The Spirit of Laws, 1748.

Democratic and aristocratic states are not in their own nature free. Political liberty is to be found only in moderate governments; and even in these it is not always found. It is there only when there is no abuse of power. But constant experience shows us that every man invested with power is apt to abuse it, and to carry his authority as far as it will go …

To prevent this abuse, it is necessary from the very nature of things that power should be a check to power …

In every government there are three sorts of power: the legislative, the executive in respect to things dependent on the law of nations; and the executive in regard to matters that depend on the civil law [the realm of the judiciary]…

When the legislative and the executive powers are united in the same person, or in the same body of magistrates, there can be no liberty; because apprehensions may arise, lest the same monarchy or senate should enact tyrannical laws, to execute them in a tyrannical manner.

Again, there is no liberty, if the judiciary power be not separated from the legislative and executive. Were it joined with the legislative, the life and liberty of the subject would be exposed to arbitrary control; for the judge would be then the legislator. Were it joined to the executive power, the judge might behave with violence and oppression.

DOCUMENT D Jean-Jacques Rousseau, French philosopher, excerpt from the novel Émile or On Education, 1762.

Once it is demonstrated that man and woman are not and ought not be constituted in the same way in either character or temperament, it follows that they ought not to have the same education. In following nature's directions, man and woman ought to act in concert, but they ought not to do the same things. The goal of their labors is common, but their labors themselves are different, and consequently so are the tastes directing them.… The good constitution of children initially depends on that of their mothers. The first education of men depends on the care of women. Men's morals, their passions, their tastes, their pleasures, their very happiness also depend on women. Thus the whole education of women ought to relate to men. To please men, to be useful to them, to make herself loved and honored by them, to raise them when young, to care for them when grown, to counsel them, to console them, to make their lives agreeable and sweet—these are the duties of women at all times, and they ought to be taught from childhood. So long as one does not return to this principle, one will deviate from the goal, and all the precepts taught to women will be of no use for their happiness or for ours.

DOCUMENT E François Marie Arouet de Voltaire, French author, Philosophical Dictionary, 1764

Fanaticism is to superstition what delirium is to fever and rage to anger. The man visited by ecstasies and visions, who takes dreams for realities and his fancies for prophecies, is an enthusiast; the man who supports his madness with murder is a fanatic …

The most detestable example of fanaticism was that of the burghers of Paris who on St. Bartholomew's Night [1572] went about assassinating and butchering all their fellow citizens who did not go to mass, throwing them out of windows, cutting them in pieces. Once fanaticism has corrupted a mind, the malady is almost incurable …

The only remedy for this epidemic malady is the philosophical spirit which, spread gradually, at last tames men's habits and prevents the disease from starting; for once the disease has made any progress, one must flee and wait for the air to clear itself. Laws and religion are not strong enough against the spiritual pest; religion, far from being healthy food for infected brains, turns to poison in them …

Even the law is impotent against these attacks of rage; it is like reading a court decree to a raving maniac. These fellows are certain that the Holy Spirit with which they are filled is above the law, that their enthusiasm is the only law they must obey.

What can we say to a man who tells you that he would rather obey God than men, and that therefore he is sure to go to heaven for butchering you?

DOCUMENT F   Jean le Rond d'Alembert, French philosopher and editor, *Preliminary Discourse to the* Encyclopedia *of Diderot*, 1772.

The mechanical arts depend on manual operation and are enslaved, if I may be permitted the term, to a species of routine, and so are left to those men whom prejudice places within the lowest classes. Poverty has driven these men to apply themselves to such work more often than taste or native genius drew them towards it, and for this reason these arts have come to be despised, so much does poverty darken what accompanies it. On the other hand, the free operations of the intellect are the lot of those who think themselves to be the most favored of nature. Nevertheless, the advantage which the liberal arts have over the mechanical, because the former demands hard, intellectual work and requires difficulty to excel, is sufficiently compensated by the far greater usefulness the latter arts for the most part provide for us. It is this very utility which forced these arts to be reduced to merely mechanical operations, so that a greater number of men could practice them. But society, in justly respecting the great geniuses which have enlightened it, need not on that account vilify the hands of those who serve it. The discovery of the compass is no less advantageous to the human race than the explanation of the properties of the compass needle is to physics. Finally, considering in itself the distinction we are discussing, how many of the so-called scholars are there for whom science is, in reality, only a mechanical art? And what is the real difference between a head filled with facts without any order, any usefulness or any connections, and the instinct of an artisan reduced to a mechanical operation?

DOCUMENT G   Immanuel Kant, German philosopher, excerpt from *'Was ist Aufklärung?' ("What is Enlightenment?"),* 1783.

If the question is put in the form: are we living in an enlightened age?, then the answer is no, but we are indubitably living in an age of enlightenment. As things now stand in the main, we have a long way to go before men may be fit to employ their own reason in matters of religion confidently and justly without the guidance of another. But there is manifest evidence that a field has been opened up to them where they may freely use that faculty, and that the obstacles to universal enlightenment or the emergence of mankind from its self-imposed minority are gradually diminishing, and in that sense this is an age of enlightenment.

DOCUMENT H   List of grievances from the Third Estate of the French city of Dourdan *(Dourdan Cahiers de Doléances),* delivered to Versailles, 1789.

The order of the third estates of the City … of Dourdan … supplicates [the king] to accept the grievances, complaints, and remonstrances which it is permitted to bring to the foot of the throne, and to see therein only the expression of its zeal and the homage of its obedience.

It wishes:

1. That his subjects of the third estate, equal by such status to all other citizens, present themselves before the common father without other distinction which might degrade them....

3. That no citizen lose his liberty except according to law: that, consequently, no one be arrested by virtue of special orders, or, if imperative circumstances necessitate such orders, that the prisoner be handed over to regular courts of justice within forty-eight hours at the latest.

12. That every tax, direct or indirect, be granted only for a limited time, and that every collection beyond such term be regarded as peculation, and punished as such....

16. That such tax be borne equally, without distinction, by all classes of citizens and by all kinds of property, even feudal ... rights.

17. That the tax substituted for the *corvée* be borne by all classes of citizens equally and without distinction. That said tax, at present beyond the capacity of those who pay it and the needs to which it is destined, be reduced by at least one-half.

DOCUMENT I Mary Wollstonecraft, British author, excerpt from A Vindication of the Rights of Women, 1792.

... Rousseau declares that a woman should never, for a moment, feel herself independent, that she should be governed by fear to exercise her natural cunning, and made a coquettish slave in order to render her a more alluring object of desire, a sweeter companion to man, whenever he chooses to relax himself. He carries the arguments, which he pretends to draw from the indications of nature, still further, and insinuates that truth and fortitude, the cornerstones of all human virtue, should be cultivated with certain restrictions, because, with respect to the female character, obedience is the grand lesson which ought to be impressed with unrelenting rigour.

What nonsense! When will a great man arise with sufficient strength of mind to put away the fumes which pride and sensuality have thus spread over the subject! If women are by nature inferior to men, their virtues must be the same in quality, if not in degree, or virtue is a relative idea; consequently, their conduct should be founded on the same principles, and have the same aim.

Connected with man as daughters, wives, and mothers, their moral character may be estimated by their manner of fulfilling those simple duties; but the end, the grand end of their exertions should be to unfold their own faculties and acquire the dignity of conscious virtue....

... I ... will venture to assert, that till women are more rationally educated, the progress of human virtue and improvement in knowledge must receive continual checks....

DOCUMENT J Thomas Munck, historian, *The* Enlightenment: A Comparative Social History 1721–1794.

Average annual output of new and reprinted works in English (books, pamphlets and smaller items) in key cities of the British Isles

	LONDON	DUBLIN	EDINBURGH	GLASGOW
1710–1719	1,705	114	160	12
1720–1729	1,378	162	144	11
1730–1739	1,446	160	147	12
1740–1749	1,345	157	214	41
1750–1759	1,567	216	201	65
1760–1769	1,693	209	379	58
1770–1779	2,038	195	249	55
1780–1789	2,434	247	207	53
1790–1795	3,472	374	316	90
Mid-century population in the thousands	675	90	57	24

DOCUMENT-BASED QUESTION 5

> *Discuss and analyze the factors that led to the European Imperialism of the nineteenth century.*

Historical Background: During the second half of the nineteenth century, and especially after 1870, Europe exercised unprecedented influence and control over the rest of the world. North and South America, as well as Australia and New Zealand, almost became part of the European world as great streams of European immigrants populated them. Until the nineteenth century, Asia (with the significant exception of India) and most of Africa had gone their own ways, having little contact with Europe. But in the latter part of that century, almost all of Africa was divided among a number of European nations. Europe also imposed its economic and political power across Asia.

DOCUMENT A Source: Denis Diderot, Eighteenth-century French philosopher, *Supplement au voyage de Bougainville,* 1772.

This country belongs to you. Why? Because you have set foot on it? If a Tahitian landed one day on your coast and he engraved on one of your rocks or on the bark of a tree: "This country belongs to the inhabitants of Tahiti," what would you think?

DOCUMENT B Source: John Ruskin, British critic, inaugural lecture, Oxford University, 1870.

There is a destiny now possible to us, the highest ever set before a nation to be accepted or refused. Will you youths of England make your country again a royal throne of kings, a sceptred isle, for all the world a source of light, a centre of peace; mistress of learning and of the Arts, faithful guardian of time-honoured principles? This is what England must do or perish: she must found colonies as fast and as far as she is able, formed of her most energetic and worthiest men; seizing every piece of fruitful waste ground she can set her feet on, and there teaching these her colonists that their chief virtue is to be fidelity to their country, and their first aim is to advance the power of England by land and sea.

DOCUMENT C Source: Lord Cromer, British government agent, "The Government of the Subject Races," 1882.

We need not always enquire too closely what these people, who are all, nationally speaking, more or less in *statu pupillari,* [student status] themselves think is in their own interests ... it is essential that each special issue should be decided mainly with reference to what, by the light of western knowledge and experience ... we conscientiously think is best for the subject race.

DOCUMENT D Source: Clement Hill, British Foreign Office official, Foreign Office memorandum, December 9, 1884.

The geographical position of the East coast lays it more within the general area of our foreign policy than that of the West Coast. ... Our alternative route by the Cape to India may at any time make it important that we should have possession of or at least free access to good harbors. The importance is not less since the French move to Madagascar. Is it not worth considering whether in view of the European race for territories on the West Coast.... we might not confine ourselves to securing the utmost possible freedom of trade on that coast, yielding to other Powers the territorial responsibilities ... and seeking compensation on the East Coast where ... we are at present, but who can say for how long, without a European rival; where the political future of the country is of real importance to Indian and Imperial interests; where the climate is superior; where commerce is capable of vast extension, and where our influence could be exercised ... in the extension of civilization, and the consequent extinction of the Slave Trade for which we have so long labored.

DOCUMENT E Source: Decree following the proclamation of a Portuguese protectorate over Dahomey, signed by Pinheiro Chagas, foreign minister, 1886.

The monarch of Dahomey, the terror of all Europeans, shows himself affable and condescending to the Portuguese alone. It was he who asked urgently that our protectorate should be established upon the coast of his kingdom. ... It is he who appears disposed to accept at our hands the benefits of European civilization, and to this design he has already borne honorable witness by abolishing human sacrifices.
The Portuguese protectorate in Dahomey is the lighted pathway that links this kingdom of darkness with Europe.

DOCUMENT F Source: American cartoon, 1888.

DOCUMENT G Source: G. W. Stevens, British journalist, Daily Mail, June 23, 1897

Up they came, more and more, new types, new realms at every couple of yards, an anthropological museum—a living gazetteer of the British Empire. With them came their English officers, whom they obey and follow like children. And you begin to understand, as never before, what the Empire amounts to. Not only that we possess all these remote outlandish places … but also that all these people are working, not simply under us, but with us—that we send out a boy here and a boy there, and a boy takes hold of the savages of the part he comes to, and teaches them to march and shoot as he tells them, to obey him and believe in him and die for him and the Queen. … A plain, stupid, uninspired people, they call us, and yet we are doing this with every kind of savage man there is. And each one of us—you and I, and that man in his shirt-sleeves at the corner—is a working part of this world-shaping force. How small you must feel in face of this stupendous whole, and yet how great to be a unit in it.

DOCUMENT H Source: Rudyard Kipling, English writer, The White Man's Burden, poem, 1899.

Take up the White Man's Burden—
Send forth the best ye breed—
Go bind your sons to exile
To serve your captives' need;

To wait in heavy harness
On fluttered folk and wild—
Your new-caught, sullen peoples,
Half devil and half child.

DOCUMENT I Source: Carl Peters, German author, Die Gründung von Deutsch-Ostafrika (*The Foundation of German East Africa*), 1906.

Manifesto of the Society for German Colonization, April 1884

In the partition of the earth, as it has proceeded from the beginning of the fifteenth century up to our times, the German nation received nothing. All the remaining European culture-bearing peoples possess areas outside our continent where their languages and customs can take firm root and flourish. The moment that the German emigrant leaves the borders of the Reich behind him, he is a stranger sojourning on foreign soil. The German Reich, great in size and strength through its bloodily achieved unity, stands in the leading position among the continental European powers: her sons abroad must adapt themselves to nations which look upon us with either indifference or even hostility. For centuries the great stream of German emigration has been plunging down into foreign races where it is lost sight of. Germandom outside Europe has been undergoing a perpetual national decline....

The Society for German Colonization aims to undertake on its own, in a resolute and sweeping manner, carefully chosen colonization projects and thereby supplement the ranks of organizations with similar tendencies.

Its particular tasks will be:

1. to provide necessary sums of capital for colonization;
2. to seek out and lay claim to suitable districts for colonization;
3. to direct German emigrants to these regions

DOCUMENT J Source: Karl Pearson, English author, National Life from the Standpoint of Science, 1907.

History shows me one way, and one way only, in which a state of civilization has been produced, namely, the struggle of race with race, and the survival of the physically and mentally fitter race.

This dependence of progress on the survival of the fitter race, terribly black as it may seem to some of you, gives the struggle for existence its redeeming features; it is the fiery crucible out of which comes the finer metal. You may hope for a time when the sword shall be turned into the ploughshare, when American and German and English traders shall no longer compete in the markets of the world for raw materials, for their food supply, when the white man and the dark shall share the soil between them, and each till it as he lists . ... The path of progress is strewn with the wreck of nations; traces are everywhere to be seen of the hecatombs of inferior races, and of victims who found not the narrow way to the greater perfection. Yet these dead peoples are, in very truth, the stepping stones on which mankind has arisen to the higher intellectual and deeper emotional life of today.

DOCUMENT-BASED QUESTION 6

To what extent was Italy's aggression in Ethiopia significant in the outbreak of World War II?

Historical Background: In October, 1935, Benito Mussolini ordered his Italian forces to invade Ethiopia, using a petty border incident as a justification for his offensive. This attack shocked the League of Nations, which was designed to protect acts of unwarranted aggression between countries. It also came at a time when Adolph Hitler was consolidating his power in Germany, and it was a real threat to European stability.

DOCUMENT A Source: Corriere alla Sera, Italian newspaper, February 13, 1935.

"The cause of Italy is that of civilization."

DOCUMENT B Source: Libro e Moschetto, Italian newspaper, on news of the Italian-Ethiopian conflict, February 16, 1935.

"Italy: a population without land. Africa: a land without population."

DOCUMENT C Source: Sir Robert Vansittart, permanent under-secretary in British Foreign Office, letter to Foreign Secretary Sir Anthony Eden, June 8, 1935.

Italy will have to be bought off—let us use and face ugly words—in some form or other, or Abyssinia [Ethiopia] will eventually perish. That might in itself matter less if it did not mean that the League would also perish (and that Italy would simultaneously perform another volte face [about-face] into the arms of Germany.)

DOCUMENT D Source: Marxist, anti-fascist pamphlet, referring to Ethiopian-Italian conflict, February 1935.

Not one man, not one cent for the African adventure of capitalism!

DOCUMENT E Source: The Times (London), on Ethiopian-Italian conflict, April 8, 1936.

If there are degrees of turpitude in the willful destruction of agreements, zero in the scale has been reached when a Power claiming the characteristics of civilization takes to the indiscriminate employment of gas against a primitive people who neither possess nor can acquire the means of defense against it.

DOCUMENT F Source: Benito Mussolini, Italian Fascist dictator, speech from balcony of Palazzo Venezia, May 5, 1936.

I announce to the Italian people and to the world that the war is finished. I announce to the Italian people and to the world that peace is re-established … Ethiopia is Italian … the diverse races of the Lion of Judah have shown by the clearest signs that they wish to live tranquilly in the shadow of the Italian tricolor. We are ready to defend our resplendent victory with the same intrepid and incontestable determination as that with which we have won it.

DOCUMENT G Source: Haile Selassie, emperor of Ethiopia, speech to League of Nations, June 30, 1936.

The Wal-Wal incident, in December, 1934, came as a thunderbolt to me. The Italian provocation was obvious and I did not hesitate to appeal to the League of Nations. I invoked the provisions of the treaty of 1928, the principles of the Covenant; I urged the procedure of conciliation and arbitration. Unhappily for Ethiopia this was the time when a certain Government considered that the European situation made it imperative at all costs to obtain the friendship of Italy. The price paid was the abandonment of Ethiopian independence to the greed of the Italian Government. This secret agreement, contrary to the obligations of the Covenant, has exerted a great influence over the course of events. Ethiopia and the whole world have suffered and are still suffering today its disastrous consequences. This first violation of the Covenant was followed by many others. Feeling itself encouraged in its policy against Ethiopia, the Rome Government feverishly made war preparations, thinking that the concerted pressure which was beginning to be exerted on the Ethiopian Government, might perhaps not overcome the resistance of my people to Italian domination …

DOCUMENT H Source: Benito Mussolini, speech to constituents, detailing week-old German-Italian alliance, November 1, 1936.

This Berlin-Rome vertical line is not an obstacle but rather an axis around which can revolve all those European states with a will to collaboration and peace.

DOCUMENT I Source: Father Messineo, Italian Jesuit, Necessità di vita e diritto di espansione, (Necessities of Life and the Law of Expansion), 1936.

We may now legitimately conclude that a state, under the pressure of vital necessity because of the narrowness of its own territories and the deficiency of the means indispensable to individual and collective life, has the faculty of appropriating a part of the earth possessed by others, in the measure required by its necessity. This power becomes even more evident if the material means necessary for freeing oneself from these straits lie inactive, in the possession of a people that does not use them, exploit them, and increase their value, whether because the extent of its territory is greater than it needs, or because of the scarcity of man power, or else because of a backwardness of its economic system. The order of nature cannot require that immense riches of the soil remain inert … while another nation overflows with population that it cannot nourish because of the absolute insufficiency of public and private means … Vital necessity can legitimize the occupation of a part of colonial territory, in order to satisfy the needs of individual and social life.

DOCUMENT J Source: British Prime Minister Neville Chamberlain, letter to Benito Mussolini, July 27, 1937.

Dear Signor Mussolini,

… Since I became Prime Minister, I have been distressed to find that the relations between Italy and Great Britain are still far from that old feeling of mutual confidence and affection which lasted for so many years. In spite of the bitterness which rose out of the Abyssinian [Ethiopian] affair I believe it possible for those old feelings to be restored, if we can only clear away some of the misunderstandings and unfounded suspicions which cloud our trust in one another …

DOCUMENT-BASED QUESTIONS SAMPLE ESSAYS

Document-Based Question 1

Defend or refute the following statement: The Protestant Reformation was a unified movement of dissent against the Catholic Church.

The Protestant Reformation grew into a powerful movement of dissent against the Catholic Church, despite the fact that it was made up of several distinct branches of revolt. Leaders such as Martin Luther, John Calvin, and Ulrich Zwingli agreed on a criticism of Catholicism for financial corruption and for perpetuating superstitions that were not grounded in scripture. Yet these men differed—sometimes sharply—in their religious beliefs and in their ambitions. Consequently, as the Reformation spread across Germany and Switzerland and then into much of northern Europe, it gave rise to a variety of Protestant churches, each with its own defining characteristics.

The Protestant Reformation was jump-started by Martin Luther's posting of his "Ninety-five Theses" on the door of the Castle Church in Wittenberg in 1517. The force and certainty of this brazen physical act is echoed in Luther's voice as he assails the corruption and ignorance that he believes informs every level of the Catholic Church (**DOCUMENT D**). Luther injects special fury into his condemnation of the Catholic Church's abuse of indulgences, or remissions of the temporal penalties imposed by priests on penitents for their sins. In fact, indulgences were regularly issued for small payments of cash, and they were used to remit not only the sins that the laity might commit in the future, but also the sins their dead relatives might be committing continually in purgatory. One of the most notorious abusers of the sale of indulgences was John Tetzel. The caricature of Tetzel (**DOCUMENT B**) uses both a visual image and verbal sarcasm to suggest the extent of this preacher's moral corruption. By contrast, Luther believed that any truly repentant Christian could seek remission of guilt without a letter of indulgence. Luther amplified his objection to the detrimental effect of indulgences in a letter to Albert of Mainz (**DOCUMENT C**). There he criticizes bishops for spending so much time encouraging Catholics to purchase grace that the bishops have little time left to preach the gospel and lead parishioners to a deeper engagement with God. Philip Melanchthon, an ally of Luther's, carries this argument one step further in *Of the Power and Primacy of the Pope.* Melanchthon condemns the pope and other Catholic leaders, and he uses words such as *demons* and *Antichrist* to suggest that the selling of indulgences is actually satanic.

While most Protestant reformers felt as Martin Luther did about the problem of indulgences, they took up other issues also in their dissent against the teachings of the Catholic Church. For instance, as Ulrich Zwingli brought Protestantism to Switzerland, he argued not only against the use of indulgences but also against the propagation of religious superstitions. Like Luther, Zwingli opposed clerical celibacy and proposed the right of clergy to marry—an idea that was later accepted among all Protestants. Zwingli differed from Luther on one crucial aspect of Protestant dogma—the presence of Christ in the Eucharist. This difference of agreement came to a head at the Colloquy of Marburg, which Philip of Hesse had arranged in order to unite Swiss and German Protestants into a single alliance. Zwingli believed that Christ's presence in the Eucharist was symbolic. As Luther made clear in a letter to his wife, he and his followers believed that Christ was present in the Eucharist bodily (**DOCUMENT F**). Neither leader was willing to compromise; as a result, the Protestant movement remained divided over this issue.

Most Protestants agreed that the power of the pope in the Catholic Church was not justified in the scriptures. Luther voiced this concern in his work *Against Catholicism,* in which he argued provocatively that—in claiming to be the head of the church—the pope effectively was unseating no less than Christ (**DOCUMENT G**). His contempt is underscored by his use of animal imagery to describe the church ("a monster") and the pope ("the cuckoo"). Luther answers critics of his ferocity by stating his wish that he had the power to discipline, if not kill, the pope with "lightning." Of course, not all critics of the central role of the pope in the Catholic Church used a tone of unbridled fury. The Protestant reformers' distaste is conveyed humorously in the 1520 parody of the Apostles' Creed (**DOCUMENT E**), which ridicules the Catholic Church for its papal abuses by adapting the format of the actual Apostles' Creed (**DOCUMENT A**)This brilliant and savage parody illustrates the deep anger Protestants felt toward what they perceived as the Catholic Church's many abuses of the sacredness of the Christian faith.

Though Luther and Zwingli could not agree on all aspects of their Protestant agendas, they shared a basic moderation in their aims. In contrast, an in response to discontent with Luther and Zwingli, various radical movements developed during the Protestant Reformation. These included the Anabaptist Movement, which Zwingli and Luther (together with Catholics) sought to suppress, and other groups, like the Spiritualists and Antitrinitarians. These diverse groups held beliefs that were incompatible with those of more moderate Protestants. Each group tended to focus more on its own emergence as a religious movement than on opposing the Catholic Church.

John Calvin brought the Protestant movement to Geneva, and by the second half of the sixteenth century Calvinism had replaced Lutheranism as the major Protestant force in Europe. Calvin believed that individual souls were pre-destined to be elected (or not elected) by God for salvation (**DOCUMENT H**). This focus differed dramatically from Lutheranism, and shifted the focus of the Protestant Reformation toward self-discipline and personal morality and away from opposition to the Catholic Church.

The Protestant Reformation contained a variety of sometimes contentious religious leaders and systems. Despite the presence of divergent theories and practices, the Protestant Reformation developed into an impressive movement of dissent that lessened the power and reach of the Catholic Church dramatically.

Document-Based Question 2

To what extent was the War of the American Revolution a European conflict?

The War of the American Revolution was not an isolated event on the American continent, but rather it was an event of international consequence that directly involved European powers, especially Great Britain and France. The American colonists made opportunistic use of the existing rivalry between France and Great Britain in waging their revolution. The colonists capitalized on the tension between these two European powers (which had flared up between 1756 and 1763 during the Seven Years' War) and took advantage of their ever-growing distrust of one another. In addition, the American Revolution was stimulated in part by the Enlightenment ideas promulgated by the philosophers and writers of England and France.

The immediate spur to the War of the American Revolution was conflict relating to revenue collection. After the end of the Seven Years' War, Britain needed to recover lost revenue, so it sought income from the American colonists for the protection and administration of their colonies. To many American colonists, this domestic taxation seemed grossly unfair, because it involved taxation from a legislative body that did not have any colonists among its members. The sentiments of John Locke, a British philosopher who had advanced many of the ideas of the Enlightenment reform in his work *Two Treatises on Civil Government,* were consonant with the colonists' views. Locke's condemnation of a government's seeking to control and destroy people's property ends with his conclusion that such actions constitute an act of war against citizens (**DOCUMENT A**). Some seventy-five years later, many of the American colonists echoed their European forebear as they protested British efforts to tax them.

The British Parliament sought additional revenue in the Sugar Act in 1764, and in the Stamp Act of 1765. These acts were particularly egregious to the colonists, who felt that Britain was forcing them to abide by laws that they had not themselves approved. Among the many stipulations in the Stamp Act of 1765, colonists were not allowed to submit any petitions to courts of law in the American colonies without paying a three-pence tax (**DOCUMENT B**). The American colonists' response to the English Stamp Act involved the organization of the Stamp Act Congress in 1765, in which they issued their official complaint that the Stamp Act had been imposed upon them by a body that did not include "representatives of the people of these colonies" (**DOCUMENT C**). This idea was fairly radical for its time, and it stemmed largely from the views of Enlightenment thinkers who, in the tradition of John Locke, believed that individuals should be liberated from the bonds of government. In addition, the colonists conceived of the English Revolution of 1688 as having established some of their fundamental political liberties, and they believed that the various taxes imposed by George III and the British Parliament were inconsistent with those freedoms.

Not all English members of Parliament felt that Britain should exclude the American colonies from representation. William Pitt, who had served as the military genius behind the British victory and gain of the American colonies in the Seven Years' War, claimed that such a condition was "the rotten part of the constitution" and encouraged that American representation in Parliament be increased (**DOCUMENT D**). This sentiment differed dramatically from American colonists, who did not seek to be incorporated into Parliament as much as they wished to have their own autonomous rule over their colonies. Thomas Paine's *The American Crisis,* along with his publication *Common Sense,* endorsed the view that the American colonies should escape "slavery" by splitting away from their British oppressors (**DOCUMENT F**).

The rising tensions between Britain and the American colonies were not restricted to a simple dispute between an imperial power and its colonial protectorate. Rather they extended to France, a country that had supported the American colonies during the Seven Years' War and that would come to its aid in its fight against Great Britain. The American colonies made a series of treaties with France that were designed to be mutually beneficial. Thomas Jefferson, in his account of June 1776 discussions in the American Congress, acknowledged the serious political calculations that went into the alliance with France, including the possibility that France could incite Great Britain to defend itself in the West Indies (**DOCUMENT E**). By bringing another European power into the War of the American Revolution, the American colonists redistributed political and military weight in what had been a delicate political balance.

For its part, France had suffered a depleted economy after its defeat in the Seven Years' War and so was eager to establish a relationship with the American colonies that could improve its economic situation and further hurt its enemy, Great Britain. In the Treaty of Alliance and the Treaty of Amity and Commerce—both signed on February 6, 1778—France effectively secured its special privileges and access in the American colonies (**DOCUMENT H**) in exchange for agreeing to ally with the American colonies against Britain in the event of another French and British conflict (**DOCUMENT G**). The Francophile Benjamin Franklin was instrumental in helping to assure the French of their special status with the American colonies; this Franco-American alliance effectively turned what had been a purely colonial conflict into a conflict of European proportion (**DOCUMENT J**).

The American colonists' perspective on taxation at the hands of their British overseers was informed by Enlightenment theories developed by Europeans like John Locke and others. The Americans' political alliance with France enabled them to squeeze Great Britain further, as it forced the British to confront the possibility of another conflict with another European power for control of the colonies. In the end, Great Britain granted the American colonies the right "to be free, sovereign, and independent States" in the Treaty of Paris in 1783 (**DOCUMENT I**). It is ironic that this treaty was signed in Paris, since the French played an important role in turning this colonial revolution into a conflict with European dimensions.

Reader's Comments on Sample Student DBQ Essay

■   The essay has a clear, well-developed thesis

- ■ The student makes use of all of the documents
- ■ The essay analyzes the documents—taking into consideration the point of view of the authors—and groups documents appropriately
- ■ The student includes additional information that is relevant
- ■ The essay effectively considers the extent to which European powers played a role in the American War of Independence

Possible student score: 8-9

Document-Based Question 3

Analyze the political and social forces that helped bring about the Paris Commune of 1871, as well as those that led to its downfall.

The Paris Commune was officially formed on March 28, 1871 when a group of Parisians elected a new municipal government that was intended to administer the citizens of Paris separately from the rest of France. In the official proclamation of its creation, the Paris Commune imagined itself as an autonomous governmental organization and used the simile "like a citizen in a free town" to describe its role (**DOCUMENT D**). There were numerous issues that brought the Paris Commune into being, but its desire for "self-administration and self-government" were high on the list. The unrest caused to the social order by the Paris Commune assisted in its downfall.

Members of the Paris Commune were, by and large, disgruntled citizens who had endured the Prussian siege during the Franco-Prussian War and were angered by the decision of monarchists in the National Assembly to permit the Prussians to remain in Paris until France paid off its war indemnity. The Prussian siege had been extraordinarily difficult for Parisians, who suffered food shortages and were forced to coexist with the enemy. The image in **DOCUMENT I** shows that the privations and shortages experienced by Parisians included the butchering of cats and dogs for meat. The Prussian presence did not affect French citizens who lived in the provinces and outside of Paris as extremely. The Paris Commune was in part a reaction against politicians who seemed ignorant of the experiences of Parisians.

France was still in the initial stages of a republic when the war with Prussia began. The Second Empire came to an end with the capture of Napoleon III at the Battle of Sedan in 1870. Shortly thereafter, the Third Republic was proclaimed, declaring "The Revolution is accomplished in the name of right and public safety," but what followed was the disaster of the Franco-Prussian conflict and the civil war brought on by the Paris Commune (**DOCUMENT A**). The participants in the Paris Commune were radicals and socialists of all kinds. Because they represented an extreme element in French society, they were feared by the monarchist government of the Nationalist Assembly headed by Adolphe Thiers. Lenin and Marx and their adherents believed in the Paris Commune as a genuine example of socialism, and Lenin praised it as "a superb example of the great proletarian movement of the nineteenth century" (**DOCUMENT J**). The Commune was never genuinely a proletarian government; it counted petty bourgeois members among its members.

Needless to say, these agitators for social reform were not welcomed by many members of the upper- and middle-classes, who believed that these extremists were anarchists rather than reformists. Edmond de Goncourt hints at this in his journal entry of March 28, 1871, the day of the proclamation of the Commune, and he equates the Communards with "Barbarians" (**DOCUMENT C**). Similarly, in her letter to her daughter, the Impressionist painter Berthe Morisot, Cornélie Morisot focuses her attention on the destruction wrought by the Paris Commune rather than its political agenda or the reforms it sought to achieve (**DOCUMENT G**). The Paris Commune did not have a broad support among upper class members of French society, who saw it as a threat to their way of life.

The threat of the Paris Commune to the French way of life assisted in its downfall.

Even as publications like the *Journal Officiel de la République Française* were arguing for the "imperative duty and absolute right" of the Commune to "take its destiny in its own hands by seizing political power," the monarchist forces at the National Assembly were gaining moral support from the provinces and from the upper and middle-classes. The Commune sought to win over converts by inveighing against the betrayal of the National Assembly: "It is now a matter, as you know, of either winning or falling into the hands of the reactionaries and clericals of Versailles, of those wretches who have deliberately handed France over to the Prussians," in an unusual reversal—calling the members of the National Assembly the "reactionaries" (**DOCUMENT E**). The Commune also sought to persuade the soldiers of Versailles to betray the French government and to come over to their side (**DOCUMENT F**). But ultimately, the National Assembly triumphed over the Commune's National Guard and restored Paris as a French city. In his declaration of the return to order, Marshal MacMahon promises "At last the fighting is over; order, work, and security will reign once more." The profound need for order and security in French society after the trauma of the Prussian occupation and the uncertain beginnings of the Third Republic helped to quash the Paris Commune.

Reader's Comments on Sample Student DBQ Essay

- The essay has a clear, well-developed thesis that is reinforced by the use of the documents.
- The student makes use of all of the documents.
- The essay groups documents appropriately and recognizes authorial bias.
- The outside information, while not abundant, is relevant to the essay.
- The essay offers a fairly nuanced consideration of the different political forces of the era during the Paris Commune.
- The essay shows time consciousness.
- The essay treats the forces that led to the Commune in greater detail than those that led to its downfall.

Possible student score: 7-8

Document-Based Question 4

Evaluate the political, social, and cultural reforms Enlightenment thinkers sought in eighteenth-century European society.

Enlightenment thinkers, known as *philosophes*, helped to inject social, political, and cultural change into traditional European institutions and traditional European ways of life. Their ability to effect sweeping changes on their society was hugely important in shaping the cultures, governments, and politics of these countries in future years. Many of these changes can be traced back to some of the works of these early Enlightenment figures. The intellectual climate of Europe at this time also contributed dramatically to the reception of these new and, in some cases, radical ideas.

One of the most important characteristics of this period was the increasing rate of literacy and the increased production and manufacturing of reading material. Europe's population was more literate than ever before, and its citizens were debating ideas that they encountered in various publications including newspaper and books. As the chart in

DOCUMENT J demonstrates, in England, the average annual output of new and reprinted works continued its ascent through the eighteenth century. It seems safe to conclude that more Europeans were buying, reading, and exploring worlds in literature that were previously unknown to them. This emergence of a print culture was significant to the success of the reforms instituted by Enlightenment thinkers.

Two of the major intellectual figures of the Enlightenment whose work profoundly influenced reformers were Isaac Newton and John Locke. (Newton had explained the law of gravitation, and Locke had articulated a vision of a government committed to individual liberty.) Locke explained human psychology in terms of experience in his work *An Essay Concerning Human Understanding,* in which he developed the idea of the human mind as a blank sheet that could gain definition and shape only with experience (**DOCUMENT A**). Locke's famous vision of humans as a *tabula rasa* was compelling to Enlightenment reformers, who interpreted his idea as evidence that human personality is changeable and could be altered by modifying the surrounding environment.

One of the first major Enlightenment works to emerge and dramatically alter the course of the social and political landscape in Europe was the massive *Encyclopedia* edited by D'Alembert and Diderot. The *Encyclopedia,* which had survived attempts at censorship and suppression, represented a towering achievement for the hundreds of *philosophe* authors whose works were anthologized in it. It included some of the most advanced ideas of the age on subjects ranging from mechanical arts to animal husbandry. Embedded in these works were revolutionary ideas and philosophical musings that questioned the *status quo,* such as d'Alembert's analysis of how economics, political power, and perceptions of native intelligence inter-relate in contemporary French society (**DOCUMENT F**). The *Encyclopedia* secularized learning and ignored the Christian tradition, preferring to focus on the application of reason over the Christian model of ethics.

Many Enlightenment thinkers were reacting against the autocratic monarchies that characterized their governments. Locke's thinking drove this reform. In his 1748 *Spirit of the Laws,* Montesquieu advocated a balance of power, and endorsed a division of the government into the legislative, the executive, and the judicial branches (**DOCUMENT C**). Montesquieu held up the example of the British constitution as the proper way to regulate a government. While some of his ideas took root in governments (Montesquieu's division of powers was adopted in the U.S. Constitution) by 1789, many of the political grievances in France reflected a frustration with the lack of democratic opportunities for citizens. As the *Cahiers de Doléances* of 1789 reveals, the Third Estate was frustrated with its unequal status in the French government (**DOCUMENT H**). The thinking of the Enlightenment was certainly responsible, in some sense, for pushing the French into the Revolution.

Enlightenment thinkers were notoriously opposed to the influence of the Church. Voltaire, whose famous *"Crush the Infamous Thing"* remark reflects a general distrust of the church and Christianity, develops these ideas in his *Philosophical Dictionary* of 1764. In his withering critique of the Catholic measures against French Protestants, Voltaire reveals his contempt for religious fanaticism (**DOCUMENT E**). Like Voltaire, Alexander Pope was drawn to the use of reason and to the focus on rational life and empirical experience, rather than the mystical aspects of religion, to understand his society (**DOCUMENT B**).

Enlightenment thinkers supported changes in education, and were fairly progressive in their attitudes toward children's need to learn. Jean-Jacques Rousseau, while a progressive in some respects, did not believe that women and men were equally suited to education (**DOCUMENT D**). His view became popular around this time, but not among more enlightened Enlightenment feminists, such as Mary Wollstonecraft, who took umbrage with Rousseau's view of women (**DOCUMENT I**). Wollstonecraft's spirited defense of women, in her *A Vindication of the Rights of Women* effectively pokes holes in Rousseau's arguments and reveals their weaknesses. Wollstonecraft was a proto-feminist, whose views continue to influence contemporary thinking about the roles of men and women.

Enlightenment thinkers strove to push their society beyond the boundaries of the *status quo*. They sought to escape the confines of religious tradition, to incorporate some of the empirical forces brought to bear during the Scientific Revolution on other areas of everyday life. This period was a time of major change, much of which came about as a result of these fearless *philosophes*, pioneers of new ways of thinking who were unafraid to expose their views to their society.

Reader's Comments on Sample Student DBQ Essay

- The essay has a clear, well-developed thesis that is reinforced by the use of the documents
- The student makes use of most of the documents
- The essay groups documents appropriately and pays attention to the significance of authorship
- The outside information is pertinent to the essay and helps to unify the use of the documents
- The essay grasps the interrelated issues faced by the Enlightenment *philosophes*, making connections among the Scientific Revolution, the religious crises, education reform, and governmental reform
- The essay shows time consciousness
- The student displays an impressive amount of erudition and a breadth of knowledge on the subject and uses the documents to great advantage

Possible student score: 8-9

Document-Based Question 5

Discuss and analyze the factors that led to the European Imperialism of the nineteenth century.

The expansion of European influence in the nineteenth century was by no means a new development. Spain, France, Portugal, Holland, and Britain had all controlled territories overseas for centuries. But over time, Britain remained the only European power with significant overseas holdings, and by mid-century, many European countries were opposed to colonization because it entailed costly military and political entanglements far from home. These attitudes changed abruptly in the last third of the century, however, and European states rapidly spread their control over as many as 10 million square miles and 150 million people—roughly one-fifth of the world's population. Social, economic, and political factors were responsible for this movement of frantic colonization that is known as the "New Imperialism."

By the mid-nineteenth century, the fruits of the Industrial Revolution were beginning to make themselves known. Thanks to improvements in agriculture, technology, transportation, and communication, European countries had achieved tremendous economic growth. Many Europeans believed that their civilization and culture were superior to those of peoples on other continents, and they justified their imperialism as a kind of social duty. In a decree announcing the new Portuguese protectorate over Dahomey, for instance, the foreign minister Pinheiro Chagas made a self-satisfied argument in describing Dahomey's willing acceptance of all the "benefits of European civilization" (**DOCUMENT E**). While it is certainly true that European colonization brought with it an investment of capital, a development of local infrastructure, and a transformation of the local culture and economy, these "benefits" were often was accompanied by European arrogance and attitudes of condescension toward the native inhabitants.

In the nineteenth century, many Europeans considered Africa the "Dark Continent" and believed that colonization was akin to a kind of salvation for the "savages" (**DOCUMENT E**). Many Christian missionaries supported imperialism because it would enable them to convert newly colonized natives to the Christian faith, enlarging the kingdom of God at the same time that they enlarged the kingdom. Rudyard Kipling, one of the most influential British writers of the era, encouraged his readers to bring civilization and culture to the unenlightened (**DOCUMENT H**).

The view held by many Europeans that the natives of Asian and African countries were culturally "backward" was reinforced by the doctrine of "social Darwinism," a quasi-scientific application of Charles Darwin's evolutionary ideas about survival of the fittest. Karl Pearson attempts to justify imperialism on these grounds; he argues that racial struggle is a natural (and *vital*) element of human progress (**DOCUMENT J**). Social Darwinism was quite compatible with many Europeans' patronizing view of the "inferior" cultures of conquered peoples. In this spirit, the British agent Lord Cromer argues that decisions should be made for "the subject race" because of their inability to make decisions in their own best interests without the "light of Western knowledge and experience" (**DOCUMENT C**).

Some used economic justifications for imperialism. For instance, in his manifesto for the society for German colonization, Carl Peters expresses the theory that foreign colonies will attract a European country's excess population. One of the goals of his Society for German Colonization was directing German emigrants to the colonies (**DOCUMENT I**). In fact, most European emigrants went to North and South America and Australia rather than colonies controlled by their countries.

Political factors were more important causes of the nineteenth century European imperialism. Leading European nations felt that colonies were essential to national security and military power. The British foreign officer Clement Hill describes the political pressure to maintain a European presence on the East Coast of Africa in **DOCUMENT D**. When the Suez Canal was completed in 1869, it made Egypt especially important to the British, because it provided them with the shortest possible route to India, the most important colonial element in the British empire. Britain purchased a major interest in the Suez Canal in 1875, and established control over Egypt soon thereafter. This was part of the "land scramble" that is satirized in the American cartoon showing England in the form of the octopus John Bull, grabbing every bit of land within its reach (**DOCUMENT F**).

For many European nations, the acquisition of colonies represented an opportunity to distinguish themselves in the international community. The Victorian critic John Ruskin articulates this vision of England's prestigious and superior destiny as " … a sceptred isle, for all the world a source of light, a centre of peace …" (**DOCUMENT B**). A similar sentiment is voiced in earnest rhetorical fashion by the British journalist G.W. Steevens (**DOCUMENT G**).

The many social, economic, and political factors responsible for the nineteenth-century phase of "New Imperialism" by European powers were complicated and different for individual powers. Nevertheless, there was undeniably a sense among the different countries that the lands they colonized were theirs for the taking. Diderot's observation that merely setting foot on foreign land seemed to justify to Europeans their right of possession is not hyperbole (**DOCUMENT A**). Nineteenth-century European Imperialism represented human greed at its most voracious and uncontrolled.

Reader's Comments on Sample Student DBQ Essay
- The essay has a clear, well-argued and developed thesis and is well-organized
- The student makes use of all of the documents
- The essay identifies the authorship and point of view of each document and takes into consideration biases on the part of authors
- The outside information is relevant and strengthens the thesis of the essay
- The essay effectively discusses and analyzes the factors involved in nineteenth-century imperialism

Possible student score: 8-9

Document-Based Question 6
To what extent was Italy's aggression in Ethiopia significant in the outbreak of World War II?

The Italian aggression in Ethiopia played an important role in the outbreak of World War II. Prior to this act, Italy had been a relatively neutral party in European affairs, despite its Fascist government under Benito Mussolini. Italy's invasion of Ethiopia and the subsequent uproar by western European nations effectively pushed the alienated Mussolini into the waiting arms of Hitler, who had long hoped for an alliance that would increase his power against the rest of western Europe.

Mussolini's agenda in Ethiopia was purely one of conquest. For years, Italy had aspired to gain colonial areas in Africa. Italy had small colonial outposts in Somaliland and Eritrea in East Africa and Libya in North Africa. In 1896, Italy had been repulsed by the Ethiopians at Adowa when it attempted to invade and conquer the country. In 1935, Mussolini used a small border incident at Wal-Wal to provoke an invasion in Ethiopia that shocked the rest of Europe. For some time, Mussolini had been advocating the spread of Italy's civilization to other areas. He encouraged women to bear more children to spread Italy's population across the globe. An Italian newspaper noted that "the cause of

Italy is that of civilization" (**DOCUMENT A**), but more accurately the cause of Italy was that of *Italian* civilization. Mussolini was not interested in preserving Ethiopian liberties or culture; he intended to wipe them out in order to spread Italian culture.

Other supportive interpretations of Mussolini's actions in Ethiopia in 1936 ranged from the argument that Ethiopian land was needed for the growing Italian population, as voiced in *Libro e Moschetto* (**DOCUMENT B**) to Father Messineo's willingness to overlook the vital necessities of the Ethiopian people as he asserted that "vital necessity can legitimize the occupation of a part of colonial territory, in order to satisfy the needs of individual and social life" (**DOCUMENT I**). Essentially, Mussolini's agenda was one of greed, and any number of apologists were willing to argue other motives for the Italian conquest of Ethiopia. There were anti-Fascist Italian dissenters to Mussolini's policies who expressed their displeasure with "the African adventure of capitalism," but these were largely shouted down by Mussolini and supporters (**DOCUMENT D**).

Italy's invasion of Ethiopia was significant to the outbreak of World War II because England and France did not want to engage in a war with Italy at a time when Hitler was conquering the rest of Europe. And so a policy of appeasement began that effectively enabled Mussolini to carry on with his acquisition of Ethiopia. Sir Robert Vansittart of the British Foreign Office acknowledges this policy of appeasement directly in saying that "Italy will have to be bought off" in order to prevent the League of Nations from collapsing and Mussolini from allying with Germany (**DOCUMENT C**). The League of Nations condemned the Italian aggression and voted economic sanctions against Italy, but—as Haile Selassie, then Emperor of Ethiopia, indicated in his address to the League of Nations, Great Britain deemed it "imperative at all costs to obtain the friendship of Italy" (**DOCUMENT G**). This friendship is further confirmed in the 1937 letter from British Prime Minister Neville Chamberlain to Benito Mussolini in which he expresses a desire for "old feelings" between the two countries to "be restored" (**DOCUMENT J**). Italy's invasion of Ethiopia rightly shocked the world, but it occurred at a time when the League of Nations was relatively powerless because it did not want to alienate Mussolini. The *Times* of London condemned in strong words the brutal attack against the Ethiopians, arguing that the Italian gassing of the defenseless Ethiopian people amounted to pure evil (**DOCUMENT E**). In his balcony speech, Mussolini couched the victorious conquest of Ethiopia in the rhetoric of peace ("… the diverse races of the Lion of Judah … wish to live tranquilly in the shadow of the Italian tricolor"). Eventually, with the League of Nations and Italy in a hostile situation, Mussolini turned to Hitler and made a pact that he referred to as the Berlin-Rome "axis around which can revolve all those European states with a will to collaboration and peace" (**DOCUMENT H**).

The Italian invasion of Ethiopia effectively demonstrated the weakness of the League of Nations in the face of the threat of Adolph Hitler. It also illustrated the dangers of appeasement, an issue that was central to the developments of World War II. Further, it pushed Hitler and Mussolini into an alliance that would dictate the conflict to come between the Allies and the Axis powers. Though the Ethiopian invasion is not usually remembered in the countdown of aggressive acts that led to World War II, it was decisive in aligning European powers against each other.

Reader's Comments on Sample Student DBQ Essay

■   The essay has a clear, well-developed thesis that is reinforced by the use of the documents

■   The student makes excellent use of all of the documents

■   The essay recognizes authorial bias and groups documents appropriately

■   The extensive use of outside information gives the essay an overall coherence

■   The essay offers a fairly nuanced consideration of the different elements involved in the invasion of Ethiopia and connects it consistently to events that led up to World War II

Possible student score: 8-9

PART IV

SAMPLE PRACTICE TEST

On the following pages are two sample exams. They mirror the AP exam in format and question types. Set aside a time to take these exams, timing yourself as you will be timed when you take the real test, to prepare you for the actual test-taking experience.

SECTION I
PART A: MULTIPLE-CHOICE QUESTIONS

1. Questions 1.1–1.4 refer to the following excerpt.

JULIUS:
What's the trouble here? Won't the gates open? I believe the lock has been changed.
GENIUS:
Better check to see if you've brought the right key. The one for the treasury won't open this door, you know. Why didn't you bring both keys? This is the key of power, not of knowledge.
JULIUS:
Why, this is the only one I've ever used! I've never seen what good the other one was.
GENIUS:
Meanwhile we're locked out.
JULIUS:
I'm losing my temper. I'm going to beat on the gate. Hey there! Somebody open this door instantly! What's holding up the doorman? Asleep, I suppose, probably drunk.
GENIUS:
(Aside) This fellow judges everyone by himself.

—Desiderius Erasmus, Dialogue: *Julius Locked Out of Heaven*

1.1 The passage above represents the employment of Renaissance learning in the service of?
   A. religious reform
   B. state building
   C. civic humanism
   D. absolutism

1.2 Based on the passage above and your knowledge, Christian Humanism led most directly to which of the following?
   A. the Catholic Reformation
   B. development of National Monarchies
   C. the Protestant Reformation
   D. the Thirty Years War

1.3 Which of the following would be most likely to *disagree* with the views represented in the document?
   A. Protestant reformers
   B. Protestant monarchs
   C. Anabaptists
   D. Habsburg rulers

1.4 Which of the following groups would be most likely to use the document to support their political beliefs?
- A. the Jesuit Order
- B. the Anabaptists
- C. Catholic bishops
- D. Nicolo Machiavelli

2. Questions 2.1–2.3 refer to the following passage.

…the French and the English had a small share of the trade in the North. But for the French this share supplied only an insignificant fraction of their material needs. As for the English, this share provided them with virtually all their needs and in addition met part of the needs of the other northern nations, for the English have always had good trade relations with the North. At first, Bruges was the principal exchange mart for this trading activity. Then the inhabitants of Antwerp took advantage of their port, facilities and attracted trade there. After the wars between the Spanish and the Dutch, the self-discipline, the moderation and the zeal of the Dutch attracted world trade to Amsterdam and to the other cities of Holland. But they were not satisfied with being the central exchange mart for all Europe and especially for the North. They decided to gain control of foreign trade at its very source. To this end they ruined the Portuguese in the East Indies. They inhibited or disturbed in every possible way the business ventures which the English had established there. They employed and are still employing every means, are exerting every effort, are applying their full resources to assume full control of world trade and to keep it out of the hands of all other nations. Their whole government is based upon this single principle. They know that as long as they maintain their commercial superiority, their power on both land and sea will keep on increasing and will make them so powerful that they will become the arbiters of peace and war in Europe. They can set whatever limits they please upon the law and the design of kings.

—Jean Colbert, French Finance Minister, *Dissertation on Alliances*, 1669

2.1. What feature of European history in this period is being described?
- A. the Enlightenment
- B. the Scientific Revolution
- C. mercantilism
- D. nationalism

2.2 What was one later development that can be directly linked to the passage?
- A. a series of Anglo-Dutch wars
- B. an alliance between the Dutch and the French
- C. an alliance between the French and the English
- D. the disappearance of piracy in the Atlantic trade

2.3 What was one practice that was common to all European states at that time that is not explicitly mentioned in the passage?
- A. discoveries of large deposits of gold in their respective colonies
- B. trade in and use of African slaves
- C. the development of power driven ships and machines

D. a decline in the volume of commerce between Europe and Asia

3. Questions 3.1–3.4 refer the following passage.

In my preceding pamphlet I had no occasion to condemn the peasants, because they promised to yield to law and better instruction, as Christ also demands. But before I can turn around, they go out and appeal to force, in spite of their promises, and rob and pillage and act like mad dogs… They practice mere devil's work, and it is the arch-devil himself who reigns at Mühlhausen, Thomas Münzer, indulging in nothing but robbery, murder, and bloodshed. Since those peasants allow themselves to be led astray and act differently from what they declared, I likewise must write differently concerning them; and first bring their sins before their eyes, as God commands.

—Martin Luther, *Against the Murderous, Thieving Hordes of Peasants* (1525)

3.1　The passage above represents a conflict over?
　　　A. the purpose of the Protestant Reformation
　　　B. the purpose of the Renaissance
　　　C. the purpose of the Scientific Revolution
　　　D. the purpose of European exploration

3.2　Which Protestant leader might well have disagreed with Luther on this issue?
　　　A. Henry VIII
　　　B. John Calvin
　　　C. Henry IV
　　　D. Elizabeth I

3.3　Which of the following might have occurred as a result of groups such as the nobility challenging monarchial authority based on religious reform?
　　　A. the Catholic Reformation
　　　B. the Edict of Nantes
　　　C. the French Wars of Religion
　　　D. the Council of Trent

3.4　Which of the following developments most likely explains the reason for the conflict that led to the production of the above document?
　　　A. the refusal of accepting Protestant teachings
　　　B. the belief that the Catholic Church was above all secular institutions
　　　C. new interpretations of Christian doctrine and practice
　　　D. the use of Jesuit teachings

4. Questions 4.1–4.3 refer to the following excerpt.

"That the various forms of epidemic, endemic, and other disease caused, or aggravated, or propagated chiefly amongst the labouring classes by atmospheric impurities produced by decomposing animal and vegetable substances, by damp and filth, and close and overcrowded dwellings prevail amongst the population in every part of the kingdom…

That such disease, wherever its attacks are frequent, is always found in connexion with the physical circumstances above specified, and that where those circumstances are removed by drainage, proper cleaning, better ventilation, and other means of diminishing atmospheric impurity, the frequency and intensity of such disease is abated; and where the removal of noxious agencies appears to be complete, such disease almost entirely disappears…

The primary and most important measures, and at the same time the most practicable, and within the recognized province, and within the recognized province of public administration, are drainage, the removal of all refuse of habitations, streets, and roads, and the improvement of the supplies of water."

—Edwin Chadwick, *Summary from the Poor Law Commissioners*

4.1 What specific type of reform did Chadwick's *Summary from the Poor Law Commissioners* help promote?
   A. hospital reform
   B. sanitation reform
   C. medical vaccinations for children
   D. government-provided medical care

4.2 What disease outbreak prompted this report by Edwin Chadwick?
   A. cholera
   B. malaria
   C. smallpox
   D. tuberculosis

4.3 What specific reforms were introduced in England in response to Chadwick's *Summary from the Poor Law Commissioners*?
   A. widespread vaccinations to prevent the spread of disease
   B. the building of new water and sewer systems
   C. new medical practices, including the quarantining of sick patients in hospitals
   D. the introduction of early air pollution controls on factories that used coal

5. Questions 5.1–5.4 refer to the following passage.

The Poor Laws 1587

Be it enacted, the churchwardens of every parish and four substantial householders there shall be nominated yearly in Easter week under the hand of justices of the peace; and they shall take order of such justices of peace for setting to work of the children of parents not be thought able to keep and maintain their children, and to raise by taxation of every inhabitant in the parish a stock of hemp, wool, iron and other stuff for the poor to work on, and also sums of money for the relief of the lame, old, blind and others not able to work, and for the putting out of such children to be apprentices…and all other things concerning the premises…

5.1   The passage above, when applied to the late 16th and early 17th centuries, represents a continued reflection of the definition of social power belonging to
A. those who had hierarchy and status.
B. the Catholic Church.
C. the monarchy.
D. the feudal nobility.

5.2   Based on the passage above and your knowledge, which of the following groups would have been most likely to have been affected by laws such as these?
A. innovators in banking
B. innovators in finance
C. displaced farmers
D. clergymen

5.3   In which of the following areas would institutions such as this be the *least* likely to be found?
A. England
B. France
C. the Netherlands
D. Russia

5.4   Based on the document and your knowledge, which of the following events most likely helped lead to the need for laws such as these?
A. Protestant Reformation
B. Price Revolution
C. Scientific Revolution
D. French Revolution

6. Questions 6.1–6.4 refer to the following images.

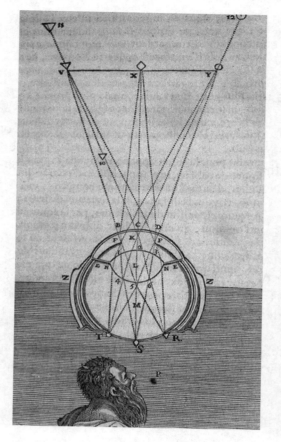

Discourse on Method, Rene Descartes   *Novum Organum,* Francis Bacon

6.1   These images are both tied to what important development?
   A. new ideas in science
   B. new ideas in religion
   C. new ideas about government
   D. new ideas about exploration

6.2   These two men were best known for their contributions to the
   A. Heliocentric Theory.
   B. Geocentric Theory.
   C. Scientific Method.
   D. Anatomy Theory.

6.3   Which of the following might have resulted from their work?
   A. the development of alchemy and astrology
   B. the emergence of the humoral theory of the body and disease
   C. the acceptance of the geocentric theory by church authorities
   D. experimentation and the use of mathematics

6.4   Which of the following men was the *least* likely to agree with the findings of these men?
   A. Newton
   B. Galen
   C. Copernicus
   D. Galileo

7. Questions 7.1–7.3 refer to the following excerpts.

"If [they] were alone in this world, they would stifle in filth…they would try to get ahead of one another in hate-filled struggle and exterminate one another…So it is absolutely wrong to infer any ideal sense of sacrifice in [them] from the fact that they stand together in struggle, or, better expressed, in the plundering of their fellow men…Not through him does any progress of mankind occur, but in spite of him."

—Adolf Hitler, *Mein Kampf*, 1923

"With particular joy I noted your assurance that for two weeks now a train has been carrying, every day, 5,000 members of the chosen people to Treblinka, so that we are now in a position to carry through this population movement at an accelerated tempo."

—Letter from General Karl Wolff [Himmler's Chief of Personal Staff and Hitler's SS Liaison Officer] to Dr. Albert Ganzenmueller [State Secretary of the Transport Ministry], August 13, 1942

7.1   All of the following terms can be linked to these two statements *except*
   A. "Final Solution."
   B. eugenics.
   C. pogroms.
   D. *lebensraum.*

7.2   Wolff was acting on the plans made at a January, 1942, conference in
   A. Berlin.
   B. Munich.
   C. Nuremberg.
   D. Wannsee.

7.3   Wolff was sending people to all of the following *except*
   A. Nuremberg.
   B. Treblinka.
   C. Auschwitz.
   D. Bergen-Belsen.

8. Questions 8.1–8.4 refer to the following document.

The Church has always understood that confession of sins was instituted by the Lord, and necessary for all who have fallen into sin after baptism; the Lord Jesus Christ, when about to ascend from earth to heaven, left his own vicars, before whom all mortal offenses into which the faithful have fallen should be carried, so that they may pronounce forgiveness or retention of sins.

Venial sin whereby we are not excluded from the grace of God, into which we fall more frequently may be omitted without guilt and expiated by other remedies. But since all mortal sins, even those of thought, render men enemies of God; it is necessary to seek pardon from God for every mortal sin, by a full confession…

—Council of Trent

8.1   The event that was most likely responsible for the Council of Trent was the
    A. Protestant Reformation.
    B. Scientific Revolution.
    C. English Civil War.
    D. Catholic Reformation.

8.2   Which of the following statements is most likely to be true based on the above document?
    A. Habsburg rulers were successful in reinstituting Catholicism in their lands.
    B. Protestant leaders quickly reconverted to Catholicism based on this document.
    C. There was a revival of the Catholic Church, but Christianity remained divided.
    D. The Holy Roman Empire was able to regain territory lost as a result of the division in Christianity.

8.3   Based on the document and your knowledge, which of the following would be the *most* likely to agree with the general tone of the document?
    A. Martin Luther
    B. John Calvin
    C. Henry VIII
    D. Jesuits

8.4   Which of the following countries or empires would most likely have agreed with the teachings found in this document?
    A. England under Elizabeth I
    B. Spain under Philip II
    C. the Netherlands under William of Orange
    D. Sweden under Gustavus Adolphus

9. Questions 9.1–9.4 refer to the following document.

Every nation engages in two types of trading activity: domestic and foreign trade. With respect to foreign trade we must understand its structure.

There are five principal categories:

(1) The movement of goods from one province to another for consumption within the kingdom.
(2) The importation from neighboring countries of goods to be sold on the domestic market.
(3) The exportation of European wares necessary to the development of the Orient and the importation from the Orient of goods.
(4) Trade with the West Indies.
(5) Exportation to Northern Europe of goods and products which are processed in Southern Europe after having been imported from the Indies, and importation from the North of the products which grow there.

—Jean Baptiste Colbert, "Dissertation on Alliances"

9.1.   The above document best represents the new economic theory of
     A. mercantilism.
     B. the guild system.
     C. scientific socialism.
     D. capitalism.

9.2.   Which of the following came about as a result of the theory presented in this document?
     A. a period of economic cooperation among European countries
     B. a period of cooperation among European trading companies
     C. the establishment of overseas empires
     D. warfare among indigenous peoples to trade with the Europeans

9.3.   Which of the following was *not* a reason that European countries were able to expand?
     A. advances in navigation
     B. advances in cartography
     C. advances in military technology
     D. advances in alchemy

9.4.   Which of the following is the most likely outcome of European countries engaging in this activity?
     A. European and American revolutions
     B. European conflicts and wars
     C. European agricultural advancements
     D. Enclosure Movements across Europe

10. Questions 10.1–10.4 refer to the following excerpt.

Jansenism made considerable progress among prominent families in Paris. They were opposed to the Jesuits and supported religious communities such as the convent in Port-Royal outside Paris. Jansenists, whose Augustinian theology resembled Calvinism, were known to live extremely pious and morally austere lives. In these respects, though firm Roman Catholics, they resembled English Puritans.

—Donald Kagan, *The Western Heritage*, p. 402

10.1. Of the following, what is the most likely explanation for the appeal of Jansenism?
   A. Louis XIV's revocation of the Edict of Nantes reassured Jansenists that they could worship without persecution.
   B. Jansenists' faith aligned with traditional "Gallican Liberties" from papal authority now combined with a resistance to royal authority.
   C. Jansenism supported the concept of "free will" and thus attracted followers from all religious denominations.
   D. Louis XIV was known to be a secret Jansenist and although officially Catholic, he demonstrated considerable toleration for religious minorities.

10.2. In what way did movements like Jansenism offer challenges to the notion of "Divine Right of Kings"?
   A. In war, such groups frequently offered aid and comfort to enemy forces.
   B. Religious conformity was considered essential to political unity and stability.
   C. Such movement often appealed to popular masses and thus threatened the existence of the state.
   D. Kings were dependent on papal authority for their status, and thus monarchs like Louis XIV had little independence on religious matters.

10.3. What development later in French history offers validation for Louis XIV's "one faith, one law, one king"?
   A. It was religious minorities that provided the main stimulus for the French Revolution.
   B. Persecution of minorities cost millions of francs and was a primary cause of later financial crises.
   C. French wars pursued religious goals more commonly than geopolitical goals, thus contributing to the draining of state finances.
   D. Nobles sought to entrench themselves in institutions like the parliaments to shield them for royal power.

10.4. What other historical development had its origins in an issue similar to the one described in the passage?
   A. the Decembrist Revolt in Russia
   B. the various "partitions" of Poland
   C. the Pragmatic Sanction of 1740
   D. the English Civil War and Glorious Revolution

11. Questions 11.1–11.3 refer to the following image.

11.1   Which group of women typically composed the work force depicted in the image above?
    A. middle class married women
    B. rural peasants
    C. young, single women and widows
    D. girls under the age of fifteen

11.2   What type of factory work did the women in the image above do?
    A. munitions production
    B. train engine construction
    C. manufactured steam engine parts
    D. textile production

11.3   How did skill requirements for women in this image differ from those in earlier home production?
    A. Women had to wait to take this job until they achieved a certain education level.
    B. Fewer skills were necessary for these jobs than were required for earlier jobs.
    C. This job required women to secure special skills that men in similar jobs did not have to gain.
    D. Both jobs required the same skills since they continued to do the same work.

12. Questions 12.1–12.4 refer to the following map.

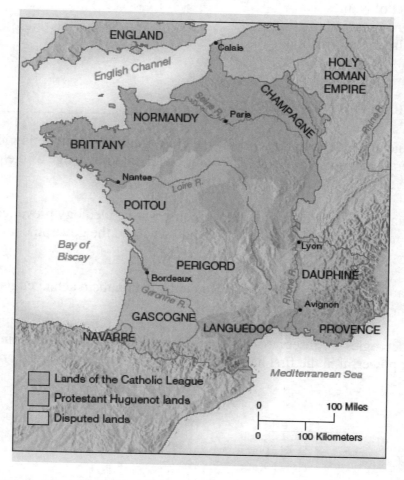

12.1   The map shows France during what period of time?
   A. the French Wars of Religion
   B. the Protestant Reformation
   C. the Renaissance
   D. the Age of Exploration

12.2   Which protestant leader had the most direct effect on France leading to this event?
   A. Henry IV
   B. Martin Luther
   C. John Calvin
   D. Ulrich Zwingli

12.3   Which of the following would most likely have supported these Huguenots?
   A. the Lutherans
   B. the Catholics
   C. the Anglicans
   D. the Anabaptists

12.4   Which of the following developments was the eventual outcome of this conflict?

A. the Thirty Years War
B. the Edict of Nantes
C. the Spanish Armada
D. the Catholic Reformation

SECTION I
PART B: SHORT-ANSWER QUESTIONS

13. During the Age of Metternich (1815–1848), there were several competing ideologies like conservatism, liberalism, and nationalism. Use your historical knowledge of the time period and these ideologies to answer parts A), B), and C) below.

A) Provide an example of one country where the conservative ideology prevailed. What challenge to conservatism did this nation face and what did the government do to limit this challenge?

B) Provide an example of one country where Romantic nationalism achieved its goals and explain what factor(s) allowed for this success.

C) Of the three ideologies—conservatism, liberalism, and nationalism—explain which seemed to be the most powerful in the first half of the nineteenth century and explain why.

SECTION II
PART A: DOCUMENT-BASED QUESTION

14. *What common ideals inspired anti-colonialists in the years immediately following World War II? To what extent were anti-colonialists inspired by Western notions of freedom and independence?*

Document 1 Decolonization since World War II.

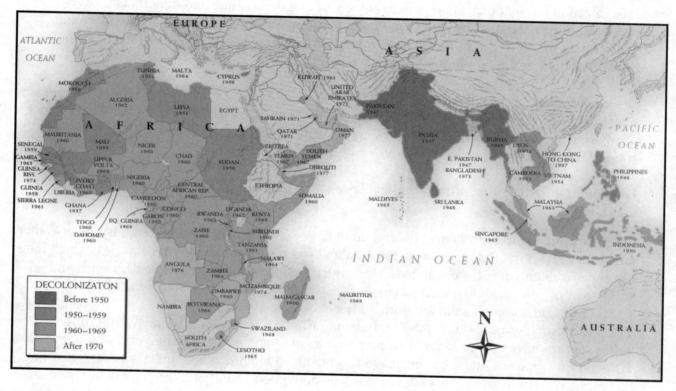

Document 2 Ho Chi Minh, "Determined to Fight to the Bitter End."

"All men are created equal. They are endowed by their Creator with certain unalienable Rights; among these are Life, Liberty, and the pursuit of Happiness"....

The Declaration of the French Revolution made in 1791 on the Rights of man and the Citizen also states: "All men are born free and with equal rights, and must always remain free and have equal rights."

Those are undeniable truths.

Nevertheless, for more than eighty years, the French imperialists, abusing the standard of Liberty, Equality, and Fraternity, have violated our Fatherland and oppressed our fellow citizens. They have acted contrary to the ideals of humanity and justice....

For these reasons, we solemnly declare to the world that Vietnam has a right to be a free and independent country – and in fact is so already. The entire Vietnamese people are determined to mobilize all their physical and mental strength, to sacrifice their lives and property in order to safeguard their independence and liberty.

Document 3 Gamal Abdel Nasser responds to the Suez Crisis, "Those Who Attack Egypt Will Never Leave Egypt Alive."

In these decisive days in the history of mankind, these days in which truth struggles to have itself recognized in international chaos where powers of evil domination and imperialism have prevailed, Egypt stands firmly to preserve her sovereignty. Your country stands solidly and staunchly to preserve her dignity against imperialistic schemes of a number of nations who have uncovered their desires for domination and supremacy....

We shall defend our freedom and independence to the last drop of our blood. This is the staunch feeling of every Egyptian. The whole Arab nation will stand by us in our common fight against aggression and domination. Free peoples, too, people who are really free will stand by us and support us against the forces of tyranny.

Document 4 India's first prime minister, Jawaharlal Nehru explains the ideas that underlay the non-aligned movement.

I speak of India because it is my country, and I have some right to speak for her. But many other countries in Asia tell the same story, for Asia today is resurgent, and these countries, which long lay under foreign yoke, have won back their independence and are fired by a new spirit and strive toward new ideals. To them, as to us, independence is as vital as the breath they take to sustain life, and colonialism in any form, or anywhere, is abhorrent....
The preservation of peace forms the central aim of India's policy. It is in the pursuit of this policy that we have chosen the path of non-alignment in any military or like pact or alliance.... Through the centuries, India has preached and practiced toleration and understanding....During these millennia of history, India has experienced both good and ill but, throughout her chequered history, she has remembered the message of peace and toleration.

SECTION II
PART B: LONG-ANSWER QUESTION

15. Explain how the theory and practice of mercantilism led to both European domination of world trade and created rivalries between various European powers.

ANSWER KEY FOR SAMPLE PRACTICE TEST

Section I
PART A: MULTIPLE-CHOICE QUESTIONS

1.1.   A   The passage represents the employment of Renaissance learning in the service of religious reform.

1.2.   C   Christian Humanism led most directly to the Protestant Reformation.

1.3.   D   Habsburg rulers would be most likely *disagree* with the views represented in the document.

1.4.   B   The Anabaptists would be most likely to use the document to support their political beliefs.

2.1.   C   Mercantilism is the feature of European history being described.

2.2.   A   What was one later development that can be directly linked to the passage?

2.3.   B   Trading in and using African slaves was one practice that was common to all European states at that time is not explicitly mentioned in the passage.

3.1.   A   The passage represents a conflict over the purpose of the Protestant Reformation. the purpose of the Renaissance

3.2.   B   John Calvin might have disagreed with Luther.

3.3.   D   The Council of Trent might have occurred as a result of groups such as the nobility challenging monarchial authority based on religious reform.

3.4.   C   New interpretations of Christian doctrine and practice most likely explains the reason for the conflict that led to the production of Martin Luther's document.

4.1.   B   Chadwick's *Summary from the Poor Law Commissioners* helped to promote sanitation reform.

4.2.   A   A cholera outbreak prompted Chadwick's report.

4.3.   B   New water and sewer systems were introduced in England in response to Chadwick's *Summary from the Poor Law Commissioners*.

5.1   A   The passage, when applied to the late 16th and early 17th centuries, represents a continued reflection of the definition of social power belonging to those who had hierarchy and status.

5.2   C   Displaced farmers would have been most likely to have been affected by laws such as these.

5.3   D   Institutions such as those described in the passage would be the *least* likely to be found in Russia.

5.4   B   The Price Revolution most likely helped lead to the need for laws such as these.

6.1   A   These images are both tied to new ideas in science.

6.2   C   These two men were best known for their contributions to the scientific method.

6.3   D   Experimentation and the use of mathematics might have resulted from their work.

6.4   B   Galen was the *least* likely to agree with the findings of Descartes and Bacon.

7.1   C   All of the following terms can be linked to these two statements *except* pogroms.

7.2   D   Wolff was acting on the plans made at a January, 1942, conference in Wannsee.

7.3   A   Wolff was sending people to all of the following *except* Nuremberg.

8.1   A   The event that was most likely responsible for the Council of Trent was the Protestant Reformation.

8.2   C   There was a revival of the Catholic Church, but Christianity remained divided.

8.3   D   Jesuits would be the *most* likely to agree with the general tone of the document.

8.4   B   Spain, under Philip II, would most likely have agreed with the teachings found in this document.

9.1   A   The document best represents the new economic theory of mercantilism.

9.2   C   The establishment of overseas empires came about as a result of the theory presented in this document.

9.3   D   Advances in alchemy was not a reason that European countries were able to expand.

9.4   B   European conflicts and wars were the most likely outcome.

10.1   C   Jansenism supported the concept of "free will" and thus attracted followers from all religious denominations.

10.2   B   Religious conformity was considered essential to political unity and stability.

10.3   D   Nobles sought to entrench themselves in institutions like the parliaments to shield them for royal power.

10.4   D   The English Civil War and Glorious Revolution had their origins in an issue similar to the one described in the passage?

11.1   C   Young, single women and widows typically composed the work force depicted in the image.

11.2   D   Women did textile production work.

11.3   B   Fewer skills were necessary for these jobs than were required for earlier jobs.

12.1   A   The map shows France during the French Wars of Religion.

12.2   C   John Calvin had the most direct effect on France leading to this event?

12.3   D   The Anabaptists would most likely have supported these Huguenots.

12.4   A   The Thirty Years War was the eventual outcome of this conflict.

Section I
PART B: SHORT-ANSWER QUESTIONS

Sample Answers

A) Countries where conservative ideology prevailed in the Age of Metternich:

- Austria – faced and attempted to contain nationalist threats from its many ethnic groups (Italians, Magyars, Czechs, Austrian Netherlands, etc.); also faced calls for liberal reforms (constitution), but Metternich's government did not implement a liberal constitution; enacted the Carlsbad Decrees to limit public (university) support for liberalism

- Russia – Decembrist Uprising by liberal military leaders who wanted to see a constitution implemented in Russia; government suppressed the revolution and enacted a very conservative government to enforce the principles of conservatism

- Spain – the attempted revolution to create a liberal government was suppressed by the Congress System and monarchy was restored

B) Countries where nationalism prevailed:
- Austrian Netherlands fought for and gained independence from Austria and became the nation of Belgium
- Greece – revolted against Ottoman control and successfully gained its independence from the Ottoman Empire; aid from European nations like Britain and France helped the Greeks achieve their objectives; Greeks were supported by Romantic writers and artists in their quest for independence; Greek independence was supported because Greeks were fellow Christians and because Greece was the home of classical democracy

C) Students can make a strong argument for both nationalism and liberalism (but not conservatism)
- Nationalism – numerous uprisings, steps toward German and Italian Unification, independence for a variety of states, including Belgium and Greece, independence of American colonies, association with the artistic endeavors Romantic artists
- Liberalism – creation of constitutions (and, therefore, the protection of natural rights) became widespread in much of Europe (not Russia), although the degree to which rights were actually protected was not always guaranteed

Section II
Part A: Document-Based Question

Sample Answer

The transformation of much of Africa and Asia from colonial domains into independent nations was the most remarkable global political event of the second half of the twentieth century. In less than a century after the great nineteenth-century drive toward empire, European imperialists found themselves in retreat around the globe. The former colonies desired independence in dramatic ways (**DOCUMENTS A, B, C, and D**).

There were common interests and experiences among the former colonies. All called for independence. All were willing to fight for that independence. The former colonies wished to preserve their own sovereignty and break free of the shackles of colonial domination **(DOCUMENTS B, C, and D)**.

The anti-colonialists evoked European models of freedom and independence. Ho Chi Minh invoked France when he used the Declaration of the French Revolution: "All men are created equal. They are endowed by their Creator with certain unalienable Rights; among these are Life, Liberty, and the pursuit of Happiness".... The Declaration of the French Revolution made in 1791 on the Rights of man and the Citizen also states: "All men are born free and with equal rights, and must always remain free and have equal rights." Those are undeniable truths. Nevertheless, for more than eighty years, the French imperialists, abusing the standard of Liberty, Equality, and Fraternity, have violated our Fatherland and oppressed our fellow citizens. They have acted contrary to the ideals of humanity and justice....

Nehru insisted that India's foreign policy was rooted in Indian history: "Through the centuries, India has preached and practiced toleration and understanding....During these millennia of history, India has experienced both good and ill but, throughout her chequered history, she has remembered the message of peace and toleration."

Decolonization was a worldwide event lasting through- out the second half of the twentieth century, often in a very compressed timeframe, and beyond (**DOCUMENTS A, B, C, and D**). It involved such dramatic moments as the Dutch being forced from the East Indies in 1949 to be replaced by the independent nation of Indonesia, the Belgian withdrawal from the Congo in 1960, the liberation of Portuguese Mozambique and Angola in 1974 and 1975, and the end of all-white rule in Rhodesia (Zimbabwe) in 1979 and most remarkably in South Africa in 1994.

Section II
Part B: Long-Answer Question

[Student Answers will vary]